W0254284

INDIAN DIASPORA IN THE CARIBBEAN

HISTORY, CULTURE AND IDENTITY

INDIAN DIASPORA in the Caribbean

HISTORY, CULTURE AND IDENTITY

edited by

RATTAN LAL HANGLOO

PRIMUS BOOKS
An imprint of Ratna Sagar P. Ltd.
Virat Bhavan
Mukherjee Nagar Commercial Complex
Delhi 110 009

Offices at
CHENNAI KOLKATA LUCKNOW
AGRA AHMEDABAD BANGALORE COIMBATORE DEHRADUN GUWAHATI
HYDERABAD JAIPUR KANPUR KOCHI MADURAI MUMBAI PATNA RANCHI

First published 2012

ISBN: 978-93-80607-38-2

Published by Primus Books

Laser typeset by Digigrafics
Gulmohar Park, New Delhi 110 049

Printed at Shree Maitrey Printech Pvt Ltd, Noida

Contents

Preface

THIS BOOK ATTEMPTS to explore the textures of Indian culture among people of Indian origin and the difficulties that they have and continue to encounter as diasporic communities. For the diaspora, debating socio-religious and cultural issues that are rooted in Indian soil is not only an intellectual necessity but also a strong identity-marker, which could not be abandoned despite varied onslaughts on their religious and cultural values from time to time. The essays featuring in this volume will discuss some of these aspects. They point towards the need to adopt a rigorous approach to the study of the Indian diaspora in the Caribbean in a more comprehensive manner. This book also provides a useful lens for both the Government of India and the Indian diaspora, specifically in the Caribbean and, in general, across the world, through which to view the complexities of the problems of the Indian diaspora and the responses it requires.

The idea for *Indian Diaspora in the Caribbean: History, Culture and Identity* took shape while I was Chair of Indian Studies at the University of West Indies in Trinidad and Tobago. The interest in India expressed by my students, many of whom represented the fourth or fifth generation of the Indian diaspora, always amazed me. The manner in which images of India, that had been passed on from one generation to another in a variety of ways, unfolded before me, not only as observed among Indian students, but also among Africans and others who have been significantly influenced by these images, deserves a keen sense of appreciation and acknowledgement. Although the poverty of pre-independent India has been a strong construct that has remained with the Indian students, yet it has never overshadowed the Indian identity they proudly cherish. This idea of putting together essays based on our regular interactions with our students also appealed to some of my colleagues. Despite their engagements, they extended their support and I wish to express my deep sense of gratitude to all those who have contributed to this volume.

It is here that I must also acknowledge a deep debt of gratitude to Dr Karan Singh, the President and Shri Suresh K. Goel, Director General of the Indian Council for Cultural Relations (ICCR), Ministry of External Affairs, Government of India for their encouragement. Shri Sunil Mehdiretta, Director, Chairs Abroad, and Mr Sunil Kumar Singh, Programme Officer at ICCR, New Delhi have always been very helpful.

My special thanks also go to Shri J.S. Sapra, the then Indian High Commissioner to Trinidad and Tobago and the present High Commissioner, Shri Malay Mishra for their generous hospitality. I also thank Dr Winston Dukheran, the present Finance Minister of Trinidad and Tobago who met me personally at Hyderabad during his visit to India in the summer of 2010. I am grateful to Professor Kusha Haraksingh and his wife, Professor Indira Singh of the University of West Indies. I benefited immensely from the discussions I had with both of them. My thanks are also due to Dr Ajay Kumar Sahoo, of Centre for the Study of Indian Diaspora, University of Hyderabad and for his useful suggestions during our interaction.

I would like to acknowledge the help of my colleagues at the Department of History, University of West Indies, particularly Professor Rita Pamberton, Dr Michel Toussaint, Dr Claudius Fergus, Dr Sherry-Ann Singh, Dr Basil Read, and Dr John Campbell.

Late Ashram Bhagirath Maharaj was a student and friend who familiarized me with the complexities of the Indian diasporic culture in the Caribbean. His enthusiasm and generosity will always be remembered. It is because of Ashram and his companion, Nalni, that exploring most of Trinidad and Tobago turned out to be a much looked-forward-to affair. My deepest thanks go to them. It pains me to know that Ashram will not be able to see this volume in print. My wonderful friends Khurshid Ganai, B.L. Betab, Professor Appa Rao Podile, Dr Gautam Sengupta, Professor Sheela Prasad, Rajesh Raina, Dr Rajgopal, Dr Srikumar, Dr Nino Kuvirikashvili, Dr Javid Wani, Dr Aijaz, Dr Altaf, Dr Durga Prasad Singh, his wife and Dr M.N. Rajesh deserve my special gratitude because they could always be counted upon to come up with solutions to my problems. My thanks to Ms. Erica Williams, the daughter of Dr Eric Williams, the first Prime Minister of Trinidad and Tobago, Professor Dominic Shellard, Pro-Vice-Chancellor, International Affairs and Dr Jennifer Lavia, University of Sheffield for inviting me to deliver the Dr Eric Williams Memorial Lecture.

My thanks also go to M. Ramakrishna, Phenish Babu, Naresh, Kimberly, Uta Ram Prasad, Radica Sukhraj, Indira, Anila Bagwat, Vade, his mother and the students whom I taught in the University of West Indies. I am grateful to Maria Peter Joseph, the then Secretary to the Department of History, University of West Indies, and her colleague Shallen for providing wonderful secretarial assistance.

My teacher, Professor Harbans Mukhia, also deserves my gratitude for his valuable ideas and new insights.

Special thanks to my family members, Shri M.L. Hangloo, Shri P.L. Hangloo, Dr Nanajee Hangloo and Arti, Suman, Sushma, Shri Jawaharlal Kaul, Professor O.N. Kaul, Phoola Kaul, Veena Kaul, Col. Ravi Bhat, Dolly, Rajinder Kaul and Rita Kaul for their invaluable support and strength.

Finally, I am deeply grateful to my wife Sharika Kaul Hangloo and our children Arkaprateem and Dr Arkapravah for their special interest in my work; without them, this book would not have seen the light of day.

Georgia RATTAN LAL HANGLOO

Editor and Contributors

ANN MARIE BISSESSAR, Professor, Department of Behavioural Sciences, University of the West Indies, St. Augustine, Trinidad and Tobago.

BRIDGET BRERETON, Professor, Department of History, University of the West Indies, St. Augustine, Trinidad and Tobago.

RATTAN LAL HANGLOO, Professor, University of Hyderabad, Hyderabad, India. At present, Chair of Indian Studies, Tbilisi State University, Georgia.

SHAHEEDA HUSSAIN, Assistant Professor, Faculty of Arts, University of Trinidad and Tobago, Trinidad and Tobago.

BENJIE MAHABIR, Professor, Department of Politics, University of the West Indies, St. Augustine, Trinidad and Tobago.

RADICA MAHASE, Assistant Professor, College of Science, Technology and Applied Arts, Port-of-Spain of Trinidad and Tobago.

NASSER MUSTAPHA, Professor, Department of Behavioural Sciences, University of the West Indies, St. Augustine, Trinidad and Tobago

BRINSLEY SAMAROO, Professor, Academy of Arts, Letters, Culture and Public Affairs, University of Trinidad and Tobago, Trinidad and Tobago.

SHERRY-ANN SINGH, Assistant Professor, Department of History, University of the West Indies, St. Augustine, Trinidad and Tobago.

Introduction

Rattan Lal Hangloo

> Overseas South Asian communities have different historical trajectories because they have developed in widely divergent historical contexts in many parts of the world. It is the fragmented nature of these contexts and experiences that complicates the use of 'the South Asian diaspora' as a transparent category.
>
> — PETER VAN DER VEER (1995: 1)

> The Caribbean is particularly striking within the larger South Asian diaspora as a distinct cultural identity has been maintained in the process of transplantation, over several generations, and in spite of the processes of colonization, assimilation, and creolization.
>
> — MARIAM PIRBHAI (2009: 110)

THE INDIAN DIASPORA constitutes an integral part of the socio-economic, political and cultural life in the Caribbean region. Having stemmed from the ugly policies and ambitious designs of British colonialism, Indians in the Caribbean have shared the suffering in a variety of ways since the beginning of their arrival on the islands (Vertovec 1992: 2). The first generation was not only the victim of poverty and inhuman treatment meted out to them at every level but also of getting uprooted from their soil in the most devastating manner that has ever been witnessed in the history of the Indian diaspora. However, since the middle of twentieth century, Indo-Caribbeans[1] have come to play a much more active role in the mainstream cultural, commercial, and political life of their adopted countries (Manuel 1997/1998: 18).

Pushing more than half a million Indians to the Caribbean as indentured labourers with absolutely false hopes and promises was the worst sort of violation of human rights and dignity by the British colonial masters (Vertovec 1992: 3). Thousands of Indians who strongly protested against the British rule during the first War of Independence in 1857 also came to the Caribbean to escape persecution (see the article by Brinsley Samaroo 2008). Steven Vertovec (1992) has been very frank in admitting that various immigration schemes were tried by the colonial authorities, including the importation of workers from Madeira, continental Europe, West Africa and China. Yet none of the groups fulfilled the needs of planters, either due to costs of recruitment and transport, unreliability of work, or a simple inability to survive in a tropical climate (see also Waite 1982). From 1834, planters in Mauritius were relatively successful in importing contract labourers from India and their model soon spread to sugar plantations around the world. The pervasive framework of British colonial administration provided the infrastructure that was needed both in India and overseas, to create what was deemed 'a new system of slavery' (Tinker 1974). Indian indentured emigration to the Caribbean was a product of uneven world capitalist development (Roopnarine 2009: 114). Given the costs of recruitment and transportation (often underwritten by local governments of the colonies dominated by sugar planters), indentured Indian migration was quickly accepted by local plantocracies as the most beneficial (profitable) solution to the post-indenture period (Vertovec 1995).[2]

> The procedure to recruit Indians was fairly straightforward but involved a hierarchy of emigration officials in India and in the Caribbean. In India, the government of India appointed Protectors of Emigration in most regions and districts to monitor and manage the system efficiently and effectively. The respective Caribbean colonial government appointed emigration agents, medical officers on the ground and on the transporting ships. The emigration agents then employed provincial and district subagents, licensed recruiters and local judges to supervise the judicial aspects of recruitment. In the Caribbean, each colonial government had an Immigration Department headed by a chief officer (called different names, Protector of Immigrants, Agent-General of Immigrants or Immigrant Agent-General). The chief immigration officer was assisted by other sub-immigration officers such as inspectors, clerks and interpreters. The Immigration Department was responsible for the distribution of Indians and the function of the indenture system. (Roopnarine 2009: 114)

Importation of Indian coolies[3] came to be regarded as the economic salvation of a number of sugar producing colonies, British or others.[4] Even though their arrival was considered economically fortunate, that was not the end of their problems, that continued to plague them generation after generation. Their new environment was predominantly Eurocentric, with traces of African values (MEA 2001: 196). The first batch of indentured labourers arrived in British Guyana on 5 May 1838 on two ships, the *SS Hesperus* and the *SS Whitby*. However, the migration was stopped for seven years and resumed with a batch of indentured labourer to Trinidad on 30 May 1845 aboard the *Fath al Razak* (Ramnarine 1998/1999). By the end of the nineteenth century, changing conditions in the Caribbean colonies, nationalist opposition in India and reformist governments in Europe put an end to the indentured contracts (Eltis 2002: 205). Although the system of importing indentured labourers from the Indian subcontinent was abolished in 1920, by this time approximately 1,43,900 Indians were already brought to Trinidad (Niranjana 1998; Klass 1991), primarily to serve a specific tenure and then be free after completing their obligations, which in most cases were agricultural. The last boat of indentured servants from India arrived in the Caribbean in 1917 (Vertovec 1992). By the time the indenture system ended officially, most workers had left the estates and settled near them in small, dispersed village communities (Khan 1994: 247).[5] Morton Klass (1961) offers a good account of the social organization of the villages of the East Indian in Trinidad.[6]

The majority of Indians who came to the Caribbean under different colonial governments (French, British and Dutch) originated from north India, primarily eastern Uttar Pradesh and western Bihar, with lesser numbers from south India, i.e. Andhra Pradesh and Tamil Nadu (Mahabir 2008). Although many of them returned to India after the abolition of the indentured labourer system, the majority remained in the Caribbean, and their descendants now constitute the largest ethnic groups in Trinidad, Guyana, and Surinam, outnumbering their Afro-Caribbean compatriots, and accounting for about 20 per cent of the English-speaking West Indian population as a whole (Manuel 1997/1998: 18). The backgrounds of Indian immigrants to the Caribbean were rather diverse (van der Veer and Vertovec 1991: 150). N. Jayaram has provided the statistical details about the religious and caste backgrounds of Indian immigrants, drawing information from various sources:

> Of the 91,691 emigrants, 78,772 (85.9%) were Hindus; 12,851 (14.0%) were Muslims; and 68 (0.1%) were Christians. Of the 78,772 Hindu emigrants, 13,242 (16.8%) were of 'Brahman castes'; 5,988 (7.6%) were of 'Artisan castes'; 27,680 (35.1%) were of 'Agricultural castes'; and 31,862 (40.5%) were of 'Low castes'... since the emigrants held several identities (regional, linguistic, occupational, etc., besides caste and sub-caste), all passing for caste, guessing which particular identity an indentured labourer invoked at the time of his or her recruitment is difficult. For example, 'Ajoodhabasi' (resident of Ayodhya), 'Halwaye' (maker of sweetmeats), and 'Kessan' (peasant) are mentioned as castes in Comins' list. (2006: 146)

Apart from the caste and religious differences, there was also a consistent major disparity between the number of men and women contracted as indentured labourers. The scarcity of Indian women in the British Caribbean was to have a profound impact on the indentured immigrant Indian community and on the status and role of women in Indian-Caribbean society (Ramnarine 1998/1999: 11). According to Rhoda Reddock (1994) the required ratio of women to men changed at least six times from 1857 to 1879. It was only in later years of the indentured period that more women were recruited from India (MEA 2001: 196). There are several push factors that caused such a large number of Indians to decide to leave for the Caribbean thousands of miles away from their homeland.[7]

With no respect for their socio-religious norms and pattern of family life and traditions, these Indian labourers were initially housed in the barracks vacated by the West African slaves, in the aftermath of Emancipation in the 60s of the twentieth century. Sometimes labourers were allowed to cultivate a small patch of land or keep a cow or pig; but despite this and the rationing of food, vitamin deficiency plagued the estates, as did malaria and hookworm (Vertovec 1995: 60). Indo-Caribbeans felt unprecedentedly isolated and, in many cases, even more consciously committed to maintaining their cultural heritage (Manuel 1997/1998: 18). Women played an important role in continuing to keep the cultural traditions of the homeland alive.

Just as women in India sing wedding songs that are central to folksong, traditions, Indian women in the Caribbean are seen as the preservers of tradition with regard to the music and dance of wedding rituals in particular. A common view is that it is due to women maintaining these Indian traditions that enabled a popular genre like *chutney* to develop. (Ramnarine 1998/1999: 12)

J.C. Jha has very rightly observed:

The Indian immigrants would have been quite familiar with the old Indian institution of extended family. However, there were several factors in the indenture days militating against a good family life. First the method of recruitment was faulty; the recruiters wanted to earn money and gave a false picture of the conditions of the country to which the Indians were emigrating and therefore many left their family behind. The women in any case were not willing to emigrate in large numbers. Some adventurous people also left India for a distant land to start a family afresh. It was only in later years of the indenture period that steps were taken to recruit whole families and sometimes from the same area. Even then the privacy of a normal family life was gone in depots and later in boats. Moreover, the dwelling conditions in the barracks were bad the immigrants were thrown together without any consideration for privacy. Naturally enough, there were conflicts and sex crimes. Also Muslim marriages before 1930s and Hindu marriages before 1946 were not recognized by Trinidad and Tobago law. (1985: 20)

The majority of Indian immigrants who settled in the Caribbean after the end of indentured contracts have permanently changed the cultural mixture of these societies (Look Lai 1993). After their arrival contact with Africans did not take place in an atmosphere of mutual goodwill. Although the Indians did not meet with any hostile reception, there was extreme timidity and no overwhelming displays of friendship on either sides. Very rarely did the Africans—the so-called natives at that time—behave spontaneously. The remarkable absence of conflict between the two could be attributed to the fact that initially both the races were not concerned to defend the personal claims to land and property. On first making contact with Indians the Africans generally refrained from aggressive behaviour but so long as the indentureship lasted the Africans did despise the Indians. The two did not mix, they lived in uneasy but non-violent co-existence (Brereton 1985: 30). According to Bates (1912: 83), 'both had a comfortable sense of superiority, the Negro because he is free to loaf while the coolie is indentured for five years, the coolie because of his traditions of his ancient civilization and the pride of caste'. Although mostly the Indians behaved peacefully at the beginning of their contacts with the African people, they had not relinquished their claim to superiority. After landing there they took care to maintain certain traditions and festivities of the homeland. This was also to indicate the superiority of their cultural heritage. The sources are too. fragmentary to permit a generalization but gradually the language of expression and gesture could overcome cultural barriers.

The reasons for transformation of contact into collision must often have been complex; they can seldom be reconstructed precisely from the Trinidad Indian accounts which are strongly partisan in such matters. However there were two main reasons for conflict: either the members of Afro-culture sensed a threat to their property and their accustomed way of life or they had ceased to respect and trust the Europeans. The entirely Indo-centric manner in which the Indians interpreted their encounters with other cultures is apparent from their failure to judge the consequences of their appearances or realize how fragile the trust of the natives to Africans was.

In order to clarify this point let me provide a representative instance. According to K.O. Lawrence (1985):

> When Indian labourers were first brought to the West Indies the possibility that they might eventually become permanent settlers was scarcely envisaged. Return passages at the conclusion of their contacts were granted to them and it was expected that they would in fact return to their homeland in due course. The view that many could and would become part of the settled population developed only slowly. When it did, it was closely related to the appearance of an Indian peasantry whose land made its ties with Trinidad obvious. Just as the old slave-owning planters had been accustomed to allowing their slaves to cultivate provision grounds on the estate in their spare time, soon after the importation of Indian labour began, some estates which had wasteland available, as the great majority did, began to permit immigrant labourers even while under indenture, to cultivate such land as they could manage on their own account without endangering their estate work, and to pasture stock on estate lands. Many Indians were thus accustomed to grow food crops and roots of their later activity as market gardeners therefore go back to the early stages of indenture system. The development of a settled peasantry, however, came slowly and it was not until the 1870s that a significant number of Indians began to own land. After Emancipation the colonial governments, in deference to planters' desire to make it as difficult as possible for labourers to move away from the estates and achieve independence, had sought to inhibit the sale of crown lands.

Diasporic identities are inherently unstable and complex entities, in which allegiances to contemporary and ancestral homelands are variously reconciled, weighted, or compartmentalized (Manuel 1997/1998: 17). In terms of African-Indian relations Trinidad, for instance, Shalini Puri finds that the colonial constructions of 'Indian' and 'African' continue to inform the contemporary formations of the two groups' identities. She notes that it is:

> ... one of the great ironies of decolonization in Trinidad that racial tensions have taken the form of horizontal hostility between blacks and Indians, rather than vertical hostility directed by blacks and Indians together against the economically privileged French Creole elite. Despite an oppositional tradition which has attempted to unite Africans and Indians on the basis of class since the 1930s, hegemonic political discourses have consistently posed African and Indian economic advancement in mutually exclusive terms. The logic of this competition has demanded the discursive production of clearly distinguishable races, along with a vocabulary of 'us' and 'them'. ... One of the striking

features of this antagonism between a racialised 'us' and 'them' is that it draws heavily on the terms of colonial racial discourse, which provides a resonant vocabulary through which Afro- and Indo-Trinidadians structure and express their relational antagonisms today. (1997: 120)

The early days of settlement were very hard and Indians could not have survived without some kind of material and moral support extended by locals. The Indians were well aware of the cultural conditions that governed the transactions for acquiring land. They noticed that the so-called natives did not cultivate land so intensively, and the colonialists had the impression that the natives had more land than they could cope with. Lacking the concept of long-term ownership the natives had never entertained the notion that land could be handed over to people of alien origin. But in course of time when they saw Indians clearing bushes and transforming the landscape in exclusive zones they felt outraged but could not do anything as exclusiveness was now vanishing fast thanks to People's National Movement (PNM) governments free housing schemes which has penetrated deeply into such areas like penal colonies, etc. Interestingly, by being shipped overseas the Africans were severed from their cultural roots more thoroughly than in any known case of international migration. Contrary to this, one finds that after being shipped abroad the Indians became more attached to their culture and religion and did everything to preserve it. It was widely held in the 1830s that Christian doctrines were to keep the indentured labourers and slaves humble and docile and also to legitimize the master's rule as a form of paternalistic guardianship. Though we need not decide whether this was true, yet the religious instruction pioneered by Presbyterians in the long run did not help them develop a genuine culture of their own. Initially, some Indians do seem to have accepted the Presbyterian religion-cultural ethos but they seem to be lost and starving for the Indian culture. In case of plantation economy their encounter did not result in the disappearance of traditional culture, for instance, the most impressive is the popularity of the *Ramayana* and Indian music in Trinidad.[8]

In the Caribbean, too, a Hinduism emerged which was unitary and capable of being followed by Hindus originally drawn from a variety of geographically, linguistically, and caste differentiated traditions. Some of the important lowest common denominators which brought Hindus together in the Caribbean were recognition of a limited pantheon of Sanskritic deities (including Vishnu and his major incarnations as Rama and Krishna, Shiva, Durga, Lakshmi, Ganesha, and Hanuman), an emphasis on Vaishnava devotionalism (bhakti) in ways significantly influenced by north Indian monastic orders such as Ramanandis (and even Ramdasis), the wide popularity of Tulsidas' *Ramayana*, and a general acceptance of the ritual authority of Brahmans. For the Indian immigrants, arriving at common religious beliefs and practices represented the first step in the development of Hinduism as an ethnic religion in the Caribbean. (van der Veer and Vertovec 1991: 153–4)

Although forced labour and punitive actions formed the keynote of the early history of indenture it exacted other types of greater sacrifices from Indians. They were menaced by the introduction and transmission of such previously known and unknown diseases as smallpox, tuberculosis and syphilis to which they were unable to build any resistance initially because of their lack of means to cure.

The historical emergence of Indo-Caribbean identity is one of the many issues that the articles in the present book deal with. A snapshot of each article is presented below.

ABOUT THE VOLUME

What makes Indian diaspora unique in the Caribbean compared to other regions in the world? Apart from constituting a significant proportion of the population in countries like Trinidad and Tobago, Guyana, and Surinam, the Indian culture has had profound influence in every aspect of Caribbean society and has thereby produced the Indo-Caribbean culture.

Radica Mahase's article examines the ways in which Indo-Trinidadian culture evolved over time. Drawing from primary and secondary sources of information from India, England and Trinidad, the article looks at the policies of the British imperial government, the colonial state in Trinidad and the independent government and how they influenced the development of 'Indian culture'. Some of the questions that the article addresses are: What constituted 'Indian culture'? What place did 'Indian culture' carve for itself in the wider society? Were there any attempts over time to syncretize the cultures of Indians with that of Africans—the other numerically dominant group in the society?

Sherry-Ann Singh's article seeks to demonstrate that the *Ramayana* has always been an intrinsic aspect of the life of Trinidadian Hindus and has functioned as both agent and mirror of developments and transformation therein. Although there are several written and oral versions of the *Ramayana,* this article focuses on the *Ramcharitmanas,* the version brought to Trinidad by Indian indentured labourers and how this has become central to the literary, cultural and religious heritage of Indian diaspora in the Caribbean.

Nasser Mustapha's article argues that although the emigration of Indian Muslims to the Caribbean as indentured labourers were small in number in comparison to the dominant group, i.e. Hindus, their emotional attachment to many Indo-Muslim cultural traditions helped in maintaining the solidarity of the group and thus a commitment to what they perceived to be Islam. The article shows how, over a period of time, Islam began to take a unique shape in countries like Trinidad, Surinam and Guyana reflecting the common experiences of the Indian Muslims in the Caribbean.

Sherry-Ann Singh's article examines how Hindus, from their early days Trinidad society, were engaged in the practice of many aspects of their religion.

Although Hindu immigrants carried a slice of their society and hence, religion with them, the uprooting from the Indian context necessitated attempts at community and religious reconstruction. In Trinidad, elements of religion were variously truncated, modified, diluted, intensified or excised. This subsequently yielded a form of Hinduism in which some of the more visible and tangible elements were markedly modified. At the same time, however, the Hinduism which emerged was unarguably rooted in the broad philosophy and general tenets of many of the strands of Hinduism practised in India.

Brinsley Samaroo's article seeks to examine the impact of the Indian Revolt of 1857 on the Caribbean history and the impact on the flow of Indian indentured labour migration to the Caribbean.

Bridget Brereton's article studies some aspects of resistance to enslavement in the Caribbean island, concentrating on the period between 1802 and 1834—the beginning of the indentured labour system. The analysis is also extended to the post-Emancipation period with a brief discussion of the 1849 riots in Port-of-Spain and tries to assess the impact of events in—and people and ideas from—the French Caribbean islands on various kinds of resistance in Trinidad.

Benjie Mahabir's article explores the contribution of Indo-Trinbagonians in an Afro-based political party, the PNM, and examines the intricacies of campaigning in the 2007 elections. It shows that sound constituency campaigning and planning and execution of an effective campaign strategy are key determinants in the winning of elections. It also shows how the Indian supporters of the PNM received benefits especially in terms of jobs, financial assistance and other forms of social assistance.

Rattan Lal Hangloo's article critically examines the economic and political crisis that the Caribbean society faced during the years of British imperialism (from the period of indenture to the period of independence) and how this has been overcome by the efforts of one of the charismatic leaders of the Caribbeans, Dr Eric Williams.

Ann Marie Bissessar's article looks at the trails and tribulations of East Indian female indentured labourers in the Caribbean. After presenting a brief historical overview of the indentureship experience the article tries to focus on the experience of East Indian females during the period of indentureship.

Shaheeda Hussain's article discusses the narratives of economic and labour activities of ex-plantation workers, specifically Indian women in Trinidad, and the role of these women in the economic diversification and development of the island. These, and a number of such issues have been discussed in the volume to throw light upon the lives of the Indian diaspora in the Caribbean.

NOTES

1. Indo-Caribbeans mainly refers to the Caribbean people with roots in the Indian subcontinent.

2. Indenture contracts agreed upon by Indian migrants to the Caribbean involved a five-year period of indenture with provision of return passage, free housing, medical attention and standard rations, in return for work of around nine hours per day, six days per week. Certain aspects of such contracts varied in minor ways between colonies and changed only slightly throughout the period of indentured migration (Vertovec 1995: 60).
3. A historical term for manual labourers from Asia, particularly China and India, in nineteenth century and early twentieth century (http://en.wikipedia.org/wiki/Coolie).
4. The Indians were the preferred choice of the planters in Caribbean, as one of the planters in British Guyana said, 'Give me my heart's desire in Coolies and I will make you million hogsheads of sugar without stirring the colony' (Bronkhrust 1883: 98).
5. Khan (1994: 247) further observes that,

   > for decades among those most subordinate in the social hierarchy, Indo-Trinidadians traditionally have been a strong presence in agricultural production. In addition to continuing estate labor, independent crop growing (notably sugarcane), and subsistence gardening, they undertook other livelihoods, particularly small-scale entrepreneurial activities and manual labor, indicative of an increasing move into a variety of urban and rural occupations.

6. In the Caribbean all persons of Indian origin are known as 'East Indians', as the whole region is commonly referred to as 'West Indies' and its residents as 'West Indians' (MEA 2001: 193). The East Indians are, along with Black Afro-Caribbeans ('West Indians'), one of the two major ethnic groups in Trinidad and Tobago, Guyana and Surinam.
7. Indian migration to the Caribbean was the product of both push/pull theory. Devastating famines, restructuring of revenue and land tenure systems, collapse of the textile industry, mass unemployment and other economic crises which plagued north-eastern India during the latter half of the nineteenth century were some of the important factors for migration of Indians to the Caribbean (van der Veer and Vertovec 1991: 150; see also Roopnarine 2009).
8. I do not deny the acculturation that also produced Indian rock music here which in certain respects lent a synthetic character to it.

REFERENCES

Bates, L. (1912), *The Path of the Conquistadores: Trinidad and Venezuelan Guiana,* Boston: Houghton Mifflin.

Brereton, Bridget (1985), 'The experience of indentureship 1845–1917', in *Calcutta to Caroni: The East Indians in Trinidad,* ed. John La Guerre, St. Augustine: University of the West Indies, Extra Mural Studies Unit.

Bronkhrust, H.V.P. (1883), *The Colony of British Guiana and its Labouring Population,* London.

Eltis, David (2002), *Coerced and Free Migration: Global Perspectives*, Chicago: Stanford University Press.

Erikson, Edgar L. (1934), 'The introduction of East Indian Coolies into British West Indies', *Journal of Modern History,* vol. 6, pp. 127-46.

Hangloo, R.L. (1857), 'A Literary Historical Perspectives in ICFAI University', *Journal of English Studies*, vol. III, no. 3, September 2008.

Jayaram, N. (2006), 'The metamorphosis of caste among Trinidad Hindu', *Contributions to Indian Sociology,* vol. 40, no. 2, pp. 143–73.

Jha, J.C. (1985), 'The Indian Heritage in Trinidad', in *Calcutta to Caroni: The East Indians in Trinidad,* ed. John La Guerre, St. Augustine: University of the West Indies, Extra Mural Studies Unit.

Khan, Aisha (1994), '"Juthaa" in Trinidad: Food, Pollution, and Hierarchy in a Caribbean Diaspora Community', *American Ethnologist,* vol. 21, no. 2, pp. 245–69.

Klass, Morton (1961), *East Indians in Trinidad,* New York: Columbia University Press.

——— (1991), *Singing with Sai Baba: The Politics of Revitalization in Trinidad,* Oxford: Westview Press.

Lawrence, K.O. (1985), 'Indians as permanent settlers in Trinidad', in *Calcutta to Caroni: The East Indians in Trinidad,* ed. John La Guerre, St. Augustine: University of the West Indies, Extra Mural Studies Unit, pp. 134–64.

Look Lai, Walton (1993), *Indentured Labor, Caribbean Sugar: Chinese and Indian Migrants to the British West Indies, 1838–1918,* Baltimore: Johns Hopkins University Press.

Mahabir, Kumar (2008), 'Introduction: An Overview of Indian Diaspora in the Caribbean', *Man in India,* vol. 88, no. 1, pp. 1–4.

Manuel, Peter (1997/1998), 'Music, Identity, and Images of India in the Indo-Caribbean Diaspora', *Asian Music,* vol. 29, no. 1, pp. 17–35.

Ministry of External Affairs (MEA) (2001), *High Level Committee Report on Indian Diaspora,* New Delhi: Indian Council of World Affairs.

Niranjana, Tejaswini (1998), '"Left to the imagination": Indian nationalisms and female sexuality in Trinidad', in *A Question of Silence? The Sexual Economies of Modern India,* Mary John and Janaki Nair, eds., New Delhi: Kali for Women, pp. 111–38.

Pirbhai, Mariam (2009), *Mythologies of Migration, Vocabularies of Indenture: Novels of the South Asian Diaspora in Africa, the Caribbean, and Asia-Pacific,* Toronto: University of Toronto Press.

Puri, Shalini (1997), 'Race, Rape, and Representation: Indo-Caribbean Women and Cultural Nationalism', *Cultural Critique,* no. 36, pp. 119–63.

Ramnarine, Tina K. (1998/1999), 'Historical Representations, Performance Spaces, and Kinship Themes in Indian-Caribbean Popular Song Texts', *Asian Music,* vol. 30, no. 1, pp. 1–33.

Rampersad, Sheila (1998), 'Jahaaji Behen? Feminist Literary Theory and the Indian Presence in the Caribbean', *Occasional Paper No. 1,* Centre for the Study of Indian Diaspora, University of Hyderabad, India.

Rao, Sandy (2000), 'India's Hidden Apartheid: The Caste system and its continuation to the Caribbean and America'. Research Paper: Website: http://saxakali.com/south asia/introduction.htm.

Reddock, Rhoda (1994), *Women, Labour and Politics in Trinidad and Tobago,* London: Zed Press.

Roopnarine, Lomarsh (2009), 'The first and only crossing: Indian indentured servitude on Danish St. Croix, 1863–1868', *South Asian Diaspora,* vol. 1, no. 2, pp. 113–40.

Tinker, Hugh (1974), *A New System of Slavery: The Export of Indian Labour Overseas, 1830–1920,* London: OUP.

Vertovec, Steven (1992), *Hindu Trinidad: Religion Ethnicity and Socio-Economic Change,* London: Macmillan.

——— (1995), 'Indian Indentured Migration to the Caribbean', in *The Cambridge Survey of World Migration,* ed. Robin Cohen, Cambridge: CUP, pp. 57–62.

van der Veer, Peter (1995), *Nation and Migration: The Politics of Space in the South Asian Diaspora,* Philadelphia: University of Pennsylvania Press.

van der Veer, Peter and Steven Vertovec (1991), 'Brahmanism Abroad: On Caribbean Hinduism as an Ethnic Religion', *Ethnology,* vol. 30, no. 2, pp. 149–66.

Waite, Gloria (1982), 'East Indians and National Politics in the Caribbean', *Comparative Studies of South Asia, Africa and the Middle East,* vol. 2, no. 2, pp. 16–28.

1

'Indian' Culture in Trinidad

Transportation, Reconstruction and Integration, 1845–1970

Radica Mahase

> A range of contemporary critical theories suggest that it is from those who have suffered the sentence of history—subjugation, domination, diaspora and displacement—that we learn our most enduring lessons for living and thinking.... It forces us to confront the concept of culture outside *objets d'art* or beyond the canonization of the 'idea' of aesthetics, to engage with culture as an uneven, incomplete production of meaning and value, often composed of incommensurable demand and practices, produced in the act of social survival.
>
> — HOMI BHABHA (1999: 190)

DURING THE PERIOD 1845–1917, approximately 1,47,900 Indians immigrated to Trinidad as indentured labourers.[1] They were brought to provide labour on the sugar cane plantations after the abolition of African enslavement. Trinidad planters saw Indian indentured labourers as a relatively cheap and regular supply of labour that would keep wages down in the colony. British colonization in India and in West Indies meant that the labour scheme would be initiated and implemented relatively easily, as it merely comprised the movement of 'subjects' from one part of the British Empire, to another. By 1920, when the indentureship system was abolished, roughly 25 per cent of the total number of labourers who immigrated to Trinidad was repatriated to the 'Motherland'. Those Indians who remained in Trinidad, for whatever reasons, along with their descendents, contributed to the development of a distinct 'Trinidadian' culture, for which the island is known today.[2] This 'Indian' culture that presently exists in Trinidad, appears to be a diluted version of the culture that Indian immigrants transported from India. It comprises traditions, practices, concepts and ideologies which the Indian immigrants developed over a period of time and which their descendents shaped to fit a society different in many ways from that in India.

This article examines the ways in which Indo-Trinidadian culture evolved over a period of time. It looks at the policies of the British imperial government, the colonial state in Trinidad and the independent government (which came into power in 1962), and how they influenced the development of 'Indian' culture. Therefore, what constituted 'Indian' culture and, what sort of place did 'Indian' culture carve for itself within society in general? Were there any attempts to syncretize the cultures of Indians with that of Africans—the other numerically dominant group in the society? The article offers tentative answers to questions such as these. It draws heavily on a variety of primary sources located in India, England and Trinidad. These include the official documents of the British imperial government and the Government of India such as the records of the Colonial Office; the Proceedings of the Government of India, the Protector of Emigrants Reports and official reports on emigration. Additionally, the censuses of India and Trinidad, newspapers and some records of the indentured labourers have been used in an attempt to reconstruct the cultural facets of Indo-Trinidadian history.

It is interesting to note that the ways in which Indian culture was viewed in India was reflected in the attitudes to 'Indian' culture in Trinidad. While early colonial policies tended to adopt a non-interference attitude, later policies were geared towards the reformation of certain socio-cultural practices such as female infanticide, widows' inability to remarry and sati. The Indians who proceeded to Trinidad as indentured labourers were seen as the 'lucky few' who had opportunity to escape from such 'negative' socio-cultural situations. As a result, when Indian indentured labourers migrated to the West Indian colonies, no particular consideration was given to their cultural practices and the Indian indentureship system was simply viewed in economic terms. Consequently, the attention given to the cultural ideology of the Indians was negligible throughout the indentureship period. In India, culture became significant when the British attempted to institute themselves as a hegemonic power but once the transportation of Indians began there was scarcely any need to place any special prominence to the culture of the Indians. This had serious implications for the manner in which the culture of the Indians was allowed to 'develop' in Trinidad.

TRANSPORTATION AND RECONSTRUCTION

An important aspect was the transportation of 'cultural slices' from India to Trinidad, which was due to a number of factors. First, it is difficult to define a common Indian culture at this point, as India boasted of a multiplicity of religious groups and castes and each village, locality and region was distinct from another. Hence, the cultural traditions that Indians practised in India were specific to their localities, villages, region, and caste and so on. Moreover, culture is not static and cultural identity evolved with time. Consequently, the 'Indian' culture that was transported to Trinidad comprised Aryan, Dravidian, Muslim and Hindu traditions and customs, each in its various manifestations. 'Indian' culture in Trinidad was an amalgam of all of these.

Second, this amalgamation was a creation of the British imperial government to a large extent as its policies towards the recruitment of indentured labourers and Indian emigration in general facilitated the transfer of Indians from a multiplicity of villages, regions, castes and religious groups. As an imperialist construct, the indentureship system emphasized the need to acquire labour, and although certain districts were susceptible to the activities of the recruiters, Indian labourers were recruited across caste, village and religious groups. By 1871, for example, Indian indentured labourers immigrated to Trinidad from a cross section of north Indian—approximately 29 per cent came from Bihar; 41 per cent from central India, Agra, and Oudh; 22 per cent from West Bengal and a handful from Madras, Bombay, Punjab and other areas.[3] A closer look at any one of these areas will make the diversity in villages, regions and localities more visible. For example, those who emigrated from Bihar came from the districts of Champaran, Darbhanga, Gaya, Monghyr, Muzaffarpur, Patna, Saran and Shahabad. With respect to caste, one can see a mixture in the groups that emigrated. In 1898, out of 1,268 emigrants who left for Trinidad from the port of Calcutta, 16 per cent were listed as Brahmins and high castes; 41 per cent as agriculturalists; 7 per cent as artisans and 22 per cent as low castes. Another 14 per cent were listed as Musalmans.[4]

This variety also existed in the religious groups that emigrated, although approximately 80 per cent of all the indentured labourers who docked in Trinidad were Hindus, the different sects of Hinduism were amply represented. Hence, Sanatan Hindus, Vedic Hindus, individuals from the Kabir Panth and Arya Samaj sects immigrated along with a small number of non-mainstream Hindus such as the Shakti worshippers. Added to this were Jains and Buddhists as well as Muslims and a few Christians. For the period 1883-4, for example, the different sects of the Hindu immigrants comprised 82 per cent of the total number of indentured labourers while 17 per cent were Muslims of diverse orientations and the remaining 1 per cent were Christians.[5] This variety in caste, religion, districts and villages meant that the notion of one common cultural tradition did not exist amongst the Indian labourers at the time of recruitment and hence 'cultural slices' were transported to Trinidad.

Third, as British imperialist activities were usually geared towards economic gratification through profit maximization, it became imperative that the cost of transferring labourers from one part of the British Empire to another should be kept as low as possible. In practice, this meant that provisions for the accommodation and shipping of Indian indentured labourers were kept as simple as possible. As a result, all impending immigrants for specific colonies were housed in the same depot. This in turn had serious implications for the cultural legacy that was brought to Trinidad for the identities and cultural traits of the different villages, castes, districts and religions were allowed to either dissolve or continued to exist in what appears to be a diluted form. This occurred as immigrants intermingled while awaiting transport to the colony. Later, when they arrived in Trinidad, they were placed in accommodation and employment areas regardless of caste, religion or district affiliations. Consequently, the mosaic of cultural traditions that were represented in India and amongst the indentured labourers was blended to a certain extent to produce a distinct 'Indian' culture in the Trinidad plantation society. A striking example is the way in which the various caste groups were now placed in situations where they interacted much more than what was possible in India. Specifically, Brahmins and Kshatriyas shared the same accommodation, were said to have slept and ate with Chamars and members of the other low castes.

Once the Indian labourers were resident in the colony, the colonial state adopted an attitude of 'benign neglect' towards their cultural practices. First, the Indians were simply perceived as labourers by the colonial state. As the main concern of the latter was the acquisition of a relatively cheap labour force—which Indian immigrants represented—its policies regarding the Indian indentured labourers in general, were more often than not geared towards the labour that the immigrants would provide. Second, the colonial state neither sanctioned the cultural traditions of the Indian labourers nor supported them. Cultural traditions and practices were curtailed but never oppressed. While every attempt was made to suppress the culture of the African slaves, less repressive measures were adopted with the Indian indentured labourers. Indians were not disallowed to hold cultural activities and occasions such as weddings and readings from the *Ramcharitmanas* (*Ramayana*) were held on plantations throughout the colony on a regular basis. While the cultural practices were never stopped, at the same time, the colonial state neglected them and did not patronize these in any way.

The cultural practices of the Indian indentured labourers were never openly repressed unless they were perceived as anti-colonial and a threat to the colonial state and the peace of the colony. There were general laws regarding the maintenance of peace and order in the colony and any activities that went counter to these laws were suppressed. For example, the colonial government's regulations stipulated that. Indian indentured immigrants were not permitted to enter the towns of San-Fernando or Port-of-Spain when celebrating the annual festival of Hosay. They were not allowed to use sticks and other offensive weapons. Torches or fire sticks were not allowed on any high or public road and they had to obtain licenses in order to conduct their processions. As a relatively large number of Indians normally gathered for the Hosay procession, the colonial state was concerned that they did not disturb the peace of the colony. Therefore, on 31 October 1884 when the immigrants attempted to make their way to the town of San-Fernando the colonial police opened fire and 21 Indians were killed.[6] The Administrator of the colony noted that while the colonial government did not mean to interfere with the religious rites connected with the Hosay festival:

> The regulations are for the sole object of ensuring order throughout the colony and the immigrants cannot, on the ground of religion, claim a right to enter the towns of

Port-of-Spain or San-Fernando, or proceed along the high roads of the colony without the prior permission of the District Magistrate.[7]

Thus, religious traditions in general were allowed as long as they were kept well within the dictates of the law of the colonial state and not seen as a contestation to the power of the colonial state.

In Trinidad, the Indian immigrants themselves were instrumental in reconstructing cultural traditions in the colony. The new 'Indian' culture which emerged appeared to be a diluted form of the culture in the 'Mother Country' (of course this is keeping in mind the fact that culture in India was not static) as certain aspects of the culture that was known in India underwent changes. Despite the fact that Indians emigrated from different villages, castes, religious groups and regions, their cultural legacy came to be viewed as the only commonality amongst them when placed in a foreign, seemingly hostile environment. Homi Bhabha has noted that, 'for victims of colonialism, culture means strategies of survival as much as heritage. . .' (1999: 170). This idea seems most appropriate in the case of the Indian indentured labourers in Trinidad as the recreation of cultural traditions became a means of survival in the host society as well as an attempt to maintain a psychological consciousness of belonging. This was especially so given the fact that the host society was perceived as a hostile one. Consequently, attempts were made to adopt cultural traditions into their everyday lives. However, given a different geographical landscape as well as a social system that was transformed upon arrival in the colony, it was difficult to fully transplant many of the traditions and practices of India. Hence, certain cultural traditions, beliefs and ideologies were modified to adapt to the new environment.

A good example of how traditions and ideologies were reconstructed emerges from a study of the caste system in Trinidad. Inter-caste relationships significantly changed to a large extent in Trinidad, as there was a conspicuous breakdown in caste endogamy. In 1893, the Protector of Immigrants in Trinidad noted that:

> Caste in the colony, though not entirely abolished, is very considerably modified, and I feel confident that were immigration from India to cease now, fifty years from this would find but little trace of caste in the colony, or what might remain so changed that the 'Brahmins' of India would not be able to recognize it. (Comins 1893: 38)

Because of the disproportion in the ratio of males to females in general and specifically within caste groups, inter-caste marriages were tolerated much more in Trinidad. Hence, traditions specific to caste were not allowed much room for growth. It must also be noted that there was a dilution of the concept of pollution which dictated the loss of caste or the unclean nature of anyone who travelled across the 'kala pani'. As the immigrants who had crossed the ocean were already polluted there was little problem with inter-caste interaction. Specifically for members of the higher caste who had already become polluted by the crossing over, he or she could have interacted with anyone, as the individual had nothing to lose in the process.

To some extent, an invention of certain traditions became characteristic of a people who had suffered a spatial history of cultural displacement. Eric Hobsbawm and Terence Ranger noted that, 'tradition which appear or claim to be old are often quite recent in origin and sometimes invented'. Also that, 'they are responses to novel situations which take the form of reference to old situations, or which establish their own past by quasi-obligatory repetition' (Hobsbawm and Ranger 1983: 1). The case of the 'bride price' in Trinidad is a clear example of one way in which the Indian immigrants responded to a 'novel situation'. Whereas the dowry system was prevalent in parts of India, in Trinidad the number of female Indian immigrants was always lower than that of the male immigrants. In fact, from 1845 to 1917, out of the total number of Indian immigrants, 69 per cent were males and 29 per cent females.[8] Therefore, parents of the girl were now able to demand a 'bride price' rather than pay a dowry upon the marriage of their daughters. Hence the dowry system was not reconstructed to any large extent while the 'bride price' instead was invented. Similarly, many immigrants elevated their status in the society by inventing new 'titles' such as 'Maharaj' meant to indicate the newly-invented high caste status of the individual.

Generally, the culture of the Indians was not disturbed to any large extent by the Africans, the other major ethnic group in Trinidadian society. In fact, by 1917, there was no significant cultural interaction between the two races primarily because of limited contact between the two ethnic groups. Reasons for this were twofold. First, the Indian immigrants lived within the plantation and the structure of the contract itself did not leave much time or space for socialization outside of the plantation. Thus, Indian immigrants were not allowed many opportunities to interact with the other races in the society.[9] Second, the movement of Indian immigrants was restricted to some extent as the Indian Immigration Ordinance stipulated that all immigrants had to carry a pass when outside of the plantation to which he or she was assigned. Therefore, whatever interaction occurred was within the confines of the plantation and was limited to that of communication with the plantation managers and overseers. The other door left open for social intermingling of the races was that of education. However, by 1900, only 28 per cent of the total Indian population was attending schools. Of this number, a mere 4 per cent was attending government schools.[10] The majority of the Indian children went to 'coolie' schools, which were established near the plantations to cater specifically for the Indian children. Normally, if the Indians were interested in educating their children they preferred to send them to schools predominantly managed and attended by Indians. In 1893 Revd Moore noted in a letter to the Governor of Trinidad,

> In my Mission Report for 1887–88, I gave it as my emphatic opinion, and this opinion is being strengthened every day, that a mixed school, i.e. for the Creoles and Indians, will be a mistake. An Indian will not send his child to a Creole school. He is afraid of

the injustice being done his child from the Creole teacher, and of ill-usage from the Creole pupils.

Consequently, there was little room for interaction between the two races and mutual feelings of suspicion between the two races began to grow. Thus, over the years a sense of distrust became common and was augmented when there was competition for political power which came with the advent of independence.

ASSERTION AND POTENTIAL INTEGRATION

In the post-indentureship period from about 1920 to 1962, the lack of any conscious attempts to encourage cultural activities amongst Indians in Trinidad by the colonial state was still visible. That the role of the colonial state primarily to promote and support the imperialist aspirations and endeavours of the 'Mother Country' and the policies of the colonial state in Trinidad, with respect to Indians in the colony, did not change to any extent with the end of the indentureship system. At this point, the colonial state became more concerned that cultural attitudes did not become synonymous with anti-colonial sentiments. The Indians had completed their indentureship contracts but most remained engaged in agricultural activities. This meant that they had not climbed beyond the lowest rung of the economic ladder and hence continued to be perceived as economically less worthy than the other groups in society. Furthermore, their culture and social behaviour continued to be seen as strange by the majority of the population mainly because of the limited contact with the Indians. By 1921, the extent to which cultural interaction between Indians and Africans or Indians and any other groups in the society occurred was still limited. The Chinese and Syrians as well as the other European groups were numerically small and tended to confine their activities within their individual group.

What is indeed clear in this period though is the emergence of the Trinidadian Indian middle classes that made conscious attempts to propagate 'Indian' culture in the colony. By 1931, 23 per cent of the total Indian population was literate and approximately 10 per cent of all Indians occupied professional positions in the colony.[11] The 'Indian' culture which they attempted to propagate had one foot deeply-rooted in India—it comprised traditions and practices which resembled those in India, and the other foot resting in Trinidad—certain traditions and practices common at the time of the arrival of the Indians, were now changed to a certain extent.

This group was in the process of attempting to construct its own identity in the wider society for which culture became key. In the first instance, the middle class was going through a process of cultural alienation and in trying to establish an identity it placed prominence on its ancestry. This resulted in a certain consciousness of being 'Indian' or of belonging to a particular ethnic group—a group that viewed itself as culturally and socially different from the other groups in society. This Trinidadian Indian middle class felt alienated in a society that it perceived as hostile and where its members were still viewed as 'coolies' despite the economic advancement it had made. It therefore reacted to what it perceived as a 'hostile environment' by attempting to promote cohesion amongst Indians and thereby asserting the 'rights' of Indians as an ethnic group in the wider Trinidadian society.

This manner of self-perception was brought about, and fuelled by the increase in the number of educated Indians in Trinidad; the emergence of Indian newspapers and organizations, and the establishment of ties with individuals and groups in India—all arising with the emergence of the Indian middle classes. In fact, by 1930, there was the emergence of Indian-only organizations such as an Indian Chamber of Commerce on the economic front. Politically witnessed the formation of the Indian Democratic League, the Young India Party and the East Indian National Congress. In the social sphere, there was much concern for the welfare of less fortunate Indians as evident by the formation of the East Indian Destitute League, the East Indian Night Shelter, the United Welfare Committee and the Home for Destitute Indians.[12]

At the same time there was the emergence of Indian-only newspapers such as the *Koh-i-Noor* (1898), the *East Indian Weekly* (1928), the *East Indian Herald* (1919) and the *East Indian Patriot* (1921) which went a long way in advocating for and encouraging cultural activities in Trinidad. Newspapers such as these did much to encourage the development of what may be called 'Trinidadian Indian nationalism', i.e. a consciousness of belonging to a particular ethnic group. The Indian middle class attempted to establish closer links with individuals, groups and organizations in India and these newspapers were instrumental in this effort. In fact, they were very active in disseminating articles and information published in newspapers in India, specifically those that told of India's struggle for independence and called upon Indo-Trinidadians to support this endeavour. Indians in Trinidad were encouraged to support the Indian National Movement and visitors to the colony included such active personalities as Pundit Jaimini Mehta and Revd Charles Freer Andrews. Some of the Indian nationalists had taken up the case of indentured emigrants in general and Mohandas Gandhi had been very active in South Africa. These visitors did much in encouraging the development and propagation of the culture of India, in the colony.

Generally the middle class Indians in Trinidad were mindful of the need to elevate themselves economically and politically in the colony and once they moved away from agriculture and started to compete for employment in the wider society there appeared to be more attempts at cohesion amongst them. Indian culture and socialization among Indians were used to appeal to the wider Indian community to stimulate integration. According to one article:

> Throughout the colony, in almost every district, there existed some kind of organized Indian group devoted to welfare, social, cultural and religious activities. The dominant principle of organization was race. Indian and even religious groups viewed themselves

as being Indians first.... Indians were the most organized community in Trinidad. (Ryan 1995: 2)

At another level, the local press was used to encourage 'Indian' cultural activities amongst Indians. There were numerous articles in the Indian-only newspapers and periodicals urging Indians to be proud of their cultural heritage, to dress Indian, to get back in touch with their 'roots' and so on. For example, the *East Indian Weekly* chastised Indian women for not reverting to the glorious past of 'Mother India' and not honouring India's traditions, adhering to her customs and obeying her laws;[13] and called on the Trinidadian Indian population to 'marry Indian'.[14] However, the Indian middle classes were most articulate in this 'cultural movement', at least at the national level. Middle class Indians were actively involved in the propagation of 'Indian' culture as this was the group that was attempting to deal with 'identity issues' arising out of a need to establish and distinguish itself in the political and economic life of the country. At the same time, the very concept of what was 'Indian' culture was evolving gradually.

Independence did not bring many changes in the status of 'Indian' culture in Trinidad. In fact, in the post-colonial era, the independent government called for cultural synchronization amongst the different ethnic groups in the society. However, at the same time cultural policies were devised in an *ad hoc* manner. On the eve of independence, Dr Eric Williams (who was to become the first Prime Minister) called on the population to unite as a nation. He said:

On August 31, 1962, a country will be free, a miniature state will be established, but a society and a nation will not have been formed.... Together, the various groups in Trinidad and Tobago have suffered, together they have aspired, together they have achieved. Only together can they succeed. And only together can they build a society, can they build a nation, can they build a homeland.... There can be no Mother India, for those whose ancestors came from India ... there can be no Mother Africa, for those of African origin.... There can be no Mother England and no dual loyalties.... There can be no Mother China...; and there can be no Mother Syria or no Mother Lebanon. A nation, like an individual, can have only one Mother. The only Mother we recognize is Mother Trinidad and Tobago, and a Mother cannot discriminate between her children. (Sutton 1981: 35)

Williams' speech shows his vision of a society where the diverging cultures interacted and where none dominated the other. However, this vision remained a purely theoretical one, as the government did not implement measures to promote cultural integration. The entire concept of cultural unity remained a myth as no concrete policies were implemented to promote cultural activities of Indo-Trinbagonians or other groups such as the Chinese, Syrians or Lebanese.

Cultural interaction between the two numerically dominant groups in society, Afro-Trinidadians and Indo-Trinidadians remained non-existent until the 1970s. This was mainly a result of the political contestation that existed in the society. The post-colonial state in Trinidad was characterized by competition for political power. At the same time, the newly independent government needed to present a neutral front in the light of the diversity of ethnic groups to establish its legitimate status. The post-colonial state was meant to be a democratic one and in this situation, all groups and individuals were supposed to have the liberty to express, actively participate in and propagate its culture. On the one hand, when the doors of colonization were closed and a country was attempting to eradicate the legacy of colonialism it might became rather easy for it to perpetuate a policy totally in contradiction to that which was implemented by the colonial government. So while the colonial state appeared disinterested in cultural policies, the post-colonial state attempted to develop a cultural policy that would advocate integration (at least in theory) of the various ethnic groups, which would encourage sentiments conducive to the further development of the nation. Hence, the idea of the nation became symbolic of a 'Trinidadian' culture—an amalgamation of the cultural legacies of all the ethnic groups in the country.

What is interesting in the case of Trinidad is that the diversity in ethnic groups and the interaction (though limited) which had developed at the grass root level meant that different types of cultural identities could be constructed simultaneously. For example, a person of Indian origin in Trinidad could be actively involved in 'Indian' cultural activities but at the same time, this 'Indian' cultural identity may overlap with the 'Trinidadian' cultural identity. Sometimes they might even come into conflict with each other. What is important to note, is that the post-colonial state did nothing to prevent the conflict that might arise from such interaction. In fact, right up to about 1970 only an ad hoc cultural policy had been developed or incorporated into the agenda of the independent government.

CONCLUSION

> Culture is everything. Culture is the way we dress, the way we carry our heads, the way we walk, the way we tie our ties—it is not only the fact of writing books or building houses. — CESAIRE (1994: 31)

The Indian immigrants brought together the ethnic, regional and religious diversity of India in one space in Trinidad. While the imperial authorities did little to encourage the reconstruction of the traditions transported from India, it allowed the practice of these customs as long as they were kept within the general laws of the colony. However, Indians persisted in the reconstruction and reinvention of the traditions of India and this led to the evolution of an 'Indian' culture in Trinidad that appears as a diluted form, different in many aspects, from what was known in India. In the post-colonial period, limited attempts have been made to syncretize 'Indian' and 'African' culture over the years (most evident with the 'Pantar'[15] and the National Best Village Festival).[16] However, there has been a contestation for cultural, economic and political space by Trinidadians of Indian origin and Trinidadians of African origin. This contestation has never become a physically violent one but it continues up to the present day.

NOTES

1. In 1888, the British colonies of Trinidad and Tobago were united for administrative purposes and Tobago became a ward of Trinidad. In 1845 when Indian indentured labourers immigrated to Trinidad almost all of the immigrants were placed on estates in Trinidad. As a result, there has been a negligible Indian presence on the island. This is the reason why Tobago is not included in this study.
2. The term 'Indian' is commonly used with reference to those who claim citizenship of or belong to the Republic of India. The politically correct term for the descendents of Indian indentured labourers in Trinidad will be Indo-Trinidadians or Trinidadian Indian. However, in everyday interaction within the Trinidadian society it is common to hear someone referred to as 'Indian', 'African' (for a person of African origin) or 'Chinee' (for a person of Chinese origin).
3. 'Annual Report on Emigration from the Port of Calcutta to British and Foreign Colonies for the year 1872'. This report was included in the Proceedings of the Government of Bengal in the Emigration Department, Revenue and Agriculture Department, Government of India, 1898, National Archives of India (hereafter NAI).
4. 'Annual Report on Emigration, 1898', NAI.
5. 'Annual Report on Emigration, 1833-1834', NAI.
6. For more on the Hosay Riots of 1884 refer to Kelvin Singh (1988).
7. Despatch from J. Scott Bushe, Esq., Administrator, Government of Trinidad to Her Majesty's Secretary of State for the Colonies, Proceedings of the Government of Bengal in the Emigration Department, 1885, NAI.
8. The remaining 2 per cent was indistinguishable as the records on the infants who immigrated did not always specify gender.
9. Immigrants were required to work from 5 in the morning to 6 in the afternoon and during the harvest period these hours were sometimes extended.
10. Percentages calculated from statistics given in the Census of Trinidad, 1901.
11. Census of Trinidad, 1931. The total Indian population comprised Indians born in India as well as those born in Trinidad. The majority of the professional Indians were employed as teachers, government clerks and proprietors.
12. This information is taken from various articles in the *East Indian Weekly* from 1928 to 1930.
13. *East Indian Weekly,* Saturday, 24 November 1928, p. 4.
14. Ibid., Saturday, 6 April 1919, p. 10.
15. This is a mixture of the music of the steel pan that is the national instrument of Trinidad and the sitar.
16. Competition based on the culture of the different villages in Trinidad. All cultures are represented in this nationwide competition.

REFERENCES

Bhabha, Homi (1999), 'The Postcolonial and the Postmodern: the question of agency', in *The Cultural Studies Reader*, Simon During, ed., London: Routledge, pp. 170–90.

Cesaire, Aime (1994), 'Address to the World Congress of Black Writers and Artists in Paris', in *The Whole World Book of Quotations: Wisdom from Women and Men around the globe throughout the centuries,* Kathryn Petras and Ross Petras, eds., New York: Perseus Publishing.

Comins, D.W.D. (1893), *Note on Emigration from India to Trinidad,* Calcutta: Bengal Secretariat Press.

Hobsbawm, Eric and Terence Ranger (1983), *The Invention of Tradition,* Cambridge: CUP.

Petras, Kathryn and Ross Petras (1994), *The Whole World Book of Quotations: Wisdom from Women and Men around the globe throughout the centuries,* New York: Perseus Publishing.

Ryan, Selwyn (1995), 'Communalism vs. Cosmopolitanism: Indian response to national politics in Trinidad and Tobago', Paper presented at Conference on 'Challenge and Change: The Indian Diaspora in its Historical and Contemporary Contexts', August, St. Augustine: University of the West Indies.

Singh, Kelvin (1988), *Bloodstained Tornbs: The Muharram Massacre 1884,* London: Macmillan Caribbean.

Sutton, Paul (1981), *Forged from the love of liberty: selected speeches of Dr Eric Williams,* Port-of-Spain: Longman Caribbean.

2

The *Ramayana* in Trinidad

A Socio-Historical Perspective

Sherry-Ann Singh

PERHAPS THE MOST celebrated product of the Trinidad Hindu community, V.S. Naipaul, described the *Ramayana* as something that 'lived among us' and as 'something I had already known' (2000: 12). Working along such assumptions, this article seeks to demonstrate that the *Ramayana* has always been an intrinsic aspect of the Trinidad Hindu society and has functioned as both agent and mirror of developments and transformation therein. Although there are several hundred written and oral versions of the *Ramayana,* this article focuses on the *Ramcharitmanas,* the recension brought to Trinidad by Indian indentured labourers. Composed by the saint-poet Tulsidas around 1574, it has been central to the literary, cultural and religious heritage of India (Lutgendorf 1991) and almost every other country of the Indian diaspora. Original neither in terms of plot nor theme, the *Ramcharitmanas* is an interpretation of the Valmiki myth of Rama, with influences and borrowings from other prominent texts of sixteenth-century India.

APPEAL OF THE *RAMAYANA*

During the period of indenture a total of 1,43,939 Indians migrated to Trinidad (Brereton 1981: 103), approximately 88 per cent of whom practised various kinds of Hinduism. Since the beginning of the Indian presence in Trinidad, the *Ramcharitmanas* has occupied the unchallenged position of '*Dharmashastra* par excellence' in all facets of Trinidadian Hinduism, providing 'the major framework of the theological edifice of Hindu migrants' (Haraksingh 1984: 19). During the indenture period, the vast majority (over 90 per cent between 1876 and 1879) of the indentured immigrants originated from regions in Uttar Pradesh and Bihar (Brereton 1981: 103), which were by then deeply immersed in the Bhakti tradition and hence permeated by Tulsidas' encapsulation of it. This can account for the *Ramcharitmanas* quickly becoming a religious, social, cultural and emotional anchor for the early indentured labour in an alien and often hostile environment.

The specifically diasporic appeal of the *Ramcharitmanas* was based on numerous factors. Its focus on the Bhakti tradition served as a link to the emotional and cultural ethos of the motherland. Its treatment of the exile theme provided immense solace and emotional support ('a balm for troubled minds') (Bahadur 1976: 11) to the immigrants who, considering their indenture as a type of exile, identified with the trials and tribulations of Rama in the text, while upholding his dignity and endurance as an ideal worthy of emulation in their own situation. The idea of exile and return that runs deep in the text provided yet another point of identification and solace, since many, especially in the earlier phases of indenture, nurtured the hope of returning to the Motherland one day.

The uncomplicated nature of the story, along with a clearly established dichotomy between good and evil rendered it an appropriate authority in the attempts of the Trinidad Hindu community at reconstruction and reconsolidation. Stories from the *Ramayana* made an impact on the Hindu, and sometimes non-Hindu perceptions of the new environment to the extent that the significant unknown 'other', or potentially threatening agents, such as white colonial oppressors and Trinidadians of African descent, were referred to as 'Ravan' (the villain of the story). The *Ramcharitmanas*' focus on interpersonal relationships provided both positive and negative models for the reconstruction of both family and community networks. Since many aspects of caste interaction in India could not be obtained overseas (Vertovec 1992: 34), the *Ramcharitmanas*' propensity for non-casteist interpretation (though this depended on the interpretor) proved extremely applicable to the Hindu community in Trinidad.

SOCIO-RELIGIOUS CONTEXT

In Trinidad, the *Ramcharitmanas* has shared the position of textual supremacy with the *Bhagvad Purana* and the *Bhagvadgita,* with other texts serving largely to reinforce or extrapolate the arguments, state of affairs and directives of these principal texts. It is possible to identify two dimensions of the textual sphere: the formal—namely the yagna forum, and the popular—namely satsangs. From the earliest post-indenture attempts at community reconstruction until the 1950s, the *Bhagvad Purana* was the primary text of focus at yagnas, which were popularly referred to as *Bhagwats.*[1] This status quo was maintained until the 1970s (Vertovec 1992: 165–6), when the *Ramcharitmanas* (and hence, *Ramayana* yagnas) began eclipsing the *Bhagvad Purana.* By the 1960s, the rise of English as the primary mode of communication among Hindus increasingly relegated the Hindi language to the more intimate, domestic and religious spheres of life. Simultaneously, the marked decline in the knowledge of Sanskrit, and rise in the popularity of other Hindi religious literature served to endorse Hindi as a 'quasi-religious language', a category previously reserved for Sanskrit. This, together with the unchallenged popularity of the *Ramcharitmanas* among ordinary Hindus, and the fact that, by the 1950s, that text was being referred to as the *Pancham Veda* or 'Fifth Veda' accounted for its ultimate ascendancy over the *Bhagvad Purana* in the formal dimension of the textual sphere of Trinidad Hinduism. While the *Ramcharitmanas* retained its position of textual supremacy, increasing trends towards a more philosophical, intellectual, spiritual and analytical approach towards religion had, by 1990, created a growing space for the highly philosophical and spiritual *Bhagvadgita* in the formal aspect of the Hindu textual tradition.

The textual tradition that developed with respect to the *Ramayana* in Trinidad can be understood within the framework of several equally active notions: that of 'text as encyclopedia', 'text without boundaries' and 'text as living document'. Text as encyclopedia hinges on the following widely held opinion that every aspect of society and daily life should be represented in it.[2] Indeed, from providing emotional solace to Indians in indenture, to forming part of the 1990s political dialogue of the country, the *Ramcharitmanas* was applied to almost every aspect of the Trinidad Hindu experience. Its capacity to cut across the restrictions of time, space, circumstance and accommodate almost any issue—due largely to its malleability to multiple meanings and interpretations—resided at the core of its function as 'encyclopedia'.

The notion of text without boundaries points to the intertextuality of the tradition; that is to say, the constant use of material from other sources to substantiate events and arguments of the text. By the late 1970s, the changing face of Hinduism in Trinidad and the increasing appearance of other versions mandated a reconsidering of the approach to the many variations of the Rama story. It was, by then, general knowledge that the *Ramcharitmanas* was but one of numerous versions of the former, and also that the Valmiki *Ramayana* was the first written version. Realizing that the various versions of the Rama story could no longer be ignored, textual exponents began including elements of the latter in their discourses. However, aspects that posed any possibility of a threat to the supremacy and major prescriptions of the *Ramcharitmanas* were either omitted or reworked. This attitude was evident in explanations such as the following:

> We need to be careful when making that kind of reference because many episodes that are present in *Valmiki Ramayana* are not in Tulsi's *Ramayana,* and some in Tulsi that are not present in Valmiki, certain details. We need to be careful not to confuse our people as to what really happened. Both are correct. It's just that Tulsi has written the details as he perceived. He has chosen the facets of life of Shri Ram that meant greatest to him.[3]

Besides versions of the Rama story, other texts too were involved in this practice of intertextuality. The recurrence of the same characters and similar events in different texts was the major source of this interconnectedness. The growing demand for more intellectual, philosophical and rational approaches to and analyses of religion to supplement and sometimes even subsume the previous focus on unquestioning faith and devotion, was a primary underlying motive for this practice of intertextuality, especially since the late 1980s. The ability to draw reference across a range of texts substantially enhanced the expounder's degree of competence and knowledge. This, in turn, augmented his appeal as a figure of religious authority.

Inadvertently, the rise of a marked number of subsects during the 1990s generated diverse attitudes to the issue of cross-referencing and intertextuality. A leading figure of the Society Working for the Advancement of Hindu Aspirations (SWAHA) for instance, saw what he referred to as 'cob webbing' of the scriptures as more applicable and beneficial to Trinidad Hinduism. Arguing that the multiplicity of texts was potentially confusing, he proposed the retention of the *Ramayana* as a doctrine on behaviour, the *Bhagvadgita* as a source of philosophy, and the *Bhagvad Purana* to support both.[4] Incorporated in Trinidad and Tobago in 1993, SWAHA is embedded in the Shankaracharya tradition in India, which is an extremely orthodox thread of Sanatan Dharma based on the Advaita Vedanta (the sixth branch of Indian philosophy). Another organization, the Chinmaya Mission, initiated in Trinidad by Swami Chinmayananda during the 1960s but revived and formally established in 1997 by Brahmachari Prem Chaitanya, has metaphysics or Vedanta as its focus. While admittedly using the *Ramcharitmanas* to promote Vedantic philosophy, and supporting Rama's divine status and the 'encyclopedic' character of the text (slipping in that 'Tulsidas intended it also'), the Mission proposed that focus on the *Bhagvadgita* and the *Upanishads* would better meet the requirements of the 'new' intellectual and philosophical approach to Hinduism. In fact one of the major objectives of this organization is the revival of these texts in Trinidad and Tobago.[5]

Members of the Sathya Sai Baba Organization in Trinidad (rejuvenated in 1983) adhere to the teachings of non-discrimination, love, peace and social service as was advocated by their guru in India. They claim to hold the *Ramayana* and all other religious texts in the same reverence as the 'orthodox' Hindus, and work the teachings of the texts into their discourses 'on Baba's advice' explaining that 'Baba is the same said Rama ... he says that devotees must go out and propagate the *Ramayana*'.[6] The Brahma Kumaris Raja Yoga Meditation Centre was founded in Trinidad in 1975 during the visit of Sister Hemlata, a senior member of the organization in India. With their focus on matters such as the mind, spirit, consciousness, soul and energies and their interpretation of 'God is light', followers of this organization view Rama as just a deity 'parallel to Christ, Buddha and Mohammed'.[7] They consequently 'look at the spiritual aspect and meaning of the *Ramayana*' instead of the 'physical (literal) meaning' and use such examples in their discourses.[8]

It is evident that each of these organization was engaged, in one way or the other, in manipulating Hindu religious texts to meet their respective objectives and orientations. That each acknowledged the primacy, if not divinity, of the *Ramcharitmanas* among Trinidad Hindus evinced both the status of the text and the recognition of the benefits to be had from its popularity and its socio-religious application. Thus, even though in theory this text may not have been as applicable to their specific orientations, the widespread and deep-seated appeal of the *Ramcharitmanas* mandated its inclusion or reworking into the ideologies of almost any religious organization that hoped to gain a substantial Hindu following in Trinidad. In summary, an absolute denial of the socio-religious validity of the *Ramcharitmanas* was not an option for Trinidad Hinduism.

DISSEMINATION

The methods of transfer of knowledge of the *Ramayana* have been considerably conditioned by the socio-economic conditions of the Hindu community. Before the 1970s, the *pathshala,* usually located in the village *kutiyas* or temples, was the principal avenue for teaching Hindi and the dissemination of scriptural knowledge. Newspaper sources since the late 1920s provided ample evidence of the presence of such institutions in areas occupied by Indians. Frequently, both young Brahmin and non-Brahmin boys and girls were tutored indiscriminately by village elders, a sadhu (or time permitting, a pundit) in Hindi. This followed a very structured system that commenced with the Hindi alphabet and culminated in the reading of texts such as the various *chalisas* and the *Ramcharitmanas.* At that point the cleavage between the formal and popular traditions took root. While the non-Brahmins continued using the *kutiya* as a base and forum for their weekly or bi-weekly discourses, the Brahmins usually enhanced this knowledge with further formal education on rites, rituals, texts, philosophy and the trade of *punditai* (Hindu priesthood) under the astute guidance of their fathers (themselves usually pundits) and gurus.[9]

From the 1930s there were sporadic attempts at promoting the *Ramayana* on a slightly more public level. For example, during the 1938 celebrations of the birth of Rama (Rama Naumi), the Sanatan Dharma Board of Control (in Trinidad) organized competitions in *Ramayana* chanting, and *Ramayana* related poetry, bhajan singing, dialogues and essay writing.[10] The establishment of Hindu primary and secondary schools by the Sanatan Dharma Maha Sabha (SDMS) and other Hindu organizations from the 1950s fulfilled the need to include religion and the *Ramayana* into the formal education system. Amidst the infusion of Hinduism into the daily school life at all SDMS schools, the primary schools' Baal Vikaas festival (a festival/competition showcasing children's skills and knowledge in various aspects of Hindu culture) initiated in 1986, added to the *Ramayana* tradition both with its *Ramayana* studies quiz and its *Ramayana* singing competition. This novel introduction of a dimension of the *Ramayana* tradition into the Hindu primary school system proved quite effective in creating an early awareness of and affinity for the tradition among the younger members of the Hindu and sometimes, non-Hindu community. Also, by the 1970s, the rise of Indian cultural and educational institutions in Trinidad provided more formal avenues for learning Hindi, a prerequisite of textual interpretation.

DIMENSIONS OF THE *RAMAYANA* TRADITION IN TRINIDAD

The *Ramayana* tradition in Trinidad comprises many dimensions, the most long-standing of which is undoubtedly the *Ramleela* (depiction of the Rama story in dramatic form). Other aspects include films, dance, dance dramas, art, literature, song and music. Each would reflect the symbiotic relationship between the Ramayana and socio-religious transformation among Hindus in Trinidad.

The *Ramayana* has also encompassed the major life cycle rituals of birth, marriage and death which comprised the important socio-religious events in the lives of most Hindus. Changes in the rituals mirrored the evolution of the socio-religious aspect of Trinidad Hinduism, and by extension, changes in the attitude towards the *Ramayana*. Until the 1970s, a vital aspect of the sixth and twelfth day birth rituals (*chhati* and *barahi* respectively) was the celebratory singing of songs, many of which depicted the birth and childhood of Rama and his brothers.

The impact of the *Ramayana* on the Hindu wedding ceremony has been substantial, enduring and diverse. While there was no direct reading of the text, the formal and informal discourse during the ceremony entailed elaborate descriptions of the marriage of Rama and Sita, emphasizing the divine couple as a role model for the newly-weds. Within this context, verses from the *Ramcharitmanas* were recited. While there may not have been much variation in the choice of verses at wedding ceremonies, there was a reworking of the points of emphasis, especially with regard to spousal relations. However, what really cemented the impact of the *Ramayana* on the Hindu wedding ceremony was the fact that, despite the transformations generated by time, place and circumstance, the core rituals and their basic format of the Hindu marriage ceremony corresponded significantly to those contained in the *Ramcharitmanas.*

The presence of the *Ramayana* in death ceremonies and rituals changed over time. Until the late 1960s, relevant verses from the *Ramcharitmanas* were sung in a suitably forlorn tone during the procession to the cemetery or, less frequently, to the cremation site. This was eventually overtaken by pre-recorded verses from the *Ramcharitmanas* played at first within the confines of the hearse, and by the 1980s, amplified for public acknowledgement of the procession. This transformation was evoked by factors such as the legalization of Hindu cremations, and the opening of cremation sites situated away from the villages (thus making the walking procession almost impossible), along with the substantial rise in vehicle-ownership and the use of heavy Western-style coffins. For about ten to fourteen days following the death of an individual, recitations from the *Ramayana* were conducted at the home of the departed by popular

Ramayanists. These nightly satsangs served as an immense source of comfort and solace for the bereaved family.

Throughout the 1990s, the revitalizing trends, attempts at introducing new India-based elements and the rise of a significant number of subsects under the umbrella of Trinidad Hinduism generated numerous less enduring manifestations of the *Ramayana* tradition. These manifestations included a *Ramayana Utsav* in 1996,[11] *Ramayana Yatras* (processions), and *Ramayana* chanting marathons and conferences. In 1995, the Divali Nagar organization had as its theme 'This *Ramayana* Country', showcasing the many facets of the local *Ramayana* tradition wherein a *Manas mandir* (temple of the *Ramcharitmanas* depicting the various elements of the *Ramayana* tradition was erected (*Trinidad Guardian,* 30 May 1996). The Hindu Prachar Kendra introduced the annual *Mantra Vimochan* (Mantra of the Year) event, wherein issues of community and national importance were highlighted through a sacred verse from the Hindu *Shaastras.*[12] In addition, in 1997, Tulsidas' 500th birth anniversary was celebrated at the *Ganga Dashara,* and a 108-night *Ramayana* reading marathon (*Gyaan Tirath*) was held, at which the *bedi* or altar for the rituals was shaped as a map of Trinidad.

THE *RAMAYANA* TRADITION AS DOCTRINE

The validity of the *Ramcharitmanas* as a social doctrine is evident in the great influence which the ethics, morals and values of the text has had on Hindus in Trinidad. Its codes of conduct are presented through concrete, convincing characters in crises, rendering them more easily comprehensible than abstract philosophical and moral expression. The major characters are faced with situations which parallel the challenges of everyday life even while they deal with real temptations. When they fall from grace, the opportunity is provided to revaluate the boundaries of ethical behaviour. Among Hindus in Trinidad, the nature of revaluation was determined by changing attitudes towards social institutions and codes of conduct, arising from social, economic and academic transformation as well as from continuous interaction with non-Hindu influences. The increasing visibility of individuals and groups advocating a more pragmatic approach to religion also led to new textual interpretations and shifts.

Furthermore, Hindu family life in Trinidad too has been greatly influenced by the values prevalent in the *Ramcharitmanas.* The text highlights various forms of interpersonal relationships, outlines acceptable tenets of behaviour and provides role models for almost all categories: Rama is the ideal husband and son; Sita the ideal wife, daughter and daughter-in-law; Bharat and Lakshman are ideal brothers; Hanuman and Sugriva are ideal friends. The transformation of the Hindu family structure from the extended to an increasingly nuclear one mandated a grudging de-emphasis of the structure and values of the traditional extended family during textual discourses. Thus, while Rama's dedication to his father and the love that existed among the four brothers were still accentuated, situations such as the four brothers living together with their respective families in the same home, and Sita's unwavering dedication to her husband either went reconsidered or downplayed. Consequently, instead of focusing on Sita's unquestioning obedience to her in-laws, as would have been done before the 1970s, now mutual respect, love and admiration were emphasized as the defining and desirable traits of that particular relationship.

During the 1970s, the increasing primacy of the sense of individualism over kinship relations further detracted from a wholesale acceptance of the traditional presentation of family relations in the *Ramcharitmanas*. By the late 1980s, family relationships, excluding perhaps those involving parents, were becoming increasingly reciprocal in nature, especially in terms of the level of respect and interaction. In this setting, even the presentation of parent-child relations as depicted in the *Ramcharitmanas* was becoming increasingly problematic. The idea of unchallenging obedience and loyalty to parental dictates emphasized in verses such as the following evoked ambiguity, though it usually went unvoiced and at times tinged with guilt:

> *Mor tumhaar param purushaarthu, swarathu sujasu dharamu paramaarthu.*
>
> For us two brothers, you as well as myself, the highest achievement of our human life, nay, our material gain, our glory, our virtue and our highest spiritual gain consist in this that both of us should obey our father's command. (*Sri Ramcharitmanas,* des. 2, verse 314.2)

Despite the increasing subscription to the more 'modern' family structure and ideologies, the strong sense of filial obligation inherent in traditional Indian society frequently generated remorseful feelings of inadequacy among offspring with regard to taking care of infirm parents.

The *Ramayana* has always had an undeniable impact on the position and role of women in both the family and society at large. The essentially patriarchal family system that developed during the early post-indenture period held Sita—chaste, submissive, faithful and loyal to her husband—as the highest ideal of womanhood. Verses such as the following also served to cement the notion of women as morally, intellectually, spiritually, physically and socially inferior to men:

> *Mahaabrishti chali phooti kiaaree, jimi sutantra bhae bigarahi naaree.*
>
> The embankments of the fields have been breached by rains just as women get spoiled by freedom. (*Sri Ramcharitmanas,* des. 4, verse 14.3)

Since then, and especially since the 1980s, numerous issues have demanded constant reconsideration of projections of women in the *Ramcharitmanas* as well as in some of the ways in which it is interpreted. Such issues included the changing concept of the ideal Indian wife and woman; the increasing sense of individualism among Hindu women; the changing role of women in rites, rituals and religion; the rapidly increasing numbers of women in almost all fields of occupation; and the shifts in priority.

Since the earliest attempts at reconstruction of community, the Hindu community has held the text of the *Ramayana* as a primary sanctioning element in religious and social matters. Thus, despite the pre-1970s dominance of the *Bhagvatpurana* in the formal yagna setting, among Hindus the *Ramayana* functioned like the Bible among Christians and the Koran among Muslims with respect to the taking of oaths. This occurred quite frequently at panchayat mediations in the village and even in the domestic sphere during more serious family disputes that occasioned the act of taking an oath. Before the 1950s, the *Ramayana* (and very rarely the *Hanuman Chalisa*) shared this sanctioning function with water (imbued with the holiness ascribed to the water of the Ganges in India) and the *lota,* the brass vessel containing the water. The eventual transplantation of this practice of swearing by the 'Ganges water' to swearing on the *lota* alone was explained by statements such as '... when they hold the *lota* it means that they swear by Ganga. Ganga does not only mean water, Ganga also means purity'.[13] Ironically enough, even though the *Bhagvadgita* had hardly performed such a sanctioning role within the Hindu community this text superseded the *Ramayana* in 1986 at the swearing in of the first Hindu Minister of the Parliament.

While the popular dimension of the *Ramayana* tradition was not greatly underscored by caste considerations, the yagna—the formal sphere of textual presentation—was the exclusive domain of Brahmin pundits until the 1970s. However, the 1980s witnessed a substantial growth in the number of non-Brahmins officiating at yagnas. The widespread practice of non-Brahmin *Ramayana* readers officiating at the less formal and informal satsangs, since the earliest days of indenture, eventually extended into the yagna forum with the entrance of the *Ramcharitmanas* into that domain. The increasing leniency towards caste considerations in ritual and religious matters, and the conscious and unconscious drive to rework Hinduism to include the values and nuances of the society and changing times accounted for this transformation.

This was met with mixed and interesting reactions from both the Brahmin and non-Brahmin population. Non-Brahmin religious aspirants and pundits focused on the seemingly anti-caste incidents from the *Ramcharitmanas* and other religious texts to validate their equal right to textual presentation. Many were quite emphatic in denouncing Brahmanic attempts at retaining their pretensions to exclusivity in this sphere. Some even referred to the association of caste with the division of labour to argue their point of view, as in the following remark: 'People who preach caste don't practice it. All pundits' sons are not pundits, but they are doing other people's occupations, due to the "almighty dollar".'[14] Within the Brahmin fold, there were two discernible attitudes towards this issue. Some, obviously considering the indisputable reality of the presence of non-Brahmins in the ritual and textual sphere and concerned with popular appeal offered views (sometimes grudgingly) such as 'many non-Brahmins are already pundits so you have to accept them, once they fulfil the role properly'.[15] However, the more orthodox Brahmins vehemently opposed this practice.

Even as early as the 1920s, there were female readers of *Ramayana* in Trinidad. The reaction towards them was ambivalent. The intrinsic love and affinity for the *Ramayana* among ordinary people served to suppress outright condemnation of female readers. However, the patriarchal norms and attitudes of the pre-1970s period, enhanced by the many ritual prescriptions restricted textual presentation by women both in terms of frequency and scope. Both the idea and the reality of female presence on the sacred *singhasan* evoked interesting responses which reflected the varying trends of thought within the community. The prevalent attitude of the priesthood, both Brahmin and non-Brahmin, was one of grudging resignation to women 'preaching Hinduism' and even reading the *Ramayana,* but only in informal settings, and definitely not on the *singhasan* at yagnas. Their arguments were largely founded upon scriptural prescriptions and the impurities associated with the menstrual cycle. Since the late 1980s, however, this has been tempered with the reality of female socio-economic and intellectual advancement, the enhanced religious position and role of women especially within many of the rapidly increasing Hindu groups. Attempts to simultaneously retain male and Brahminic monopoly in this sphere, and accommodate the mindset of the contemporary Hindu woman and society at large, elicited responses such as the following:

> When we look at our scriptural texts we are hard-pressed to find evidence of women holding priestly positions. Women have been assigned a very honorable position, a very high position in that they are the *Devi,* the very Goddess in our homes. ... It is not to say that women are debarred from elevating themselves spiritually.[16]

Notwithstanding the more liberal approach to women of some new Hindu organizations such as the Hindu Prachar Kendra and the Trinidad Academy of Hinduism, popular opinion, until the 1990s, revealed reservations towards (though not as deep-seated or as endemic) or outright acceptance of women acting as ritual and textual specialists. Non-acceptance was more marked especially in the yagna setting. This echoed both a characteristic reluctance in the religious sphere to effect such a monumental transformation and the still evident though often denied patriarchal tendencies of the Hindu community. Nevertheless, the 1990s witnessed the advent of the first woman to conduct formal *Ramayana* yagnas.

HINDU LEADERSHIP

Since the period of indenture, Hindu leadership was largely directed by Hindu religious texts, especially by the *Ramcharitmanas.* As a text that revolves around polity, administration, diplomacy and war, it also details the benefits of good government and democracy as exemplified in the *Ramrajya* (the reign of Rama; an Utopian state) while the contrary is shown under the rule of Ravan. This political dimension has always played an important role in both the reconstruction and sustenance of Hindu life in Trinidad. While the obvious difference in time, place, social and political contexts did not allow for the wholesale application of the political systems and codes of the *Ramayana* in Trinidad, the principles of good government and leadership outlined in the text were very interestingly worked into the local situation. Rama's embodiment of the perfect leader was constantly alluded to in the community's search for and affirmation of its own figures of authority. The principles of *Ramrajya*—peace, justice and reverence of socio-religious authority—were presented and seemingly accepted as the ideal among local Hindus. Conversely, the text's anti-hero, Ravan, illustrated the epitome of corrupt leadership.

Before the 1940s, *Ramayana* politics was apparent only within the Hindu community, influencing matters such as constitution of panchayat and its decisions, and the selection of immediate community leaders. However, there were sporadic instances when *Ramayana* politics was extended beyond the boundaries of the Hindu community. For example, in a 1939 newspaper article reporting that local Indians 'unanimously passed a resolution of loyalty to the British Raj', the political situation in the *Ramayana* was analogized to World War II as follows:

> The love of the Mother of Bharata was that of Hitlerism. She was rebuked by her son because it was based on deceit; so the righteous sons of Germany are saying (or will someday say) to Hitler: we do not thank you for the throne of Poland (and other countries). Britain, like unto Lachmana is being told (and will be told) to do its duty by assisting France, for therein lies the support of righteousness. (*Port-of-Spain Gazette,* 1 October 1939)

In the panchayat's function as mediator and judge of social problems, the *Ramayana* provided a source of reference, guide and confirmation in decision making, and also a source of divine yet human role models for both community and family life. Thus, for example, the very troublesome but socially sanctioned issue of oral promises would be supported by reference to Rama's renouncing of kingship to fulfil his father's promise, and by quoting verses such as the following:

> *Ragukul reeti sadaa chali aayee, praan jaayee baru vachana na jayee.*
>
> It has always been the rule that one's plighted word must be redeemed even at the cost of one's life. (*Sri Ramcharitmanas,* des. 1, verse 27.2)

Conflict among siblings over issues of inheritance frequently evoked references to the relationship between Rama and his brothers and how they dealt with succession. Marital discord almost always occasioned a lauding of Rama and Sita's 'ideal' relationship, with an intrinsically patriarchal focus on

Sita's unwavering dedication to her husband, even in the face of substantial odds.

Since the 1980s, however, the steadily increasing Hindu presence in the political arena culminating in the election of a Hindu Prime Minister and a government comprising a significant percentage of Indians, imparted national significance and ramifications to '*Ramayana* politics'. Both national and community figures and leaders (pundits, gurus, counsellors and socio-religious leaders) began highlighting and reworking ideas in the *Ramayana* such as *Ramrajya,* Rama's ideal portrayal of kingship, leadership, loyalty, nature and functions of ministers, political harmony, selflessness, cooperation, and the primacy of the state and subjects in their bid to influence their audience. The merits of both Rama and his rule were often attributed to leader and party respectively, while opposing parties were inadvertently 'Ravanized'. Comparisons between the ideals of *Ramrajya* and the local political situation were common at both yagnas and satsangs, as well as at rum shops. That both young and old, whether at yagna or rum shop, regardless of the varying levels of formal education, related to and analysed current affairs within the framework of the *Ramayana* highlights the pervasiveness of the *Ramayana* text and tradition.

The permeable lines between the sacred and the secular, together with the pervasiveness of Hinduism in all dimensions of life, led to an increasing use of yagnas and satsangs as political platforms. Hopeful political aspirants capitalized on the religious atmosphere of these gatherings to gain the support of the Hindu audience, and usually correlated their own political ideologies to that of the *Ramayana.* Not surprisingly, this mixing of the sacred and the secular in that particular framework generated considerable conflict.

TEXTUAL PRESENTATION

The actual occasions for presentation of religious texts have provided some level of elucidation on what the Hindu community held as important enough to warrant association with the divine, and also on some aspects of its evolving social and religious lifestyle. They also mirrored the changing boundaries and relationship between the sacred and the secular. Since the earliest days of indenture, satsangs were an important aspect of both the religious and social life of Hindus. These weekly or fortnightly readings hosted in rotational fashion among different families persisted in the villages during the early post-indenture period. The Presbyterian missionary K.G. Grant testified to the popularity of such satsangs, noting that '... snatches or *slokas* from this great epic (the *Ramayana*) are often heard in song, accompanied by cymbals and drums, when the days work is over...' (1923: 71). By the 1930s, the substantial rise in the number of temples and *kutiyas* (Prorok 1988) provided another setting for such communal readings, both as an extension of the existent weekly or fortnightly system, and by hosting the very popular monthly communal 'full moon *katha'* (puja performed on the full moon day of each month). Such readings also formed an integral part of the annual 'ritual complex' (Vertovec 1992: 115) of pujas extending from Friday through Sunday, and performed in almost every Hindu household. That the puja held on Saturday was dedicated to Hanuman, a major character in the *Ramayana,* also accounted for the inclusion of readings from that text on Saturday nights.

As mentioned earlier, the death of an individual also occasioned readings and chanting from the texts. Popular and pertinent verses from the *Ramcharitmanas* were chanted by members of the funerary procession on the way to the cemetery, and readings were conducted by laymen for between 10 and 14 days afterwards, and at the six month or one-year death anniversary. These provided a measure of spiritual and emotional solace for the bereaved family. Finally, the fulfilment of 'promises' made in the quid pro quo style characteristic of divine-human relations especially regarding events such as a fruitful agricultural season, a child's outstanding academic achievement, recovery from a serious illness, and travel overseas occasioned both satsangs and, less frequently, yagnas.

By the 1970s, economic advancement and the increasing influence of non-Hindu ideas both increased the frequency and altered the spectrum of occasions for textual discourses. Added to pujas, promises and death, the emphasis on birthdays, wedding anniversaries and personal achievements and successes variably provided increasing forums for satsangs and yagnas. Individuals were also more economically equipped to simply fulfil a desire to host both satsangs and yagnas; the latter unavoidably leading to a simultaneous decline of the panchoutie yagna. Reflecting the infusion of the religious essence of Hinduism into practically all other dimensions of life, textual discourses, in this sense, trod on the heels of the social, economic and political ascension of the Hindu community as well as expansion—both within the community and in relation to the wider society.[17]

During the first half of the twentieth century, the Hindu attitude towards religion was marked by an overall unchallenging and almost fatalistic acceptance of religious texts, rituals and customs. The rare instances of serious interrogation of matters pertaining to religion would almost certainly be quelled and satisfied by textual quotation or a reference to time-honoured traditions, or by the actions and teachings of religious figures. All of the aforementioned factors influenced the style and content of textual presentation. Until the 1980s there was a marked emphasis on the narrative content of texts, that '... meant everything to our elderly mothers and fathers'.[18] Despite the popular, though questionable view of the earlier narrative style being just 'story-telling', this traditional approach functioned as a vehicle for both moral and spiritual teachings, and emotional and psychological solace.

From the 1950s, social, economic, academic and religious transformations generated a gradual amelioration in the status of Hindus, and consequently, created a need for more than just the 'story' and devotional aspects of the text. Hence, by late 1970s, there was a gradual yet accelerated move away from the predominantly narrative mode to one that simultaneously and variously reflected the rise of Hindu philosophical probings, a decline in subscription to superstitions, taboos and certain traditional practices and more practical and analytical approach to religion in general. In addition, the cases of conversion which arose among the Hindu community during the late 1960s and 1970s served as a catalyst for what was described by anthropologist Morton Klass as a period of 'revitalization' in Trinidad Hinduism (1991). Thus, by the 1990s, the traditional narrative style was being either infused with or sometimes superseded by a focus on the philosophy inherent in the text, and connected to contemporary social operatives and issues.

Knowledge of the social, physical, emotional, economic and even political disposition of the respective audience is a crucial component in the presentation of the religious texts. Such insight is compulsory both in the formal and popular spheres with regard to such matters as style, focus, topic, context, language and level of reverence. Inasmuch as they were contingent upon the contemporary conditions, preferences and needs of the Hindu community, such presentation skills and techniques varied throughout the twentieth century, and hence, have functioned as a definite indicator of Hindu socio-religious change in Trinidad. Even during the pre-1960s, wherein extremely reverential attitudes towards religious matters left little need for conscious efforts at making the proceedings 'appealing', many factors were taken into consideration by those expounding the texts. One popular pundit who had conducted yagnas from 1945 confirmed his application of certain tactics.

> You look at the people ... the type of people (in the village), their temperament, their taste, their ways and habits. I read to suit your village. ... If I go to Port-of-Spain, the people have a different understanding, so I need to suit them now. ...Things that I know will be too difficult for you, I wouldn't apply it right away, will do it gradually. ...That is where you as a pundit have to study human psychology for at least three years, how to deal with people when you meet them; the method of approach.[19]

One particular reader's strategy also involved singling out the most socially or intellectually prominent individual in the audience and procuring his approval on what was being presented, either verbally or by the use of eye contact. Such techniques are reflective of both 'the interactive milieu essential to good performance in the Indian context, and a reminder of the archaic sense of *hatha* as "conversation"' (Lutgendorf 1991: 189).

While almost all dimensions of the *Ramayana* tradition in Trinidad succumbed to considerable variation, elements of the earlier approach were still noticeable, albeit with varying degrees of modification. Indeed, one can safely say that, since the 1980s, textual interpretation and presentation evolved into an institution that borrowed variously from the schools of Art, Science and Psychology. The community was studied beforehand, goals were set, and this largely determined the choice of content (which was prepared in advance in great detail). This was accompanied by an assessment of the nature and composition of the audience (with age and the perceived intellectual level being the major underlying factors). Consequently this determined how the content was pitched, the level of language used and, the balance or bias between the narrative and philosophical modes. Generally, and in keeping with conventions of the earlier period, a congregation predominated by persons over 50 years of age entailed an emphasis on the story of the *Ramayana* with simple references to mundane occurrences and minimal emphasis on the philosophical and 'technical' aspects of the content. References were made to the more popular verses of the text with which members of the audience were able to identify. Verses from the text were sung in the more traditional melody reminiscent of earlier decades, and evoking memories of the solace gained from these verses in the early days of toil and hardship. A predominance of younger individuals in the gathering consequently mandated an inversion of the foregoing. The commonality of mixed audiences, moreover, demanded an admixture of the narrative and the thematic as the most popular contemporary approach to textual presentation. A typical session comprised bhajan singing, a period of narration from the text, an emphasis on love and devotion to God, and a bit of related *Bhagvadgita* philosophy, all expertly tied together at the end of the discourse. In this resulting holistic approach '... dramatics, body language, speech, everything is compacted in that so you cater to the entire congregation'.[20]

CONCLUSION

That the *Ramcharitmanas* has had a time honoured and intimate relationship with the local Hindu society and history cannot be denied. From the earliest days of indenture until the present time, the vicissitudes of the Hindu experience drew upon the authoritative and affective functions of this text in its continuous search for solutions and solace. The occasions for textual readings, the attitude towards the associated paraphernalia and the treatment of related issues collectively evinced the symbiotic relationship between change in the textual sphere and wider socio-religious transformation.

The endurance and dissemination of the *Ramayana* tradition within the multicultural society of Trinidad through the periods of indenture, community reconstruction, conflict and affirmation echoed the dynamism and flexibility that has enabled the tradition to flourish globally throughout the Indian diaspora. Judging by the endurance and function of the more long-standing *Ramayana* traditions in India, Asia and other countries of the Indian diaspora, one can conclude that the last 163 years has been a period essentially of establishment of the *Ramayana* tradition. During this time it has emerged as an integral dimension in the life of Trinidad Hindus but one which is still substantially influenced by the values, cultural nuances and systems of the Indian subcontinent. The stage is now fully set, in the twenty-first century, to explore whether the *Ramayana* tradition in Trinidad—immersed in the country's swirl of socio-economic, socio-cultural and political transformation—will engage in a higher level of 'Trinidadianization' and shed even more of its exclusively Hindu application. Conversely, nostalgia for the traditional that is continuously fed by the propensity of Hinduism for continuity amidst the change could work to deter the weaning away of the tradition from its ancestral homeland, India. Either way, the *Ramayana* tradition in Trinidad will undoubtedly continue to act both as mirror and metaphor of the Hindu experience in Trinidad.

NOTES

1. This term, when used orally, referred not just to the text, but encapsulated the entire gamut of the socio-religious activity, which was usually a seven, nine or fourteen day affair, with readings and all of the associated rituals being performed three times daily. This extension of the name of the text, in popular oral use, to connote the entire event with all its accoutrements exemplifies the intimate dialogue between text and tradition, and the textual tradition and society.
2. Pundit Hardath Maharaj, personal interview, 24 November 2002.
3. Pundit Khemraj Vyas, personal interview, 27 November 2002.
4. Pundit Prakash Persad, personal interview, 5 October 2001.
5. Brahmachari Prem Chaitanya, personal interview, 23 November 2001.
6. Lall Paladee, personal interview, 22 November 2001.
7. In Hinduism, non-Hindu religious icons like Buddha and Mohammed, while not accepted as the Divine or as an avatar, are considered figures imbued with substantial levels of divine attributes and capabilities, who act as agents of the Divine.
8. Sister Krishna Gupta, personal interview, 22 November 2001.
9. Pundit Khemraj Vyas, personal interview, 27 November 2002.
10. *Port-of-Spain Gazette,* 20 March 1938.
11. A week-long celebration of the *Ramayana* which featured depictions in song, dance, drama, dance-drama, chanting, painting and other art forms.
12. Hindu Prachar Kendra, Mantra Vimochan 2003 Invitation.
13. Boodram Ramgoolam, personal interview, 16 December 2002.
14. Pundit Doodnath Rampersad, personal interview, 5 January 2002.
15. Pundit Prakash Persad, personal interview, 5 October 2001.
16. Pundit Khemraj Vyas, personal interview, 27 November 2002.
17. In the year 2001, yagnas were held for 'the political stability' of the country; and in 2002, in commemoration of the Sanatan Dharma Maha Sabha's fiftieth anniversary at various SDMS primary schools. In one instance, a *bedi* (consecrated altar) in the shape of the map of Trinidad was constructed and consecrated as the ritual altar for the duration of the yagna. Another prominent contemporary concept was the 'answer back yagna' which attempted to disseminate information to the adherence of Sanatan Dharma and to simultaneously combat the attacks launched against Hinduism.
18. Pundit Khemraj Vyas, personal interview, 27 November 2002.
19. Pundit Hardath Maharaj, personal interview, 24 November 2002.
20. Pundit Brahmanand Rambachan, personal interview, 22 November 2002.

REFERENCES

Bahadur, K.P. (1976), *Ramcharitmanas: A Study in Perspective,* Delhi: Ess Ess Publications.

Brereton, Bridget (1981), *A History of Modern Trinidad 1783–1962,* Portsmouth USA: Heinemann International.

Grant, K.G. (1923), *My Missionary Memories,* Halifax, Nova Scotia: Imperial.
Haraksingh, Kusha (1984), 'The Hindu Experience in Trinidad', Proceedings of Conference on 'East Indians in the Caribbean-beyond survival', 28 August–5 September, St. Augustine: University of the West Indies.
Klass, Morton (1991), *Singing with Sai Baba: The Politics of Revitalisation in Trinidad*, San Francisco: Westview Press.
Lutgendorf, Philip (1991), *The Life of a Text,* Berkeley, California: University of California Press.
Naipaul, V.S. (2000), 'Reading and Writing: A Personal Account', New York: *New York Review Books.*
Prorok, Carolyn (1988), 'Hindu Temples in Trinidad: A Cultural Geography of Religious Structures and Ethnic Identity', Ph.D. Dissertation, University of Pittsburgh.
Vertovec, Steven (1992), *Hindu Trinidad: Religion, Ethnicity and Socio-Economic Change,* London: Macmillan Education.

3

Muslims in the Caribbean

Nasser Mustapha

According to most historical sources, the first Muslim to enter the Caribbean were the Africans who were brought to provide slave labour on the plantations from as early as the sixteenth and seventeenth centuries.[1] They were mostly from the Mandingo, Fulani and Hausa nations. The subsequent breaking up of families during slavery meant that it was extremely difficult for them to transmit Islam to their descendants. This accultural process took place systematically throughout the period of slavery and might have varied in intensity from one Caribbean country to another as Melville Herskovits has observed.

Afroz (1995) indicates that African Muslims attempted to resist acculturation and were at the forefront of many slave rebellions. Contrary to popular opinion, there were many among the slaves who were highly educated in their faith, some of them knew the Koran by heart. Robert Madden (1958) wrote, 'They could all read and write Arabic, and one of them showed me a copy of the Koran written from memory. One of them, Benjamin Cochrane, practised as a doctor in Kingston.' Nevertheless, aspects of Islam continued to exert an influence on African-Caribbean linguistic, musical and religious forms (Diouf 1998: 184–205).

The conditions of plantation slavery made it difficult to retain African ancestral beliefs and Islam as a distinct religious tradition seems to have disappeared. However, the slaves' unswerving attachment to the religions of their homeland led them to maintain a latent sensitivity to their ancestry. After Emancipation, the suppression of African Islam continued by subtle and effective means, mainly through the socialization of the Africans through Christian-Western education, and laws that prohibited the practice of non-Christian faiths and cultural forms.

Though within a few generations, all significant traces of Islam virtually disappeared in the Caribbean, the latent, suppressed attachment to African ancestral religions resurfaced. And in one of the ironies of Caribbean history, many Afro-Caribbean people later converted to Islam, centuries after all traces of this religion were destroyed by the European cultural dominance faced by their ancestors.

INDIAN MUSLIMS IN THE CARIBBEAN

After Emancipation, the planters sought other sources of labour. The second major entry of Muslims into the Caribbean was from India. Approximately 15 per cent of the Indian indentured immigrants were Muslims. The largest numbers were sent to Guyana, Trinidad and Surinam, while smaller numbers were sent to other territories. Though the conditions of indentured immigration were difficult, they nevertheless were more amenable than those of slavery to the survival of immigrants' cultural traditions, as long as it did not affect the performance of their work and the security of the estates. The planters were generally satisfied with the productivity and work ethic of the Indian immigrants.

There were few among them who had received extensive religious training, but in general Indian Muslims had a rudimentary religious education. As such, they attempted to reconstruct aspects of their faith as they knew it, sometimes without textual proof. Because of the need to preserve their faith in an alien environment, they became very defensive and introverted. Their emotional attachment to many Indo-Muslim cultural traditions helped in maintaining group solidarity, and thus a commitment to what they perceived to be Islam. Looking backwards and clinging to the past in response to the pressures of indentured labour made these early Muslims suspicious of any socio-cultural or religious change. The idea that they would return to India after the termination of their contracts provided further impetus for cultural persistence.

By the early years of the twentieth century, Islam began to take a unique shape among Indians in the Caribbean. For this reason, many early Indian Muslims disagreed with some Indian missionaries whose ideas and practices were at variance with those they had adopted in the Caribbean. There were many similarities among Muslims of Trinidad, Surinam and Guyana, reflecting their common experiences and the interpretations of Islam dominant in north India, partly due to the influence of Hinduism and tribal religions there.

There were mainly Hanafi Sunnis, a few Shias and followers of other schools of thought among them. Over a period of time, however, the culture of the Indian Muslims in the Caribbean stabilized as differences among them were reduced. In Surinam, further differentiation was introduced by the significant influx of Javanese immigrants, bringing with them their own Islamic beliefs and practices. Annemarie de Waal Malefijt (1976) documents the existence of the seemingly incompatible doctrines of monotheism and animism among Muslims in Surinam. In other territories where the number of Indians was smaller, they were easily assimilated into the culture of the wider society, although evidence of strong resistance to assimilation exists among Indians in Jamaica (Khan 1998).

Most research has so far focussed on Trinidad and Guyana, where large Muslim communities exist today. In both territories, similar versions of Islam exist. This is not surprising, since most of the immigrants came from the

Gangetic plains of India bringing similar interpretations of Islam, had similar experiences on the ships and on the plantations and shared similar contacts with India through the arrival of missionaries. The Indian immigrants tried to remember their religion as they knew it and to re-establish it under new and challenging circumstances in the Caribbean. They reactivated and often modified various religious practices and social events that they had known in India. The close-knit Indian family system also helped in the transmission of cultural norms, values and traits to the younger Indians. Under the circumstances, they viewed the culture of the wider society with suspicion. Their settlement in isolated rural villages and the condescending manner in which they were treated by the rest of the society, worked in their favour. The bonds of ethnic solidarity were strengthened and they adapted successfully to the new society. The circumstances were more conducive to cultural persistence than among their African predecessors.

RELIGIOUS PRACTICES AND TRADITIONS

The 'traditionalist Sunnis', by far make up the largest group in the Caribbean today, accounting for more than 50 per cent of the Muslim community. The older generation is more familiar with all the detailed aspects of traditional Islam, and efforts are being made to promote its transmission to younger generations. Officially they are Hanafi Sunnis, indicating that they follow the school of law developed by Imam Abu Hanifa, and adopt the *Ahle Sunnah wal Jamah* approach as advocated by Ahmad Riza Khan of Barelwi in nineteenth-century India (Sanyal 1996). They subscribe to Indian cultural practices such as *niyaz* or *fatiha, moulood* and *tazeem,* and are wary of Muslim groups that do not support these practices. They are often suspicious of interpretations of Islam which vary from their own, and even censure foreign missionaries to ensure their compatibility. They are highly insular and there is a notable lack of desire to propagate their faith to non-Muslims. The traditionalists are also known to lend strong support to the existing political authority and to seldom oppose the status quo.

Among this group there have been efforts to promote the Urdu language. Though Urdu is an integral part of the Muslim legacy, some Muslims today disassociate themselves from it, due to its Indian cultural origins. Such persons consider Arabic as the only medium for religious instruction. Many traditional Muslim practices in the Caribbean make use of the Urdu language. These include *moulood* (singing of *qasidas* or Urdu songs), *tazeem* (prayer sending salutations to the Prophet), *niyaz* (prayer over food), milad-un-nabi (celebrating the Prophet's birthday) and *miraj* (observing the Prophet's ascension to Heaven).

Debates concerning these rituals have created deep rifts among Muslims in the Caribbean from the 1940s to the present. Some Muslims consider these practices to be *bida'h* ('innovations') which have not been practised by the

Prophet or his companions. Within the last decade or so, these debates have subsided somewhat as Muslims of different orientations are showing increased tolerance of each other's differences. 'Traditionalist' Muslims continue to support these practices, while 'fundamentalist' or 'purist' Muslims consider them to be *bida'h* and hence undesirable.

The *qasida* ('song of praise') evolved from the Arab and Persian traditions, and it spread from the heart of Arabia to the Islamic periphery. The Arabic language impacted heavily on the vocabulary, grammar and literary prose of other languages, including Turkish, Persian and Urdu. *Qasida,* like poetry, became a popular form of expression among Muslims in South Asia. These renditions, largely in Urdu, were an integral part of religious functions among the early Indian Muslims in the Caribbean. Today in Trinidad, there is an attempt to revive this tradition. However, there is a lack of enthusiasm from the younger generation, many of whom prefer to learn Islam from its original Arabic sources rather than from Indian traditions.

Tazeem is a song of praise to the Prophet Muhammad. It is usually rendered towards the end of a reading or prayer function when all present are required to stand and recite: *Ya Nabi salaam alaika, Ya rasul salaam alaika* (Oh Prophet, Peace be unto you, Oh Messenger, Peace be unto you.) Whereas traditionalist Muslims emphasize the necessity of observing *tazeem*, the purists claim that it is not Islamic. Several Islamic scholars from the subcontinent have provided justification for *tazeem*, claiming that it is in accordance with Islam and is highly commendable (some even consider it obligatory) and does not conflict with the Koran and the Sunnah.

Milad-un-nabi is the celebration or commemoration of the birth, life and achievements of the Prophet. Many Sufi orders support this celebration, claiming that the event is the Muslim community's expression of love for the Prophet. It is an effort to show gratitude to Allah for His favour of blessing humanity with such a *Nabi* (Prophet), and to the *Nabi* for bringing humanity out of the darkness of ignorance. The essence of milad-un-nabi is to remember and observe, discuss and recite the event of the birth and the advent of the Prophet. Opponents of this practice have called it *bida'h* or an innovation. They quote the Prophet, 'Whoever brings forth an innovation into our religion which is not part of it, it is rejected,' and again, 'Beware of innovative matters for every invention is an innovation and every innovation is misleading' (*Hadith, Sahih Bukhari*, vol. 3, Bk. 49, no. 861).

The visits of Maulana Ansari and Maulana Siddiqi to the Caribbean in the 1950s provided religious legitimacy for the practice of *qasida, tazeem* and *milad-un-nabi.* These scholars endorsed these practices and refuted claims that these were evil innovations. They were able to convince many local Muslims that based on the Koran, the Hadith and the *fiqh* (the tradition of Islamic jurisprudence), these traditional practices were within the parameters of Islam, and are *bida'h hasanat* ('good innovations').

Shi'ah Muslims also, brought their cultural traditions to the Caribbean. They believe that the fourth Caliph Ali should have been the successor to Muhammad of the leadership of the *Ummah*. Their most important religious symbols are Husayn and Fatima, the grandson and daughter of the Prophet respectively. Every year they observe the martyrdom of Husayn, which occurred in 680 AD on the tenth day of the month of Muharram. It is a very emotional event involving mourning, the expression of grief and the chanting of prayers as devotees conduct a street procession of *taziyah*, or representations of the tomb of Husayn. Shi'ah Muslims also utilize this event to atone for their sins.

The 'Hosay' festival, as this practice has historically been called, was introduced into the Caribbean by early Indian immigrants. Though Shi'ah Islam was largely submerged into the wider Muslim community, Hosay persisted in a Caribbeanized or 'creolized' form. Though it mostly lost its religious significance (Mansingh and Mansingh 1995), Hosay represented a visual display of resistance by Indians, sufficient to cause fear on the part of the colonial authorities. Several historians (including Ken Parmasad and Kelvin Singh) have documented the importance of the 1884 Hosay Riots in Trinidad. The Hosay festival continues to attract interest as an important cultural event, and has received much popular support in India and in Trinidad and Tobago. People of various religious and cultural persuasions participate in the festival, providing additional modification of its form. However, all orthodox Muslim groups have distanced themselves from its observance. Furthermore, the small Shi'ah community that resurfaced in Trinidad in the 1980s, has also condemned the manner in which Hosay is currently celebrated, with drinking alcohol and a carnival-like atmosphere. This Shi'ah group observes the martyrdom of Husayn in what they claim is the truly Islamic manner, as a time of mourning. Shi'ah Muslims have also been strongly condemned by Wahhabi Muslims for their veneration of saints, visits to tombs and shrines and commemoration of death anniversaries. Certain practices associated with the Shi'ah tradition are also observed by Sufi Muslims.

Sufi Muslims are also found in the Caribbean today. This popular religious group is found throughout the Muslim world, including the Arab countries, Africa and South Asia (Riyazul Islam 2002). It is a mystical tradition that seeks to emphasize the inner spiritual development of the individual. Sufis follow an ascetic life of simplicity, purification, denial and detachment from the material world. Rarely addressing what they view as the mundane issues of society, they spend much of their efforts in prayer, singing, fasting, meditation and *dhikr* ('remembrance of God'). Though initially having an elite following, the Sufi movement attracted persons from all levels of society. Over the years, Sufi activities came under the influence of Christian hermits, Buddhist monks and Hindu sadhus. Many orthodox Islamic scholars have rejected the Sufi movement for its 'excesses'. Wahhabi Muslims have even described it as heretical or a blasphemous deviation that compromises people's *iman* ('faith'). Sufi Islam finds support especially among the 'traditionalist' Muslims in the Caribbean, including the Hanafi Sunnis and the Tabligh movement.

Syncretic practices involving Islam and magical cures were also brought to the Caribbean from India. In several communities in Trinidad today, persons perform exorcism using Arabic prayers. Sometimes Arabic phrases are inscribed on paper and given to clients to ward off evil spirits. Services such as fortune-telling, healing of ailments and detection of thieves are also offered. In the performance of this role, many parallels can be found with the Orisha priest or Obeah-man.

Indian Muslims have therefore been able to maintain their religious identity amidst the pressures of a plural society, while making several adaptations in the process. Minor theological differences were brushed aside as survival was uppermost on their agenda. They were largely united as they successfully resisted integration into the wider society. Smith (1963) concludes, on the basis of studies conducted among the Muslims of Trinidad: 'To the present time, family organization and organized religion have engaged the forces of assimilation and acculturation and won ...'.

Although Indian Muslims adopted a common version of Islam, the diversity found in Indian society and in the Muslim world generally started to resurface in the Caribbean from the 1930s onwards with the return of Maulvi Ameer Ali from studies in Lahore followed by Maulvi Nazeer Ahmad Seemab who was allegedly a Wahhabi. The views of the latter two scholars were at variance with the then leader Hajji Ruknudeen, a traditionalist Sunni.

'SYNCRETIC' PRACTICES

Common external pressures led to greater mutual respect and acceptance between Indian Muslims and Hindus in the Caribbean. Despite marked differences in beliefs, there was cordial relationship between these two groups. Around the time of Partition of India and the formation of Pakistan, Hindu-Muslim relationships became somewhat strained. However, the relationship was long and intimate enough to lead to the borrowing and sharing of customs. This mutual transfer of cultural traits began in India, and continued in the Caribbean.

According to Khan (1987), some Muslim rituals in Trinidad have been a result of Hindu contact. These include the three-day and forty-day mourning rituals and *niyaz,* an offering for the dead. Another relatively new practice involves the reading of the Koran for several nights during which sweets are served. The event culminates in a full meal being served to a large gathering. In format, this practice closely resembles the *Ramayan Yagh* function of the Hindus. Culinary practices among today's Muslims reveal a high degree of acculturation, with almost any type of dish, including Afro- or Chinese-Caribbean food, being served. While vegetarian dishes are served at all Hindu functions, usually on a leaf to be eaten by the hands, most Muslim functions serve meat (usually goat meat for the more affluent), rice, roti and numerous vegetable side dishes. Many of today's Indo-Caribbean dishes are supposedly of Muslim origin. These include the paratha roti, made with ghee or butter. The halwa of the Muslims of Middle Eastern origin is similar to the Hindu *parsad.* During Diwali and Id-ul-Fitr similar types of sweets are served. The popular

Trinidadian street-food 'doubles' originated among Indo-Trinidadian Muslims around the Usine-St. Madeline Sugar Factory in south Trinidad.

CONFLICT AND CHANGE

After the period of indentureship, most of the debates among Muslims in the Caribbean focused on cultural practices that Muslims brought from India. There have been two major 'camps' on this issue, one comprising the younger generation who prefer to abandon the Indian cultural heritage, and the other comprising the older generation who desire to preserve this tradition. Today, those of the younger generation who have studied in the Arabic-speaking world prefer Arabic over Urdu, and link the Indian Muslim tradition to Hinduism. A continuous attempt has therefore been made to purge 'cultural Islam' of 'un-Islamic' innovations. As Samaroo (1995: 23) states, 'In modern day Trinidad and Guyana, where there are substantial Muslim populations, there is much confusion, often conflict, between the two types of Islam.'

A major religious conflict among Muslims in the Caribbean was posed by the introduction of *Ahmadiism* in the 1930s. Towards the end of the nineteenth century in India, Mirza Ghulam Ahmad had laid claims to prophethood, claiming at various times to have been a reincarnation of religious personalities of Hinduism, Christianity and Islam. Sunn'i Muslims did not recognize his followers, known today as *Qadiani* and *Ahmadi* Muslims. There are no records of *Ahmadi* Muslims in the Caribbean until 1921 when Maulana Durrani, an Ahmadi missionary from India, arrived in Trinidad (Samaroo 1987). After being bitterly opposed by the local leaders, he soon returned to India. He was nevertheless instrumental in persuading a Trinidadian, Ameer Ali, to take up a scholarship at an Ahmadi institute in Lahore.

When he returned to Trinidad, Ameer Ali claimed that he was not an Ahmadi, but a *Ghair Mukallid* ('non-conformist'). He adopted a 'modernist' approach to Islam, encouraging the free participation of women in religious activities and criticizing some of the local institutionalized traditions. His liberal views were strongly condemned by local Muslim leaders. He eventually formed his own organization in 1947, the Trinidad Muslim League. This organization was formally affiliated with the worldwide Ahmadi movement from 1969 to 1976, but today identifies itself as *Ghair Mukallid*. The attractiveness of 'Westernization' was difficult to resist and by the 1960s, many of the younger and more educated Muslims became assimilated into the culture of the wider Caribbean society. The Islam that was being taught as a body of rituals and traditions was irreconcilable with what was being taught in the 'secular' educational system. Also by this time, most of the youth, having been educated in the English language, were unable to understand and speak Urdu. Many religious sermons were still being delivered in the Urdu language, while there was very little Islamic literature available in English. The subsequent arrival of learned persons who were able to teach Islam in the English language and the increasing availability of literature in English led to a reawakening of the local Muslims. This revival took place in Guyana and Trinidad simultaneously, and was further strengthened by the return of qualified locals from abroad and contact with Muslims in North America.

The Wahhabi movement, often called 'fundamentalist' in contrast to the 'traditionalist' Hanafi Sunn'i tradition, was introduced into the religious landscape of the Caribbean initially from India and later from Saudi Arabia. This Muslim group has grown in size over the last two decades, but by no means is it homogeneous. The work of Muhammad Ibn Abdul Wahhab (1708-92) has inspired many of today's revivalist movements. Abdul Wahhab's major focus was on the removal of accretions and innovations that crept into Islam over a period of time. He was appalled by some religious practices found in his time, including the veneration of saints and their tombs. He saw such acts as *shirk* (polytheism)—considered the most serious sin in Islam. Wahhabi Muslims are usually critical of popular interpretations of Islam, especially when they condone cultural practices which were not found among the Prophet's generation. This movement advocates a return to the 'fundamentals' or original sources of Islam, namely the Koran and the Sunnah. They reject Sufi practices and destroy all idols, icons, tombs and shrines, or anything that they believe comes between God and humanity.

The Wahhabi movement has been very influential, inspiring not only revivalism in the Arabian Peninsula, but also Uthman dan Fodio's reform movement in Nigeria and the Sanusi movement in Libya. This trend in Caribbean Islam was initially influenced by an early missionary from India, Nazeer Ahmad Simab, who came to Trinidad and Tobago in 1935. He did not find favour with the local Muslims, and was ostracized for his rejection of some of their allegedly 'un-Islamic' practices. He was even condemned for saying that the Prophet was a man like us. This missionary was instrumental in obtaining government recognition for the first non-Christian denominational school in the West Indies.

Subsequently, several groups in the Caribbean have advocated a return to the 'fundamentals' of Islam. Like the Wahhabis, these 'neo-revivalists' generally show high levels of religious commitment. Originally inspired by movements in South Asia and more recently by Middle Eastern and North American contact, they often find themselves at odds with 'traditionalist' Muslims over the latter's apparent overemphasis on ancestral traditions as opposed to *faraid* ('obligatory') acts of worship. Many neo-revivalists are actively engaged in propagating their faith among both Muslims and non-Muslims. Generally, members of this group do not follow the rulings of any one of the four recognized schools of Islamic law, and some find *ijtiad* ('personal judgement' in the implementation of the law) to be acceptable.

The Tabligh (literally, 'preaching') movement, based in India and found throughout the diaspora, was introduced in the Caribbean in the early 1970s. It also advocates a rigid system of adherence to the 'fundamentals' of Islam, and is dedicated to the propagation of Islam but only among Muslims. Although members of this group are Hanafi Sunn'i like the 'traditionalists', they do not follow Indian cultural practices which they consider to be *bida*'. They refrain from polemics and adopt a fixed, literal and cautious interpretation of Islamic texts. They seem indifferent to contemporary social and political issues, and avoid conflict with established authority and controversial issues. Most of them are highly active in religious observance. Nevertheless, their rigid stance on many issues often contributes to their lack of popularity among both 'traditionalists' and other 'fundamentalists'. Their activities are centred around the mosques and require little resources. Their missionary work follows a fixed format, which rarely involves the use of modern technology. They made it possible for a number of locals to obtain scholarships to pursue Islamic studies in India. Today, as a result of the efforts of the Tabligh movement, there exists a multi-million dollar complex in Trinidad, the Dar-ul-Ulum Institute of Islamic Studies. The clientele of this institute comes from several Caribbean territories.

Recently, an extreme form of Wahhabi Islam has been introduced into the Caribbean, the Salafi movement. They advocate a literal 'back to basics' approach to Islam, and are often criticized for making peripheral matters into central issues. Though rather small, they have grown over the past decade, being influenced mainly by the return of Saudi-trained Shaikhs over the last two decades.

THE RETURN OF AFRICAN MUSLIMS

In one of the ironies of Caribbean history, many Afro-Caribbean people converted to Islam—centuries after all traces of this religion were destroyed among their ancestors. With little or no missionary effort on the part of the Indian Muslim community, a few individuals of African descent converted to Islam from as early as 1940. Among these were Pir Robinson and Yusuf Mitchell, both of whom became leaders in what was perceived then as an Indian religion.

The significant influx of African converts began in the early 1970s with the increased black consciousness among the Afro-Caribbean community. This phenomenon was inspired by events in North America, and particularly by Malcolm X. While the Nation of Islam did have a small following in Port-of-Spain, Trinidad and in other Caribbean territories, the majority of Africans in the Caribbean who accepted Islam joined the orthodox Muslim community. These new African Muslims came mainly from grass roots urban communities and did not find ready acceptance by the middle class leadership of the traditional Muslim community. However, among the younger members of the Muslim community who were generally more fundamentalist in their religious orientation, there was no significant race or class barrier.

Though African Muslims were accommodated warmly by the Islamic Missionaries Guild of the Caribbean and South America (with branches in

Guyana, Barbados and Trinidad) and the Islamic Trust of Trinidad and Guyana, as a group they were still uncomfortable with the Indian Muslim community. They were especially concerned with the Indian cultural baggage which they felt was influenced by Hinduism. In February 1977, African Muslims in Trinidad established their own group under the influence of the Islamic Party of North America. The Jamaat-al-Muslimeen evolved out of this group. After the July 1990 insurrection, many of the Jamaat's members left to form the Islamic Resource Society. This group has very cordial relations with the Indian Muslim community and belongs to the United Islamic Organizations, a coordinating body of Muslim groups in Trinidad. African Muslims frequently worship at most of the Indian-dominated mosques in Trinidad and Tobago and in Guyana, but there are a few urban mosques that are predominantly African in their congregation. The other Muslim communities in the Caribbean, with the exception of Barbados, are predominantly Afro-Caribbean in their membership.

MIDDLE EASTERN INFLUENCE

There were Muslims, Jews and Christians among the early Syrian and Lebanese immigrants to the Caribbean. Those who remained Muslims often intermingled and sometimes intermarried with Indian Muslims. One of the first Muslim missionaries from the Middle East was Abdel Salaam from Egypt. He taught Arabic at several centres in Trinidad. In the 1970s, nationals from Trinidad, Guyana and Barbados were awarded scholarships to pursue studies in Egypt and Saudi Arabia. Their return provided a new turn of events for the Muslim community in the Caribbean. As might have been expected, their interpretations of Islam did not find favour with the traditional Muslims. They nevertheless found tremendous support from the youth who were largely disenchanted with the leadership of traditional Muslims. These new and radical approaches to the practice of Islam provided an exciting escape from the traditionalism of the mainstream Muslim community. The Iranian Revolution of 1979 further kindled the flames of fundamentalism among Caribbean Muslims. Young Muslims took pride in identifying openly with Islam. It was only around the mid-1970s that Muslim women began wearing the *hijab* or veil. Prior to this, the *ohrni,* an Indian head covering, was worn by older women only (Niehoff and Niehoff 1961).

In some Caribbean countries, organizations bringing together different Muslim traditions have been established. These 'ecumenical' attempts have achieved some degree of success at the formal level, where groups of different orientations sit together to address the needs of the Muslim community. However, the older Muslims show little inclination to change traditional religious practices. In countries such as Guyana, Trinidad and Tobago and Surinam the major strength of the community lies in its numerous institutions. There are Muslim cooperatives, a credit union, a housing cooperative, several primary and secondary schools and three religious institutes. The mosques of the region have also served as important institutions over the years. As of 1998, Guyana had 154 mosques; Trinidad and Tobago, 112; Surinam 100; Jamaica, 6; and Barbados, 4. In addition to serving as places of worship, many mosques serve as educational institutions, known as *maktab* or *madrasah*. In most of the smaller Muslim communities of the Caribbean, members, largely of African descent, have attempted to form a regional body to coordinate their activities. This body was known as the Association of Islamic Communities of the Caribbean and Latin America (AICCLA). They have received some financial and other forms of assistance from outside the Caribbean.

The Muslim community in the Caribbean has successfully struggled to maintain a visible presence in the face of numerous forces that threatened their very existence. And yet a marked diversity exists within the community, even among those who claim to have the same orientation. There is need for further research on the historical background and unique characteristics of Caribbean Muslims.

NOTE

1. A.H. Quick (1990) cites numerous sources to illustrate that Muslims arrived in the Caribbean before Columbus.

REFERENCES

Afroz, S. (1995), 'The Unsung Slaves in Plantation America', *Caribbean Quarterly,* vol. 41, nos. 2 and 3, pp. 30–44.

Caribbean Islamic Secretariat (1998), *Muslims in the Caribbean,* Port-of-Spain: CIS.

De Waal Malefijt, A. (1976), 'Animism and Islam among the Javanese in Surinam', in *Peoples and Cultures of the Caribbean,* M. Horowitz, ed., New York: Natural History Press.

Diouf, S. (1998), *Servants of Allah: African Muslims Enslaved in the Americas,* New York: New York University Press.

Hadith: Sahih al Bukhari (1980), Chicago: Kazi Publications.

Hamid, A.W. (1978), 'Muslims in the West Indies', Paper presented to the Muslim Minorities Seminar, Islamic Council of Europe.

Herklots, G.A. (1931), *Islam in India,* London: Kurzon Press.

Kasule, O. (1986), 'Muslims in Trinidad and Tobago', *Journal of the Institute of Muslim Minority Affairs,* vol. 7, no. 1, pp. 195–224.

Khan, F. (1987), 'Islam as a Social Force in the Caribbean', Paper presented at the Conference of the History Teachers' Association of Trinidad and Tobago, June.

Khan, N. (1998), Personal Communication, September 1998.

Mansingh, A. and L. Mansingh (1995), 'Hosay and its Creolization', *Caribbean Quarterly,* vol. 41, no. 1, pp. 25–39.

The Muslim Standard, no. 3, Trinidad: The Islamic Trust, December 1975.

Niehoff, A. and J. Niehoff (1961), *East Indians in Trinidad and Tobago,* Milwaukee: Public Museum Publications in Anthropology, no. 6.

Quick, A.H. (1990), *Deeper Roots: Muslims of the Caribbean before Columbus to the Present,* Nassau, Bahamas: AICCLA.

Riyazul Islam, *Sufism in South Asia,* OUP, 2002.

Samaroo, B. (1987), 'The Indian Connection: The Influence of Indian Thought and Ideas on East Indians in the Caribbean', in *India in the Caribbean,* D. Dabydeen and B. Samaroo, eds., London: Hansib Publishing House.

——— (1995), 'Early African and East Indian Muslims in Trinidad and Tobago', in *Across the Dark Waters,* D. Dabydeen and B. Samaroo, eds., Warwick University.

Sanyal, U. (1996), *Devotional Islam and Politics in British India,* Delhi: OUP.

Smith, R.J. (1964), 'Muslim East Indians in Trinidad: Retention of Ethnic Identity under Acculturative Conditions', Ph.D. dissertation, Anthropology Department, Michigan State University.

4

Trinidad Hinduism, 1917-1945:

Religious Transformation and Identity Construction

Sherry-Ann Singh

During the period of Indian indenture close to 1,43,939 Indians migrated to Trinidad (Brereton 1981: 103), approximately 88 per cent of whom practised various kinds of Hinduism. Of this number, 12.03 per cent belonged to the 'Brahmins and other high castes', 36.82 per cent the 'agricultural castes', 6.39 per cent belonged to the 'artisan castes', and 33.16 per cent belonged to the 'low castes'[1] (Vertovec 1992: 33). Despite the trying conditions experienced under the indenture system,[2] about four out of five Indian immigrants chose, to settle down in Trinidad at the end of their contracted periods of indenture (ibid.: 73). From their very entrance into Trinidad society, Hindus were engaged in the practice of many rites of their religion. This was especially so of the more private rituals which could be observed within either the home or the immediate Hindu/Indian community. However, although Hindu immigrants, as it has been argued, 'carried a slice' (Haraksingh 1985: 163) of their society and, hence, religion with them, uprooting from the Indian context necessitated attempts at community and religious reconstruction.

In Trinidad, elements of religion were variously truncated, modified, diluted, intensified or excised. Thus, reconstitution and telescoping (ibid.: 163), rather than transplanting, were two of the dominant processes that could be observed. This subsequently yielded a form of Hinduism in which some of the more visible and tangible elements were modified substantially. At the same time however, the Hinduism which emerged was unarguably rooted in the broad philosophy and in the general tenets of several strands of Hinduism practised in India. This applied to the caste system, Hindu priesthood, the institution of marriage, gender roles, and many of the religious rites, rituals and observances.

Since Indian indentured immigration encompassed a wide sweep of the Indian subcontinent, there was a remarkable degree of social, religious and cultural diversity within the immigrant population in Trinidad. This was evident in such areas as language, kinship ideology, social and economic structures, values, and general attitudes, lifestyle and behaviour. This social and geographical diversity also underscored a 'jumbled medley of beliefs, doctrines, rites, experiences, relationships, restrictions, polities, economies and orientations regarding matters supernatural and spiritual' (Vertovec 1992: 106). Specific regions in India yielded particular religious traditions which, inevitably, were transported—albeit often in highly attenuated forms—to the Trinidad context. The Bengal, Bihar and Orissa regions were dominated by Shaktism (worship of the Mother Goddess) and, to a lesser extent, by *Vaishnavism* (worship of the various forms of the God Vishnu). Eastern and western Uttar Pradesh were also primarily *Vaisnavite* and permeated by the Bhakti tradition. Yet, some of these regions were also strongholds of Shaivism (worship of the God Shiva) (ibid.: 106).

Regions in the south of India also provided a high concentration of Shakti traditions. Compounding this religious melange was the presence of numerous socio-religious subgroupings specific to the different religious traditions. In his 1893 *Note on Emigration*, Surgeon Major W.D. Comins identified the presence of sects such as the *Ramanund Phunt*,[3] the *Kabeer Phunt*, the *Oughur Phunt,* and the *Sewnarain Phunt.*[4] The diversity among these four groups was very evident. He described the *Ramanand Phunt* and the *Kabeer Phunt* as being 'very clean' and not consuming meat, alcohol or fish. On the other hand, the *Oughur* and *Sewnarain Phunts* were characterized as groups in which the followers ate and drank 'everything' and ceremonies often entailed the use of alcohol. All four groups comprised mainly non-Brahmin individuals. Interestingly though, the 'headmen' of both the *Sewnarain Phunt* and the *Ramanund Phunt* were described as 'now a Brahmin'. Since their names indicated non-Brahmin origins, it can be assumed that the stature of Brahmin was assumed by the headmen to enhance their status as socio-religious leaders of these sects. In addition to the main or 'higher' deities, there were a host of lesser gods and goddesses, and district or village godlings, saints, spirits and supernatural (Vertovec 1992: 107). Much of this diversity was situated in the presence of elements of both the Great and Little Traditions of Hinduism[5] in Trinidad. Caste distinctions also added to the religious diversity. However, by the beginning of the twentieth century most of these minor traditions were being subsumed by the drive for a standardized form of Hinduism; namely the Sanatan Dharma as practiced in Trinidad.

This article endeavours to examine the various levels of religious transformation that were evident within the Hindu community during this period from the end of Indian indenture in 1917 to the year 1945. Though neither as socially visible as the period of indenture, nor ripe enough as a community, the period from 1917 to 1945 was a turning point in local Hindu history. By the 1920s, factors such as the acceptance of Trinidad as their homeland by those immigrants who had opted to remain in the colony, the leavening out of the male-female ratio and the age imbalance, and the noticeable, increase in the birth rate of Indians contributed to the characterization of the Indian population as 'a "whole" population, a vehicle and a receptacle for cultural ferment and effort' (Haraksingh 1988: 117). This 'wholeness' would facilitate the establishment of the community, which would, in turn, generate a focus on and acceleration of social and religious change. Ultimately, this would contribute to the process of identity formation within the Hindu community. The unfavourable economic conditions that dominated the period (Pemberton 1996) collectively impacted on the society, providing both the backdrop and a changing context, which acted as a potent force of such transformation.

By 1921, Indians comprised 33 per cent of the entire population, with a rise to 35 per cent in 1946.[6] Interestingly, the figure for Hindus showed a gradual decline during these years. In 1921, Hindus comprised 72.7 per cent of the Indian population; in 1931, 67 per cent; and in 1946, 64.5 per cent (Ramesar 1994). However, by 1938, J.D. Tyson, reporting on the conditions of Indians in Trinidad, was of the opinion that 'the Hindu community on the island ... has undoubtedly been "quickened" in its Hinduism during the last few years'.[7] With most of the fundamental, inherently Indian social, religious, economic and political structures in place, the drive towards personal and communal advancement witnessed a dynamic interplay between 'Indian' and 'Trinidadian', the traditional and the modern, the religious and the secular, retention and transformation, between the theory of being 'free' and the reality of restrictions. The article examines this social intercourse in the areas of religion, internal organization and social change within the traditional caste system, and the attempts of the Hindu community at visibility, mobility and self-definition within the larger Trinidad society.

REWORKING RELIGION

This period witnessed a number of key developments that contributed to the restructuring of certain aspects of Hinduism. Although by the 1920s, the Hindu community had undergone some amount of homogenization, the continued influx of Indians from India and the return and visits of Trinidad Indians to India provided a substantial level of transience and variation to the situation. During this time, the Brahmins assiduously attempted to cement their position at the top of the socio-religious hierarchy. The consolidation of a standardized form of *Sanatan Dharma* (literally, 'eternal duty, order or religion' but in this context, the generalized form of Hinduism that evolved in Trinidad) (Vertovec 1992: 245) as a representative body of Trinidad Hindus, was possibly the major struggle in which Hindus were engaged.

In addition, tentative steps were taken in the direction of formal organization. Both goals were achieved by 1945. The beginnings of the slow yet prominent move towards the notion of a 'Trinidad Hinduism' characterized this period.[8] This idea of 'Trinidad Hinduism' can best be defined as the synthesis and retention of the fundamental tenets, beliefs and rituals of the various strands of Hinduism brought and reconstructed by the indentured immigrants. The inevitable adoption, omission or altering of certain dimensions essentially mirrored the conscious or unconscious movement towards a 'Trinidad idea of religion'; that is to say, what Hinduism could or should constitute in Trinidad. Many of these changes echoed the aspiration for both individual and communal identity and mobility.

This period also came to incorporate what was popularly referred to by the Indian middle class in Trinidad as the 'Indian Renaissance', and saw the local move to reinterpret and present Hinduism (Sanskritic ideology) as more of a universal religion, whose principles and practices could apply to and, in some aspects, parallel those of the wider society. The concept of universal religion apparently played itself out in Hinduism, not as the acceptance *by* all of one religion, but as the acceptance *of* all the religions by everyone (Sharma 1998: 135). Locally, this concept was more evident in the gradual emergence of a highly simplified and uniform culture, one that tended to incorporate all the varying strands of Hinduism present in Trinidad. Thus, vegetarianism, practised by the priestly caste, was upheld as the ideal towards which one should strive in the quest for a more healthy and beneficent way of life, and within the Hindu community, as a signifier of greater ritual of purity, and hence, of higher religious and social merit. The principle of *ahimsa* (non-violence) advocated by Gandhi and strongly highlighted by the local press provided another essentially Hindu approach upon which Hindu and Indian leaders and political aspirants could base their arguments.

The worship of a multiplicity of deities was always a characteristic feature of both popular and Sanskritic Hinduism (pertaining to the Great Tradition in Hinduism, which is embedded in the culture of the 'twice-born' castes). Since Hinduism was seemingly polytheistic in an otherwise monotheistic society, the pressure for recognition and status saw a move by community leaders, priests, and other local figures to reinforce the idea of a single Supreme.[9] While Hinduism could never fit into the Western definition of monotheism, there was increasing emphasis on the principle of one God with multiple forms and names; this was especially evident in the emergence of various socio-religious groups. Nothing, however, was allowed to detract from the divinity of any of the various deities. Hindus based their choice of a 'special' deity on personal preference, while simultaneously worshipping a miltitude of others.

Nevertheless, several aspects of Hinduism, usually originating in the Little (folk) Tradition, were rejected by some of those who aspired for a higher status. Practices such as animal sacrifices and the 'fire pass' ritual, and the worship of deities connected to these events were toned down, modified or dropped altogether, and both publicly and privately denounced. Thus, even a folk ritual such as the Dee puja[10] began to elicit mixed reactions towards what was heretofore a vital aspect of the performance, namely, the sacrifice of a rooster. In an attempt to emulate the ritually higher Sanskritic practices such as performing yagnas (a series of religious rites and ceremonial readings spanning five to fourteen days) and observing only certain religious festivals and occasions, the common practices by the south Indians (and non-south Indians) of smoking ganja (marijuana), consuming alcohol during and after *Ramayana* satsangs, and even consuming meat on Diwali day were also abjured. Interestingly enough, the south Indians practised their own refinement of the caste system, with those engaged in 'hog-puja' (religious ritual involving the sacrifice of a pig) relegated to the lowest position. Many south Indians refused to attend such pujas, deeming them 'dirty and low'.[11] However, some other south Indians practices, notably those not directly contingent on Sanskritic Hinduism such as Kali worship, and some funerary and wedding rituals were not totally expunged.

The Bhakti form of worship (Hindu religious orientation of loving devotion to God), prevalent in the Ganges basin during the period of recruitment for indenture, and hence, widely subscribed to by Hindus in Trinidad, posed a formidable challenge to Sanskritization (the process by which 'low' Hindu caste, or tribal or other group, changes its customs, ritual ideology, and way of life in the direction of a high and frequently, 'twice-born' caste).[12] The excision of the intermediary between the devotee and God—the hallmark of Bhakti—promoted the awareness that priests were not necessary for the acquisition of spiritual merit and that anyone, not just Brahmins (and including women), could perform the necessary rituals. This would eventually contribute to a decrease in the ritual monopoly and social importance of the Brahmins some of whom, it must be said, responded by adopting several features of the Bhakti form of worship.

In addition, while Brahmins were still the principal holders of the proverbial trump card in ritual performance and the knowledge of Sanskrit mantras, their jealously guarded monopoly even in this vital area was increasingly challenged. The Arya Samaj, the reformist Hindu sect formed in India in 1875 and existing in Trinidad since around 1910, initiated the translation of Sanskrit mantra's into both Hindi and English, making them more accessible to the population at large. Those who considered the sound of the Sanskrit words integral to these chants questioned whether the translation was appropriate as some of the mystery was obviously lost.

Persons aspiring to improve their social status adopted what can be termed as 'personal Sanskritization'. This involved the adoption, in varying degrees, of various elements of a Sanskritized lifestyle such as vegetarianism, teetotalism, and becoming particular about the performance of such religious activities as regularly reciting from the holy texts, attending and participating in religious discourses, and joining religious groups. This usually led to the individual rising in the esteem of his relatives, friends and community. Sometimes, however, especially if the individual hailed from a very low caste, he might become an object of ridicule. It was not uncommon for a non-Brahmin, especially those who functioned as priests of their respective castes, to officiate at the smaller scale satsangs and readings of the holy texts. Such individuals however, in preparation for the role of priest, would engage in 'temporary Sanskritization', abstaining from meat-eating and other 'vices' for several days, and would also meticulously dress the part. Many shared the view that pundits then could be 'any capable person, not just Brahmins'.[13] The larger scale yagnas and weddings however, were still the exclusive domain of the Brahmin priest, though they had to share the space (but not the ritual status) with non-Brahmin pundits with regard to performing pujas.

Possibly the most blatant, though singular, example of the challenge to Brahminic supremacy was the initiation in 1943 of a non-Brahmin woman, Deokie Devi, as a pundit (*Trinidad Guardian,* 31 January 1945). Although the first formal initiation and recognition of a woman as a priest, this isolated incident simply echoed the common presence of female saintly figures and healers in Hinduism. Such individuals also had to subscribe to the previously noted elements of a Sanskritized lifestyle and through these means acquired a certain aura of holiness and evoked an appropriate level of community respect. The ascension of non-Brahmins to the status of religious and social leaders was substantially facilitated by the egalitarianism of Bhakti worship. Some contribution to this development, though, came from the fact that many Hindu socio-religious (often non-Brahminic) organizations emerged during this period, and also from the absence of any authoritative body or formal structure to pronounce on religious claims or pretensions.

During this period the qualities and requisites of leaders, both spiritual and lay, were being redefined. While among the general Hindu population Brahmins (priests and non-priests) continued to receive respect and adulation, newer factors were added to the customary, largely ritually ascribed list of prerequisites of Hindu leadership passed on from generation to generation. These included the level of English education, personal and family financial status, personal credibility and appeal and the individual's potential as a credible representative or spokesman of the Hindu community in the eyes of the wider society. In addition, an understanding of the philosophical aspect of Hinduism rather than just ritualism, personal reputation based on one's own religious competence, and other factors such as if, and how many times, the individual had visited India all acted as hierarchical markers among Brahmins. Pundits who had acquired an English education and had a working knowledge of the non-Hindu community tended to look down upon others as ignorant and unschooled. For example, Pundit Capildeo, grandfather of V.S. Naipaul, refused to perform a wedding ceremony with another pundit citing his reason as: 'I don't want him to say that he did a wedding ceremony with me, for he is an illiterate man' (DeVerteuil 1989: 132).

While in India the process of Sanskritization has normally been initiated by the lower groups, in the diaspora it has proven to be two-dimensional, initiated variously by both the lower and higher groups. In Trinidad, this move was discernible, albeit with great variation, and more so during the latter part of the 1940s. While it was reported that certain Brahmins absolutely refused to perform Sanatan rituals at the homes of Chamars (low caste of leather workers within the traditional Hindu caste system) and other low caste individuals, most agreed to do them out of fear also of losing 'control of their flock' to the non-

Brahmin pundits. They would, however, refuse to take part in the ritual feast associated with the event.[14] This attitude on the part of the Brahmins echoed the nature of competitive politics within the Hindu community, and the 'love-hate relationship' between the Brahmins and the lower castes. The Brahmins needed the numbers of the Hindu masses to support their dominant position, and in return, the lower groups gained a higher level of recognition and respect from having a Brahmin perform at their functions. The Brahmins, however, were careful to limit the boundaries of their participation, so that their relative status would not be compromised.

During this period, Hindu rituals and festivals were also undergoing change. While not a new phenomenon, non-Brahmin pundits were also increasingly taking advantage of the economic and educational opportunities to enhance their social and ritual status. Frequent notices in the local press such as that of Pundit Seusankar Seunarine, Secretary of the Sanatan Dharma Pratinidhi Sabha, going abroad to study medicine provided evidence of this development (*Trinidad Guardian,* 3 January 1945). There was a steady, notable rise in the quantum and scale of rituals and celebrations performed at a community level. This was facilitated by a marked increase in the appearance of temples in almost every major area where Hindus lived. Activities organized by groups usually reflected an awareness of the perceived need to revive, reform and promote Hinduism in a manner that would impart a greater degree of visibility and acceptability of both the religion and its adherents.

Temple-based collective worship became more noticeable in Trinidad during this period due to a remarkable growth in the construction of temples. The durability of the material being used (stone, clay, bricks and wood), the addition of the kutiya (small, hut-like structure usually made of rudimentary material) alongside the traditional temples, and the increasing use of temples for the purposes of preaching and political activities provided additional indicators of changes in Hindu society. According to Carolyn Prorok, 'changes in temple form reveal changes specifically associated with the Hindu population ... changes which indicate processes of Sanskritization and Westernization' (1988: 74–5). Temples also served as the preferred meeting places where issues relating to the Hindu community, often in relation to their social mobility as a group, were discussed, debated and sometimes resolved. Thus, they functioned as both the basis and markers of the increase in Hindu organizational development during this period.

The inclusion of non-Hindu elements and observances, while reflecting the accommodative and assimilative nature of Hinduism, exemplify attempts—though very possibly not deliberate—at incorporation into the wider society. During the period of indenture, the *La Divina Pastora* deity (a Roman Catholic saint) was adopted into the Hindu pantheon as *Sipari Mai* (Mother of Siparia). This was facilitated through the goddess-worship aspect of Hinduism and the prominence placed on spiritual-curative aids. Since then, Hindus continued to journey to Siparia to make offerings to the statue, which was quite similar in appearance to some *murtis* (image or small statue of deity) of female Hindu deities. The deity was worshipped in the church in a recognizably Hindu manner. The primary purpose of visits to *Sipari Mai* was to secure relief from illnesses, and to pray for offspring. Many Hindus often conducted the first ritual shaving of a child's hair at that location and symbolically offered the shaved hair to *Sipari Mai*. The inclusion of *La Divina Pastora* into the Hindu pantheon also instigated the observance of Good Friday as an auspicious day. All Saint's day was also incorporated into the rituals pertaining to the dead. On that day, many Hindus cleaned the graves of their dead, decorated them with flowers, and lit candles on the graves in the evening.

The religious texts, primarily the *Ramayana* and the *Bhagvad Purana,* assisted in the dissemination of knowledge about the Great Gods, and in the spread of a common culture throughout the country. Through the medium of the stories of the Puranas (sacred writings in Sanskrit on Hindu mythology and folklore) certain basic theological ideas of Sanskritic Hinduism were made available to ordinary folk. These texts also filtered out many, usually questionable, and in the quest for social mobility, often undesirable elements of the local folk tradition, such as animal sacrifice and the associated deities. The promotion of essentially Sanskritic ideals in areas such as family life, social organization and politics using the actions of the characters in these epics as the model, further prompted the Hindu population to aspire towards such values and behaviour, and to relinquish those that did not conform. The advent of Indian films in Trinidad brought the texts and gods to life through films, thereby deepening aspirations for the Sanskritic culture exalted in these films.

Any examination of mobility within Hindu society demands some insight into the existent (or non-existent) dynamics of caste within the specific geographical, historical and cultural context. Much work has been done on the caste system within the diaspora, and it has been established that, rather than a full-blown transplantation, there was more of an attenuation and reworking of the traditional system, resulting in emphasis on the basic and very diluted gradation of the four main varnas (caste groupings). The various restrictions encountered in the attempt at adjusting and reconstructing an Indian social system in an overseas setting saw, among many other modifications, the almost total dissolution of the concerns, restrictions and boundaries of the numerous jatis or sub-groups within the four major varnas (Brahmin, Kshatriya, Vaishya and Shudra). The system of power relations encountered in Trinidad proved to be at variance with the traditional caste system, itself a system of power relations based on very clearly defined occupational categories permeated by the notion of ritual purity and pollution. In these circumstances, the recreation of the traditional caste system was virtually impossible. Thus, rather than a fixed 'caste system', what emerged by the end of the nineteenth century can more aptly be described as a very modified and fluid ideology or sentiment of caste, becoming even more diluted and modified through constant interaction with divergent systems, lifestyles, values and beliefs. The often suspect nature of the authenticity of claims to Brahminism also further the situation.

The issue of naming provides an interesting dimension to the process of Sanskritization. A number of the interviewees reported that, until the 1920s, caste was a major deciding factor in the assigning of names to individuals. The Brahmins reserved special names for members of their caste, and gave 'lower caste names'[15] (such as naming persons according to the day of the week on which they were born) to the non-Brahmin population. By the 1930s many were opting for names with such prefixes as *'Ram-'*, and *'Jag-'* (a variation of yagna), and for the names of the gods and deities such as 'Krishna', 'Sita', 'Latchman'. The tendency for children to assume the first name of the father as their surname[16] made it more possible for persons, and eventually their families, to acquire a ritually higher name.

INTERNAL ORGANIZATION AND SOCIAL MOBILITY

Though not as noticeable to the wider society as some of the Indian organizations others such as the Sanatan Dharma Board of Control (SDBC) and Sanatan Dharma Association (SDA) were already serving as representatives of the Hindu population by the beginning of the twentieth century. This was evident in the rallying of the pundits throughout the island into a 'national panchayat' in response to the flogging to death of an Indian during the strikes of November and December 1919 (DeVerteuil 1989: 138). As historian Kelvin Singh has explained, the Hindu priest was viewed as 'extremely important in giving the mass of the Indians psychological protection in a society basically hostile to them, racially, culturally, economically...'. (1974: 41).

During the 1920s, there emerged numerous organized Sanatanist groups usually labelled 'Hindu Sabha' throughout Trinidad (embedded in the generalized, orthodox form of Hinduism which evolved in both India and Trinidad). By 1928, there were various attempts at integrating these organizations and the larger Hindu community into a more united body. There was also an All Trinidad Hindu Conference geared towards 'unifying Hindu Sabhas throughout the country' (*East Indian Weekly,* 24 November 1928). By the 1920s however, the increasing adoption of the classically-based and communally-shared Sanatan Dharma, by most of the smaller subsects of Trinidad Hinduism, left the Arya Samaj as the only potential adversary to Sanatanist, and hence, Brahminic religious authority (Vertovec 1992: 112). Formally established in 1934, but existent in Trinidad and Tobago since around 1910, the Arya Samaj posed a most direct and formidable challenge to one of the major structural and ideological pillars of Hinduism at that time: caste ideology. This organization espoused a paradoxical admixture of Western organizational forms and procedures, and selective, often reinterpreted Vedic ideology aimed at Sanatanists and their existent religious belief systems. Its negation of the idea of caste by birth provided the platform from which many of the extremely low caste individuals could achieve both religious and social mobility. Its followers, leaders and priesthood (some of whom had failed to win acceptance by orthodox Brahmins) comprised mainly non-Brahmins. Younger persons, with some degree of formal English education, usually of the middle class, were prominent in the group.

The Samaj challenged the foundation of the existing Sanatanist system of power relations, the *Guru-Chela* (preceptor-disciple) system, which had as its basis the precedence of personal loyalties over communal or principle-based loyalties, and which ensured Brahmin socio-religious and political authority regardless of personal and public behaviour. This system was regarded by the Samaj as the root of factional conflict and as greatly responsible for the lack of mobilization, solidarity and consequently, social mobility of the Hindu society as a group in the larger society. The attempt of the samaj to adhere to democratic, constitutionally regulated organizational forms and procedures provided a possible avenue out of the stranglehold of the priestly caste and towards social and religious uplift, both for individuals and for the group as a whole.

In response, the Sanatanists embarked on their own drive towards mobilization of their followers. Sanatanist pundits and supporters organized themselves, so that by April 1938 more than 21 local Sanatan Dharma Sabhas had been established (*Port-of-Spain Gazette,* 10 April 1938). Community meetings and lectures were regularly held, and Sanatanist scholars from India were invited to Trinidad (*Port-of-Spain Gazette,* 25 April 1937). In the drive for Hindu social mobility and visibility, the Hindu community eventually rejected the input of Christian Indians, which was previously welcomed, or, at the least, tolerated.

The 1930s entailed a great deal of organizational activity among Hindus. The SDBC put forward strong proposals to the government for the allocation of ecclesiastical grants to the Hindu community. The legal recognition of Hindu marriages, the language issue in relation to adult franchise, and divorce, formed the core of debate among Hindu organizations. In addition, the drive towards Indian independence, the collection of funds for the Bengal famine and the lobbying for the construction of Hindu and Indian denominational schools, all led to collective action among Hindu organizations otherwise wrought with strife and conflict. Both the efforts and successes enhanced the pride and sense of visibility of the Hindu population. This was especially the case with the opening of the Hindu-Muslim school in 1930. In 1937, the East Indian Advisory Board, chaired by the Protector of Immigrants, was formed for the purpose of advising '[the] government on all matters relating to East Indians in the colony'. Of a total of 10 members, at least three were Hindus (*Port-of-Spain Gazette,* 22 April 1937). In 1938, there was an amalgamation of the two major organizations, the SDBC and the SDA (*Port-of-Spain Gazette,* 20 November 1938). Attempts at cooperation were made even by the Sanatanists and Arya Samajists (*Port-of-Spain Gazette,* 4 June 1939).

Such attempts at cooperation notwithstanding, Hindu leadership during this period was defined by factionalism and a general lack of solidarity and unanimity, which was quite often reflected in, and even obstructed the pursuit of many official matters pertaining to Hindu social mobility. Almost 20 years after the introduction of the Hindu Marriage issue into the Legislative Council, the Hon. T.M. Kelshall, a member of the appointed committee, concluded that 'the question of priests' was a major problem while reflecting both his and the wider society's misunderstanding of Hindu organizational function and structure. 'Every sect of priest objected to every other sect of priest' (Hansard 1944: 434). In 1945, the Governor, Sir Clifford Bede stated that if 'the Hindu bodies were more closely united they would become eligible for capitation Grant' (*Trinidad Guardian,* 22 February 1945).

Within the Hindu community however, this issue of factionalism elicited seemingly contradictory attitudes. While in the eyes of the larger society and on the administrative level, factionalism did prove to be a problem, many Hindus, entrenched in the *Guru-Chela* system and not bothered about religious diversity, were not too concerned. When verbal or physical altercations did erupt, it was more a reaction to condemnations of aspects of their religion and religious practice, rather than due to any innate animosity with a certain organization. The newness of and uniformity inherent in essentially Western forms of organization, in reality, could not cater to the diversity of the ideology, practice and structure of Hindu. This was noticeable in the ongoing lack of unanimity, despite the official 'resolutions' of many issues. Essentially, the conflict was, in a sense, an 'outside' imposition; a result of trying to impose a framework which made sense to the wider society but which could not fully accommodate the divergences of Hindu systems and structures.

The institution of marriage emerged on a national level as possibly the most contentious of Hindu issues in the form of the Marriage Bill, highlighting, yet again, the conflict between Hindu and Western ideologies, the Hindu attempt at being accepted as equally valid members of the Trinidad society, and the reluctance of the Brahmins to endanger their stronghold on their followers. This issue was taken up from as early as 1923, at the seventh meeting of the Ordinary Session of the Legislative Council (*Port-of-Spain Gazette,* 5 May 1923). Conflict was multifaceted. The problem was, however, more deeply ensconced in the conflict of religions, ideologies and cultures.

In addition to the disagreement about marriage officers, several other concerns variously related to religion were raised within the Hindu community. The registration of marriages, a civil ceremony, was far removed from the sacred nature of the Hindu ceremony and rituals. As far as the Hindu community was concerned, once their ceremony had been performed, and hence, sanctioned by their gods and other major characters of the religious texts, no further validation was needed. Many aspects of the ceremony such as the *Kanya Daan* (gift of a 'virgin') were being undermined by the conditions of the proposed Marriage Bill. In keeping with the Western notion of a virgin as someone who had not had sexual intercourse, the suggested age of sixteen for marriage seemed reasonable. However, since according to the Hindu interpretation, *kanya* meant not literally a virgin but, rather, a (female) child who had not yet started menstruating, the age of sixteen directly contradicted the innate significance of this ritual. In addition, the actual ritual involved the child sitting on the lap of her father, which ought not to be done if the girl was no longer a *kanya*.

Connected to the issue of the legalization of Hindu marriages, was the 'illegitimacy' of persons born of such unions. Within the boundaries of the Hindu community, neither was viewed as an issue since their traditional marriage ceremony was all the validation needed for both the union and offspring. However the need to ensure inheritance rights was a key push factor in that direction, since, in addition to lengthy and expensive court procedures, there were many cases of property being escheated to the state upon the death of the owner (Hansard 1941: 117). The removal of the stigma of illegitimacy would also serve to enhance the status of the Hindu community in the wider society.

The acquisition of education in both Hindi and English was another major agent of social mobility within the Hindu community and on a wider level. In 1921, only 12.6 per cent of the Indian population was classified as being able to read. In 1931, this number rose to 22.8 per cent, and in 1946, to 40.2 per cent (Ramesar 1994: 114). The 1946 census classified as illiterate (either able to read only or unable to read and write English) 50.6 per cent of Indians. In the same year, just over 25 per cent of pupils attending both primary and intermediate schools were Hindus (*Colony of Trinidad and Tobago Census Album,* 1948). Despite the economic and social constraints, suspicions, fears and taboos, it was clear that the desire for both individual and communal mobility resulted in the increasing gravitation towards acquiring an education in both English and Hindi.

The desire to educate Hindus in both Hindi and Hindu ideology and culture led to the appearance of numerous Hindi schools and *pathshalas* (localized village schools engaged in the teaching of Hindi and aspects of Hindu religion and culture) in almost every Hindu residential area. From as early as 1928, meetings were held to discuss the inclusion of Hindi and Urdu into the Western school curriculum (*East Indian Weekly,* 13 October 1928).[17] In order to sensitize the Hindu community on the issue, public lectures on the importance of education were held. One wealthy merchant even began distributing Hindi primers free of charge to the population (*East Indian Weekly,* 31 August 1929). In addition to the localized *pathshalas* and Hindu schools, this period saw the emergence of the first few formalized Hindu schools with a curriculum mirroring that of the wider educational system. The forerunner in this development was the much prized Hindu-Muslim school established in Chaguanas in 1930, which though identified in the popular mind with the Arya Samaj, was rather a collective effort on the part of non-Christian Indians.

The emphasis on organization had a profound impact on the existing condition and structure of local Hinduism. Formal organization now allowed for a wider networking, and hence, the opportunity for mass consultations among pundits and leaders and for more standardized decisions. Large-scale yagnas were now being arranged and advertised through the press. Amidst the prevalent factionalism within the Hindu community during the 1930s and 1940s, each subgroup resorted to varying degrees of borrowing from the other to increase their viability and status both within and beyond the boundaries of the Hindu community. Thus, while the Samajists promoted several essentially Western and Christian forms, many Sanatanists began adopting some of these forms, such as daytime weddings, 'Sunday Services', and Western clothing.

The traditional Hindu panchayat system (a group—usually five—of village elders which, based on a combination of intelligence, and social, economic and religious status, is entrusted with the responsibility of resolving both family and communal disputes) also demonstrated evidence of social mobility and change. Internally, being a member of the panchayat meant occupying the highest social position in the village; one accorded possibly the greatest degree of respect and authority. Judgements of the panchayat could have direct bearing on the status of both individuals and entire families in the village. The most outstanding evidence of this was the application of the state of *kujat* (outcaste) which involved the barring of the offender(s) from any kind of social interaction with fellow villagers; with the duration of the ban dependent on the gravity of the offence. Such offences included intra-village, inter-religious, or worst of all, inter-racial marriages; and the time period could range from a few months, to a few years, to life.[18]

Until the early 1920s the composition of the panchayat was based on a flexible combination of caste, age, moral uprightness, scriptural and religious knowledge and a sound sense of judgement. By the late 1930s, however, factors such as English education and economic status were added to, and sometimes even superseded, the more traditional determinants. In addition to the presence of wealthy non-Brahmins, the age restriction was being broken with the infiltration of some comparably younger members on the basis of their level of English education. However, the one enduring prerequisite for members was good character.

As with most tradition-based systems and institutions, the authority of the panchayat remained unquestioned as long as the traditional order which sanctioned its role remained intact and its rulings could be enforced. Thus, as the period came to an end, the increasing awareness and adoption of the alternative (State Law), resulting from the increasing entry of individuals into the wider society, generated a gradual reduction of the authority of the panchayat's decisions, since individuals could now override unfavourable decisions, and appeal to a much higher order.

It is evident therefore that the Hindu community in Trinidad possessed its own, unique systems and values, neither exclusively Indian, nor exclusively Trinidadian, but which rather, was a checkered combination of both. Along this perspective, the proposed theory of selective Sanskritization works to best elucidate social mobility within this religious group. It is clear that in this period the defining characteristics of Hinduism such as it being a 'way of life' (rather than a 'religion' in the Western sense), the inextricable interaction of the religious and the secular, the diversity and flexibility of the tradition and the precedence of group dynamics over individualism were at work in almost all spheres of Hindu life. This led to unavoidable conflict when faced with, more often than not, opposing Western and secular values, institutions and procedures.

While factors such as caste, level of subscription to the dominant Sanskritic culture landownership, economic position, and the *Guru-Chela* and panchayat systems of power relations were still the major determinants of social rank and mobility, they were being increasingly tempered by the gradual infiltration of Western, elements such as education, urbanization, and secularization. This of course was most evident among those, individuals or groups, usually the higher class/castes, engaged in a conscious bid for social mobility and the creation of a Hindu identity.

The process of natural filtration and the desire to emulate the socially higher groups gradually guided this interplay into the lives of the larger Hindu community. However, the diversity of both the Hindu religion and the local Hindu population generated great variation in the degree, rate and adopted factors of this interplay of cultures, lifestyles, and structures.

NOTES

1. These numbers were derived from the Annual Reports of the Protector of Emigrants, Calcutta 1874–1917. However, according to Vertovec, the categories are rather crude and artificial and reflect more the conceptions of colonial administrators than the indigenous social categories.
2. See Laurence (1994) for a detailed description and analysis of the system of indenture.
3. The term *phunt* is a corruption of *panth* which refers to a religious sect or group.
4. IOR Official Series V/27/820/10: Note on Emigration from India to Trinidad by Surgeon Major W.D. Comins, Calcutta: Bengal Secretariat Press, 1893.
5. In Hinduism, the Little Tradition refers to those aspects which have evolved independently of the Great Tradition. These are usually embedded in orality, and are geographically localized and linguistically restrictive. The Great Tradition refers to the essentially Sanskritic/Brahminic strand of Hinduism which is embedded in the Vedas and other Sanskrit literature.
6. Colony of Trinidad and Tobago Census Album, 1948.
7. IOR Public and Judicial Department Records L/PJ/8/338: Royal Commission on the West Indies, Deputation of J.D. Tyson to the West Indies; Tyson's Report on the Condition of Indians in Jamaica, British Guiana and Trinidad; Labour Conditions in the West Indies (1938–43), p. 27.
8. Some interviewees, mainly those in leadership positions, are still quite reluctant to accept this idea, primarily due to political purposes, or the desire to maintain 'purity and exclusivity'.
9. Crystallized towards the end of *Rig Veda Samhitas*, and fully developed between the *Samhitas* and *Brahmanas*.

10. Propitiation of the deity believed to be the protector of one's residential and agricultural property.
11. Moonsammy, personal interview, 7 November 2001.
12. This term was coined by Indian anthropologist M.N. Srinivas in his work *The Cohesive Role of Sanskritisation and Other Essays,* Bombay: OUP, 1989.
13. Ramdial Boodram, personal interview, 10 October 1999.
14. Pundit Lutchmie Persad, personal interview, 9 February 2002.
15. Hardeo Ramsingh, personal interview, 7 October 2001.
16. The surname was essentially a concept imposed on/adopted by Indians in their attempts at conforming to the policies and practices of the larger society.
17. By the 1940s, it was acknowledged that Hindi was being taught at the Canadian Mission schools for 90 minutes each week. The government schools had very little or no Hindi at all.
18. Pundit Lutchmie Persad, personal interview, 21 July 2001.

REFERENCES

Brereton, Bridget (1981), *A History of Modern Trinidad 1783–1962,* USA: Heinemann International.

DeVerteuil, Anthony (1989), *Eight East Indian Immigrants,* Port-of-Spain: Paria Publishing Co. Ltd.

Haraksingh, Kusha (1985), 'Aspects of the Indian Experience in the Caribbean', in *Calcutta to Caroni: The East Indians of Trinidad,* ed. John la Guerre, St. Augustine: Extra Mural Studies Unit, University of the West Indies.

——— (1988), 'Structure, Process and Indian Culture in Trinidad', in *Immigrants & Minorities,* London: Frank Cass and Company Limited.

Laurence, K.O. (1994), *A Question of Labour: Indentured Immigration into Trinidad and British Guiana 1875–1917,* Jamaica: Ian Randle Publishers.

Pemberton, Rita (1996), 'The Evolution of Agricultural Policy in Trinidad and Tobago 1890–1945', Ph.D. Dissertation, University of the West Indies.

Prorok, Carolyn V. (1988), 'Hindu Temples in Trinidad: A Cultural Geography of Religious Structures and Ethnic Identity', Ph.D. Dissertation, University of Pittsburgh.

Ramesar, Marianne (1994), *Survivors of Another Crossing: A History of East Indians in Trinidad, 1880–1946,* St. Augustine: University of the West Indies, School of Continuing Studies.

Sharma, Arvind (1998), *The Concept of Universal Religion in Modern Hindu Thought,* New York: Palgrave.

Singh, Kelvin (1974), 'Indians and the Larger Society', in *Calcutta to Caroni,* Trinidad: Extra Mural Studies Unit, University of the West Indies.

Vertovec, Steven (1992), *Hindu Trinidad: Religion, Ethnicity and Socio-Economic Change,* London: Macmillan Education.

5

The Caribbean Consequences of the Indian Revolt of 1857

Brinsley Samaroo

THE IMPACT OF the Indian Revolt of 1857 on South Asian and imperial history has been very extensively studied and continues to be a subject of heated debate. This article seeks to examine one further dimension of that period of turbulence, namely, its significant impact on Caribbean history. The Revolt occurred at a time when vigorous attempts were being made on this side of the water to replace/displace African labour in the wake of British abolition and of subsequent efforts to end the enslavement of Africans by those leaders who had delayed abolition. For the British West Indian plantocracy particularly in the newer areas of settlement—Demerara, Belize and Trinidad—the source of supply was to be Asia, hence the high demand for coolies from China and India. Indian immigration to the Caribbean had started in 1838 with the delivery of 396 labourers to Demerara. Complaints about ill-treatment caused a temporary cessation in 1839 but in 1845 the body trade was resumed with full force, extending its tentacles over a period of time to Jamaica, Grenada, Trinidad, Belize, St.Vincent, St. Croix and St. Kitts. Soon the French joined this lucrative trade and from 1853 thousands were brought to French Guiana, Martinique and Guadeloupe from Pondicherry.

In the midst of this thriving commerce in human beings, the Great Revolt rocked large parts of India. This event had a major impact on the movement of immigrants in that the period after 1858 witnessed a distinctively noticeable increase in the number of Indians destined for the Caribbean. Among the large increase of labourers to this region there could have been many who had actively participated in the Revolt. The problem of identifying such persons is necessarily a difficult one. Participants in the Revolt who wished to migrate were forced to hide their identities or places of residence since the British Indian bureaucracy and militia, actively sought out such persons to hang them from the nearest tree or to blow them out of the mouths of cannons. On 20 June 1857, for example, the *Roorkee Garrison Gazette* proudly proclaimed:

Ten mutineers of the 54 Regiment R.I. were tried at Umbala yesterday, convicted and blown away from guns.

After the most difficult phase had passed, Queen Victoria was minded to a policy of clemency. Her 1858 proclamation assured that:

> Our power has been shown by the suppression of that rebellion in the field. We desire to show our mercy, by pardoning those whom have been this misled, but who desire to return to the path of duty.

However for the men on the ground 'the monarch was an abstraction to be venerated; what had to be safeguarded was their personal stake in the longevity of the Raj' (Oldenburg 1989: xix–xx). Behind every bush these executors of British rule saw revolution and further mayhem and were hardly lenient:

> Thus Rajah Jye Lal Singh the Commander in Chief of the Begum of Oude was hanged on 1st October 1859; even later Khan Bahadur Khan of Bareilly was captured and hanged on 8th September 1862. Years after the events the British Press was noting the capture and sentencing of rebels. (Taylor 1996: 147)

In the state of Oudh, a major centre of Revolt and perhaps the primary supplier of indentured Caribbean labour, there was an 'obsessive witch hunt for disloyal nawabi nobles', that is, those who had shown faithfulness to the last nawab Wajid Ali Shah (Oldenburg 1989: 248). More than half a century after 1857, the British used the standard of the revolt to judge Indians. The recruiting handbooks still classified Indian social groups according to the stand they had adopted during the Uprising (Omissi 1994: 30). In such circumstances it was only logical that those seeking to escape British vengeance had to move incognito. It would be the argument of this article that the Revolt was directly and indirectly the cause of a considerable increase in the numbers of destitute and desperate Indians who were forced to leave their ancestral place. Second, among such people there appears to have been a fair number who had participated in that momentous uprising against British rule.

PRECURSORS TO 1857

The years 1757 and 1857 stand out as perhaps the two most significant dates in the history of modern India. The former, 1757, in fact led directly to 1857. It was in January 1757 that the East India Company's troops under Robert Clive finally retook Calcutta and its major defence centre, Fort William after a year of skirmishing against of the Nawab of Bengal Siraj ud Daulah who had expelled the British from there in June 1756. In order to press his advantage, Clive conspired with some of the Nawab's trusted lieutenants led by Mir Jaffar and led a march towards the Nawab's capital at Murshidabad. In June 1757 the betrayed regent was easily routed at the Battle of Plassey, just outside the capital city. The Nawab was captured and beheaded and the Company took control of Bengal. Clive was not unaware of the value of this new acquisition; he compared it with the opulence of London. He found Murshidabad to be:

As extensive populous and rich as London, with individuals possessing infinitely greater property than those in the English metropolis. One of its palaces situated on the Western bank (of the Bhagirathi River) was big enough to accommodate three European monarchs. (cited in Majumdar 1905: 7)

In that same report Clive noted that the inhabitants of the city were so numerous that if they had been inclined to destroy the British, they could have done so easily with sticks and stones.

In July 1757, hardly a month after Plassey, there arrived in Calcutta the first consignment of Murshidabad's treasures: Rs. 76 lakh (7.6 million) as well as coined silver packed in 700 chests laden on 100 boats. In another six weeks coins worth Rs. 40 lakh (4 million) again arrived in Calcutta to meet the losses sustained by the British army. An Englishman in Calcutta, recalling these events during the early twentieth century commented that 'never before did the English nation obtain such a prize in solid money' (Cotton 1909: 60–1).[1] Mir Jaffar who had so treacherously replaced Siraj ud Daulah rewarded the senior employees of the Company handsomely; Clive's share being £234,000. Clive later acknowledged the largesse which he received:

I was amongst the many who benefited by his favour. I never sought to conceal it; but declared publicly in my letters to the Secret Committee of India Directors that the nawab's generosity had made my fortune easy, and that the Company's welfare was now my only motive for staying in India. The Company had acquired £1-1/2 million and revenue of £100,000 per annum from the success of the forces under my command. (cited in Majumdar 1905: 296)

A grateful British nation heaped honours on their new hero. Clive was knighted at 34, made Baron of Plassey and later Governor General and Commander-in-Chief of Bengal. At the end, though harassed by his detractors, he committed suicide in November 1774. Nevertheless, his statue now adorns a prominent plinth in London's historic Westminster borough, adjacent to other creators of Empire. Therefore, 1757 must be seen as that crucial point when the Company made its major breakthrough in the conquest of Bengal, gateway to India's fertile Gangetic plain. After 1757, the *diwani*, that is the power to administer civil government and collect revenue, passed on to the English *sarkar* (government). Therefore, the subcontinent was milked relentlessly as Britain proceeded apace, combining West Indian and (East) Indian resources in a vast mercantilist triangle which created the first links between India and the Caribbean.

As mentioned earlier, the exploitation which became entrenched in 1757, led straight on to 1857. A century after Plassey there had arisen a widespread belief in India that events had gone on far enough. Even before 1857 this anger was being expressed in numerous uprisings. I shall now look very briefly at a few examples during the period immediately preceding 1857. The Moplahs of Malabar, a determined Islamic group was a constant thorn in the British flesh.

In 1843 and again in 1849 they revolted and had to be suppressed forcibly. They seemed a highly motivated people who stored and passed on their military tradition through songs and ballads. This tradition was transferred through their *cheeror* ballads which celebrated the prowess of ancestors and promised celestial rewards to those who maintained the heroic tradition. One British magistrate called these ballads 'the most frightfully fanatical and murder-inciting chaunt that can be imagined. The mosques are the repositories of these exciting ballads' (IOR 1857a).

In 1857 the Moplahs were again on the warpath, harassing and plundering British settlements in the Madras area. One Moplah leader was convicted for singing 'the songs which incite to deeds of violence and blood after the example of former fanatics' (IOR 1857a). In northern India around Patna, a major source for the recruitment of indentured labour, the turmoil was continuous. A nineteenth century Commissioner for the Patna region considered Patna 'a seat of disaffection and intrigue' and noted that the conspiracy of 1846 was but a branch of a more general plot, namely, 'the destruction of the English, the overthrow of British government' (W. Taylor, cited in Nath 1980: 3). Equally important was the Santhal Movement (1855–7) in which these tribals from Bihar waged constant warfare against the British. They were the cause of such exasperation to British Indian interests that the *London Times* strongly suggested that they be transported to some distant Caribbean colonies (*Port-of-Spain Gazette* (*POSG*), 11 October 1857). Finally in 1856 a frustrated British officer requested military assistance in East Bengal:

> In no part of India is the proportion of Mahomedans so great as in Eastern Bengal and of late years a great number of them have formed themselves into a strong, energetic and growing sect. Since I have been in India there have been three serious disturbances in the country between Calcutta and Dacca. (IOR 1856)[2]

In the same document there is a February 1856 complaint from the indigo planters of Bengal about increasing tension among the people around Dacca and the great insecurity felt by the indigo producers. These fields of indigo had replaced extensive areas previously dedicated to food crops which had provided sustenance to hundreds of thousands of peasants in East Bengal. Now there was anger against the large-scale conversion to a non-edible commercial crop. In 1917 Mahatma Gandhi had, once again, to take up the plight of the indigo workers, this time in Champaran, Bihar. The argument of his account of pre-1857 unrest is that the Revolt of 1857 did not come as a bolt from the blue. The build-up was present; the cartridge case lubricated with a mixture of beef and pork fat was the spark which ignited the fire of revolt.

THE PROBLEM OF DEFINITION

Since 1857 there has been considerable debate on the definition of 1857. On the one hand, the creators of the English language have persistently sought to change the nature of the discourse relating to 1857. For the British establishment, 1857 was no more than a sepoy mutiny, an uprising of disgruntled soldiers who did not desire any fundamental change of the system of governance. According to this view, those who took up arms in 1857 wanted change within the system, not change of the system. There is, on the other hand, a significant school of subaltern thought which sees 1857, not as a mutiny but rather as a revolt which demanded a return of rule to the people of India. Even among the British ruling class this difference of definition was very noticeable. As we enter the debate in this article, let us begin by looking at the manner in which contemporary nineteenth century observers and participants described the events.

Lord Canning, Governor General in 1857 repeatedly wrote, not of a Mutiny, but of 'the revolt of the Native Army' (IOR 1858c).[3] In March 1858 the Secretary to the Chief Commissioner of Oudh where the action was most explosive, wrote unequivocally of 'The revolt of the native army of India' (IOR 1858c, IOR 1858d). Again in September of 1857, the President of the London-based Board of Commissioners for the Affairs of India wrote to the Secretary of State for the Colonial Administration, requesting him to convey the Board's thanks to the Governor of Mauritius for his assistance in extinguishing 'the formidable insurrection of the Bengal Army' (IOR 1851/58). Whereas the men on the spot appeared to have no illusions about the serious, revolutionary proportions of the uprising, both in its intensity and its widespread nature, the British government and the Western press did their utmost to downplay the event. Queen Victoria's proclamation in 1858 called it a 'rebellion', in the Parliament and Canning was castigated for being caught unawares and for his clemency in putting down a sepoy mutiny. Letters from officials in India headed 'Revolt of the Bengal Army' were responded to by the English counterparts under the heading 'Sepoy Mutiny' or 'Mutiny of the Bengal Army'. The more persistent the British-Indian description from Calcutta, of the events as a revolt, the more adamant were responses from London to the mutiny. The men on the spot were accurately reporting what they were witnessing. Officialdom clearly understood the power of language as well as the language of power. Now, that language became the major medium of information. But there were times when the guard fell. The London correspondent of the *Port-of-Spain Gazette* praised the British people for contributing liberally to the Indian Fund aimed at compensating the dependants of British soldiers who had fallen in India: *'One of the best results is seen in the Christian liberality which was then evinced towards the sufferers by the Indian revolt'* (POSG, 17 October 1857) [emphasis mine].

Canning seemed quite certain that he was not dealing with a mere mutiny. A full year after the outbreak of the Revolt he emphatically stated that he could not send a single European soldier to assist in the war against China:

> It is with much regret that I find myself unable to comply with the Major Generals' request. The needs of India are almost as pressing as ever, and it is impossible without obstructing the operations now in progress for the pacification of the country to spare the services of a single European soldier. (IOR 1858a)

By June 1858 the situation regarding the 'mutiny' had deteriorated even further. Canning was now urging the lowering of entry requirements for recruits in Britain and Ireland because of the very urgent need for Europeans in India. At the present rate of recruitment of 100 men a day, Canning argued, only about 36,000 to 40,000 men would be recruited in a year. At that rate India would have to wait for four to five years to meet its manpower requirement; an impossible wait if the country was to remain British. For British Indian troops therefore, both the height and age requirement should be lowered since 'Light men will be necessary for the Cavalry and as Artillery drivers and in the Infantry no soldier had to carry his own knapsack' (IOR 1858a, 1858e). Knapsacks of course, could be carried by Indian porters! One is forced to wonder, whether such serious preparations would have been necessary had this event been a mere mutiny. One also wonders whether the suppressors of a sepoy uprising would have been so splendidly honoured as these were, half a century after 1857 at the Delhi Durbar in 1903. On this gala occasion the veterans of 1857 entered the arena with the Governor General Lord Curzon as well as the Duke and Duchess of Connaught:

> The soldiers were old men; some were blind, and others lame; many had to be helped along—but all received a magnificent ovation as they completed their sedate lap of honour, proudly wearing their red and white medal ribbons. (Omissi 1994: 69)

On the international front too the British took ample precautions which belie their description of the event as a mutiny. They demanded and received from the Russian government an assurance that the latter were not supporting the revolutionaries (IOR 1857c) as Russian intentions towards India were deeply disturbing. At that same time the British thanked another rival in South Asia, the French, for their support against insurgents in Pondicherry. The French were to gain from this show of solidarity in that they were allowed to subsequently satisfy their need for indentured Indians in the frenzy which took place in the aftermath of the Revolt. Studying these events from London in the mid-nineteenth century, Karl Marx described 1857 as the 'First War of Indian Independence'.

THE CARIBBEAN LABOUR SCENE REVISITED

One year before the Revolt, the plantocracy in Trinidad and Demerara were in a state of depression since there seemed a dearth in the supply of labourers from India. The Colonial Emigration Agent at Calcutta, Thomas Caird had indicated that there was a scarcity of persons willing to leave India and that this did not augur too well for the future. The *Port-of-Spain Gazette* mouthpiece of the planters claimed that the emancipated African population and their descendants contributed little to the production of the colony, beyond the food, which they themselves consumed, adding nothing to the quota of exportable produce. 'The future development of the resources of the Island must therefore depend mainly on the introduction of labourers from the East' (*POSG,* 25 July 1857). What was particularly galling to the West Indian plantocracy was that they had carefully prepared the way for increased immigration:

> By 1854 the West Indian had largely secured the system of contractual immigrant labour they had always wanted. Fifteen years of agitation and experiment had finally secured a seemingly satisfactory system.... An immigration begun as a short term remedy for falling production had become permanent and regular. (Laurence 1994: 6)

By this time too immigration was no more a burden on the general revenue but was supported by a tax on indenture paid by the planters and by a duty on rum. In early 1856 there was a credit £36,000 in Trinidad but there were few Indians to be found. In the midst of all this preparedness for new immigrants there came the news of the Great Revolt. The earlier depression gave way to deep gloom. A notice sent out by Caird in November 1857 warned that 'in consequence of the disturbed state of the Upper Provinces of India he has been unable to obtain immigrants for the West Indies' (Government Notice, *POSG,* 14 November 1857). But this shortage was only temporary. In suppressing the revolt the British army had followed a scorched earth policy in many of the major scenes of revolt. In this way they forced many thousands out of their homes and fields, in search of alternative employment. The razing of the city of Lucknow, capital of the medieval State of Oudh and major source of Caribbean labour, bears some telling. For this account we are grateful to William Howard Russell of the *London Times* who came to India in 1858 and remained until 1859. He travelled extensively during and after the Revolt and accompanied the British army. The result of his acute observations were his two volumes *Diary in India in the year 1858–59* published in London in 1878. His description of Lucknow just before its destruction in 1858 reminds us of Clive's earlier description of Murshidabad:

> Spires of god glitter in the sun. Turrets and glided spheres shine like constellations. There is nothing mean or squalid to be seen. There is a city vaster than Paris as it seems and more brilliant, lying before us. Is this a city in Oude? Is this the capital of a semi-barbarous race erected by a corrupt effete and degraded dynasty? Not Rome not Athens not Constantinople, not any city I have seen appears to me so striking and beautiful as this. (Russell, cited in Taylor 1996: 198)

As it was being finally re-taken by the British in 1858, Russell was also there to record the pillage. The looting of Lucknow was second only to the sack of Delhi, officers packed their kits and ammunition pouches with jewels and gold mohurs snatched from the burning houses of Oudh's aristocracy. The total take from Lucknow's palaces and vaults and wells was estimated over one million pounds. Officers now eagerly sought home leave so that they could sell these treasures. As soon as the looting was over a few citizens of Lucknow started to return but Russell accurately predicted that 'tens of thousands will never return' (Russell, cited in Ward 1996: 501). These tens of thousands of Lucknautis were to be found later in the cane-fields of Demerara and Trinidad, Fiji, Mauritius and Natal. Many of them spoke the Avadhi or Bhojpuri languages common to that region. Their names, music, *kheesas* (folk tales) all spoke (and still do) to the diaspora from Oudh.

Even those who had returned to Lucknow could not remain for too long. Not content with the looting and destruction of the city, the British further razed sections of the city which were still standing in order to create an architecture less favourable to the urban guerrilla warfare adopted by Lucknow's erstwhile defenders. Captain Robert Napier of the Bengal Engineers who had arrived with the force which had recaptured the city demolished a further two-fifths of the city. 'Hardship' he conceded 'will no doubt be inflicted upon individuals, property may be destroyed, but the community will generally benefit, and may be made to compensate the individual sufferers' (cited in Oldenburg 1989: 33). In addition, Lucknautis had to pay heavily through a series of impositions for the restoration and reconstruction works (see Chapter 5 in Oldenburg 1989). Despite natural increase, the population of Lucknow declined from around 3,00,000 in 1800 to 2,56,000 by the end of the century (Llewellyn-Jones 1985: 12). But this was not the end of degradation faced by Lucknow. This came in 1877 when Oudh was amalgamated with the North-West Provinces to form one administrative unit and Allahabad replaced Lucknow as the new capital of a reformed administration.

If the destruction of Lucknow gives a micro-view of the devastation wrought during the Great Revolt there are other indicators of the larger damage done to the Indian economy. This became a major push-factor, forcing hundreds of thousands to find their way—by bullock, boat or on foot to Calcutta or Madras and thence to the Americas. Administrators in India and in the Caribbean were quick in seeing a great boost to immigration due to India's problems. Trinidad's Attorney General, for example, assured the island's Council of Government that they could anticipate a large influx from Madras since Lord Harris (Governor of Madras and a former Governor of Trinidad) had written saying that 'an immense number of people had been thrown out of employment by the suspension of public works' (*POSG*, 23 April 1859). Even before Harris' letter of comfort, the *Port-of-Spain Gazette* had accurately and happily summarized the Indian scenario:

> Owing to the suppression of public works and the general unsettlement consequent upon the thorough disorganization of the Indian community, there will be a vast amount of idle pauperism throughout Hindostan, which can only find relief by an extended emigration; and there is moreover, the sanguine expectations, raised upon the possibility of expatriation being made the punishment of the less obnoxious of the mutineers. By this way, we may profit to a degree far greater than anything we have yet experienced. (*POSG,* 23 January 1858)

In the planter's view, India's loss was to be the Caribbean's gain. They now moved in for the kill. Even starvation and its resultant emaciation were not to be an excuse for refusing to indenture Indian peasants. Early in 1858, Caird, the Agent in Calcutta reported that he had sent back a number of Indians who had wished to be indentured because 'of their miserable state from want of food in their own country' (Council of Government meeting report in *POSG*, 7 April 1859). This 'misdemeanour' on Caird's part was the cause a spate of anti-Caird resolutions and letters from the Demerara Planters, their counterparts in Trinidad and interest groups such as the West India Association of Glasgow. Even the *London Times* joined in, accusing Caird of causing deaths during the passage from India by giving the travellers impure Hooghly water and biscuits which were alien to the Indian diet. Caird was also accused of favouring Mauritian over West Indian Planters (*POSG*, 18 August, also 20 February and 15 May 1858). The result of this campaign was the removal of the Caribbean from Caird's portfolio and the appointment of two Caribbean agents at Calcutta and one at Madras. The *Port-of-Spain Gazette* praised Secretary of State Stanley for effecting this change, thereby ending Caribbean suffering 'from the want of zeal, partiality, obstinacy and irresponsibility of Mr Caird and his agents' (*POSG* Editorial, 14 July 1858). Now the floodgates were open; by April 1859 the London reporter for the *Port-of-Spain Gazette* was sending the happy news:

> The total immigration from the British Indian possessions must be now something immense. The draughts for Jamaica, Trinidad, Demerara, Mauritius, the French colonies, Ceylon, not to enumerate smaller and less noticed places, may all of a sudden be found too urgent to meet and the bank stopped altogether. (*POSG*, 23 April 1859)

The feeding frenzy was not limited to all those places mentioned in the above dispatch. In 1859 legislation was quickly passed to enable Natal to join the queue. In 1860 when the first batch of Indians arrived in Natal there was famine in the North-West Provinces and in that year 17,899 persons left Calcutta (Henning 1993: 16).

There seems to be little doubt regarding a direct relationship between the Revolt and the large exodus from India; this is particularly true of the northern Indo-Gangetic plains from where the bulk of the immigrants came. One researcher (Professor Gaffar) who comes from this region observes that the north Bihar district of Arrah was witness to the heroic resistance of Koer Singh during the struggle of 1857 which affected Shahabad, Arrah and Azamgarh. However, Koer Singh's resistance was repressed with the help of the sepoys. The sepoys in the Company's regiments had been recruited from the upper caste peasant families of eastern Uttar Pradesh and Bihar (Malik 1988). In addition, Malik cites a Calcutta Emigration Department Minute of 29 September 1859 pointing clearly to the influx of new applicants to this new form of slavery: 'Prior to the Mutiny the monthly average of Mauritius emigration was about 700, it was even less than average but suddenly shot up to two times and then three times by the end of 1859'. Another, written on 24 October 1859 points out that 'especially during last year, superior class people crowded in depots unaided and offered to emigrate' (Malik 1988: 31–2). Equally interesting are the insights provided by Kingsley David regarding pre- and post-1857 migration from India (Davis 1968: 99).

TABLE 5.1: Estimated Total Migration from India for Selected Years

Year	*Number of emigrants (in '000)*
1836–40	188
1841–5	240
1846–50	247
1851–5	357
1856–60	618
1861–5	793
1866–70	976

Finally there are convincing statistics connecting mass exodus with the Revolt in a Royal Commission Report on emigration from India to the crown Colonies and the Protectorates presented to the British parliament in June of 1910.

The largest number of emigrants that ever sailed from Calcutta (27,779) was in 1858, immediately after the Mutiny; and it has been conjectured that the two circumstances are not without connection; next to that year came the following one, 1859 when 25,337 persons left the Hooghly; but after these two years, those (years) when scarcity or famine prevailed in the areas of recruitment are found to have yielded the largest number of labourers for the Colonies. (Cd. 5192, 1910; 8 and 10)

Prior to this large-scale exodus the figures were substantially lower, in 1856, for example, the migration from *all* Indian ports was 14,555 persons. Now Calcutta alone was easily topping that number.

But how many of these increased numbers were revolutionaries? From late 1857 there arose a lengthy debate regarding the future of those who had participated in the Revolt. Whilst condemning these disaffected persons in the most despicable terms, there were shareholders from the Caribbean, Australia and British India who were eager to possess these recalcitrants and turn them to a good profit. I will first briefly study the Australian initiative. In November 1857 a group of landholders from western Australia led by John Hutt requested that those Indian convicts sentenced to transportation for life with hard labour be sent to western Australia to be employed in public works. There were many advantages in this scheme, the petitioners argued. There would be little objection since Australia was already accustomed to English convicts, the distance from India was short and the climate of western Australia was good—like that of the northern and central provinces of Bengal. These would-be deportees had little chance of escape since on one side of the proposed settlement there was the sea and on the other 'a perfectly wild and in many places desert and uninhabitable country'. The costs of this operation were to be borne by the Imperial and Indian Government and 'should not under any plea be made chargeable upon them or their resources' (IOR 1857b). The *London Times* report of this request sought to put a positive spin on the petition. This was a group of western Australian gentlemen, landlords and others who had volunteered to receive transported rebels and employ them in their healthy western Australian climate (*Times,* 19 November 1857, cited in Ward 1996: 537). As we shall see, nothing came of this scheme.

The west Indian requests were argued forcefully and over a longer period of time. The campaign was pursued with vigour at many levels, in the Caribbean in India and in the United Kingdom. In August 1857, even before the Australian move, a correspondent of the *London Times* argued that 'these miscreants' should surely be transported to the West Indies:

> Transportation to the high-caste East Indian is, in anticipation as dreadful a punishment as death.... In the British West Indian colonies, far from the scenes of their horrible crimes these misguided men, dangerous in their own country would in the course of time become useful members of the community. (*Times,* 24 September 1857, cited in Ward 1996: 537)

In October 1857 the West India Committee, the major club of West Indian investors in Britain, informed the Secretary of State that prominent West Indian planters had met with some directors of the East India Company and had arrived at a general agreement that those who had participated in the events of 1857 should be sent to the Caribbean. The Company should bear costs of transportation but reception, employment and control should be borne by the West Indian colonies. The rebels should be allowed to bring their families at the cost of colonial funds which they would repay through their labour. Unlike the normal indentured labourer, these prisoners would not be able to return to India and their family (transportation) dues were to come for their wages (Jha 1973: 7). In Trinidad, the Standing Committee on Immigration of Trinidad's Council of Government wrote to the London-based Board of Land and Emigration arguing that at least 10,000 convicts would be required per year for several years because of the need to build railroads, cultivate new fertile lands and open up potentially promising mining areas in the colony. If the British Government was willing to secure a guaranteed loan for Trinidad, all persons sentenced to deportation could be accommodated here (Jha 1973: 8). In June 1858 planters in St. Mary's in Jamaica made a similar request for Indian deportees. This request did not go down well with the planters of the southern Caribbean.

Among the Caribbean colonies there was lively debate about the disposal of these former soldiers now unwanted in their own country. In Demerara the Combined Court supported by the Court of Policy laid out a programme for the receipt of these Indians:

A large number of those implicated in the East India rebellion who have been led or forced into the revolt by others, but who nevertheless, have not taken part in any acts of great atrocity might be safely and advantageously received into this colony with their wives and families. Also a number not exceeding 1,000 of the graver class mutineers or other Indian convicts who may be sentenced to penal servitude for life or for long terms might with advantage be transported to this colony, to be employed on Public Works on the understanding that the cost of their passage shall be defrayed by the Government of India and that of their maintenance here from the time of their arrival, by the Government of the colony. (reported in *POSG,* 26 June 1858)

Meanwhile, that colony had already applied for 6,000 Indians for the years 1858–9. Jamaica's aforementioned attempt to cash in on the Indian misery was strongly opposed by the Trinidad interests. The *Port-of-Spain Gazette* praised Trinidad for having taken advantage of Indian immigration: 'had we failed we would be in a worse position than Jamaica is. Jamaica that did not export this year scarcely one-tenth of what it had done formerly' (*POSG* Editorial, 2 September 1854). One month later the same paper commented on Jamaica's willingness to accept Santhal rebels and Bengal mutineers. But Jamaica's record had shown that 'immigration was of little importance. So far as coolie or Asiatic immigration is concerned, Jamaica has signally failed to gather any advantage from the supply' (*POSG,* 11 October 1857). The *Gazette* commended Jamaica's *Morning Journal* for advising that the colony should first observe how the others were dealing with transported fighters before making its own application.

In the interim Demerara and Trinidad should be given the advantage since these colonies had already shown that they could use Indian labourers properly. Trinidad and Demerara worked hand-in-hand and generally without conflict in agitating for Indian labourers; they even drew up a common plan to set up a joint immigration office in Bombay, hitherto a non-existent source of labour for the Caribbean (*POSG,* 10 April 1858). However this proposal did not find favour with the Bombay administration. The proposal for importing soldiers who revolted was extensively discussed in the *Demerara Colonist* and the *Grenada Chronicle.* One correspondent to the *London Times* even suggested that initially the convicts should be brought to Barbados where they would be weaned from their 'idolatrous, their priests and heathen practices' before being redistributed in the other colonies (Jha 1973: 9).

An important initiative concerns the efforts to introduce unwanted sepoys and their dependants into the colony of Belize. This effort was an offshoot of the West India Committee's campaign to bring the sepoys to the Caribbean. Stephen Cave, Deputy Chairman of the Committee, had in December 1857, sent a letter to Frederick Seymour, President of Nevis proposing the transportation of 'certain sepoy mutineers to the West Indies' (PRO 1858a).[4] By the time of Seymour's receipt of the letter however, he had been transferred as Superintendent of Belize who was subordinate to the Governor of Jamaica from whence Belize was administered. Seymour put Cave's letter to the Belize House of Assembly in February 1858 with the warning that whilst considering the advantages of such a scheme, the House should not forget 'the dangers which might attend the introduction of another element of disturbances to our population'. The matter was debated and the House resolved in favour of the importation of 1,000 'Indian mutineers with their wives and families'. Seymour in his covering letter to the Governor-in-Chief based in Jamaica did not support the idea:

> I wish her Majesty's Government to be aware that opinion is much divided in the community as to the propriety of receiving the Indian Mutineers and that my own feelings are hostile to the project. (PRO 1858b)

Upon receipt (via Governor Darling) of this correspondence, Secretary of State Stanley requested Darling to inform Seymour that 'he will in future occasions perceive the propriety of declining to enter into such correspondence as that to which he was invited by Mr Cave's letter'. Four years later as India's misery poured many thousands into the Caribbean, Belize changed its tune. The same Frederick Seymour made an urgent plea for East Indians. After complaining about the frequent rebellions of Central American Indians he waxed in praise of Belize:

> At present in spite of many adverse circumstances and difficulties I know not a country in the world where material well being is so universal, and I should therefore have been well contended to leave the increase of numbers to natural action. But the proprietors of land wish to increase the value of their estates, the shopkeepers look forward to an influx of purchases and finally in raising revenue by indirect taxation which is so easy here that all parties are anxious that the experiment which has answered so well in British Guiana and Trinidad should have a trial here. (PRO 1862a)

When in late 1862 Belize did receive permission to import labours, the source was to be China, not India (PRO 1862b). Soon the Chinese were found to be less than suitable. In 1872 a request was made by leading landowners for 500 indentured East Indians. A small number appears to have been imported since the census of 1881 showed 175 persons born in India (Aschroft 1968: 77). From the late nineteenth century too, Belize's East Indian population was augmented by Indians from Jamaica who settled just outside Belize City and from Calcutta. From the late nineteenth century too, Belize's East Indian population was augmented by getting Indians from Jamaica and from Calcutta (Mansingh and Mansingh 1999: 86).

Whilst all this debate and activity was taking place in the Caribbean and through the British press, British authorities in London and Calcutta were in a dither: What do we do with rebelling soldiers? The debate was a difficult and protracted one conducted during a period when revolt was still raging. In early March 1858, for example, alleged plots were being uncovered by sepoy spies and arms were being discovered hidden in tanks (IOR 1858b). Lucknow was not taken until 21 March while in Jhansi, the heroic Rani at the head of her troops was not killed until the middle of June. In the midst of the military consultation on the fate of the disarmed Bengal sepoys the Hon. H.B. Pocock pointed out that 'at this very moment Rohilkhand is in the hands of the Rebels and 37th Regt. is threatened at Azamgarh, and has been obliged to confine itself to entrenchments'. Additionally, while discussions regarding the fate of the soldiers were pending there was the threat of large-scale death among thousands of native soldiers whose huts had been razed to make way for barracks for European soldiers. These men were being exposed to rain and heat and 'will probably die in numbers on account of increased sickness' (IOR 1858f). The new settlement of Barrack-pur (Soldiers' haven) now replaced the native villages north of Calcutta.

The arguments among members of the Council in Calcutta veered from clemency to vengeance. The Hon. H.B. Pocock, argued that whilst there was no legal evidence to convict the sepoys there was sufficient moral evidence to prove 'that they would have joined in the mutiny if their arms had been left on their hands' and if they had found a suitable opportunity for intervention. They were aware of what was happening and would have told their officer had they been loyal. But then, they could not be merely disbanded since there were 23 Native Regiments consisting of 16,000 to 20,000 disaffected men, trained to arms and without the means of gaining an honest livelihood. Such men would be a constant source of terror and would 'endanger the tranquillity of the country'. If they were allowed to return to the lower provinces, there would not be sufficient Europeans to guard them, they would therefore rob and plunder the peaceable inhabitants, destroy telegraphs (a major advantage which the British possessed) and assist the rebels. Pocock's solution was the banishment of these sepoys to a place where they could become peaceable and useful members of society. 'Many of our West India colonies would be glad to receive them and with the consent of the home authorities and of the Colonial Government I would send them there.' Their families would be allowed to accompany them and after a decade they would be allowed to return if by their industry and good conduct they had saved enough for the return journey. At the end of the decade, Pocock felt, their character would have been so altered that no danger was likely to arise from allowing them to return. Should there be difficulty in sending them to the West Indies then they should be sent first to the Andaman Islands and subsequently induced to go the West Indies. Pocock's colleague on the council, J.P. Grant felt that the men should be paid off and sent to their homes. The banishment proposed was unjust, and would foment discontent among the masses. The sepoys would not submit to a fate, which to many of them was worse than death without attempting to avoid it even at the risk of their lives. The result would be a 'shocking massacre' engineered by men who were not being sent home with a feeling of security and savings but 'men driven by despair'. The British Army, he said, had done very well in restoring India to quiet times and must now not appear to be frightened by 20,000 men armed without ramrods:

I think that there is a wide disfunction between dispensing with the services of a man and banishing him as a culprit and unconvicted.... I fear if we were to transport 20,000 men who have committed no offence our reputation for fairness and justice which has been no immaterial element strengths to us even in the late terrible times, would hardly survive.

A third council member, J. Grant said that he believed that the disarmed but organized bodies of men at Barrackpore are in mortal dread 'of some sudden stroke such as transportation en masse'. Such desperate and fearful men would be prepared to pay heavily to avoid that hidden purpose. Then there was the question of cost:

We must be paying at the rate of at least 25 to 30 lacks of rupees a year to people for carrying about ramrods, not to speak of what we pay for Europeans to watch them, who however much their services may be needed elsewhere, cannot be spared till the disarmed Regiments are broken up.

Grant felt that 'a free grant of discharges would tend strongly to tranquillise the minds of all'. Finally there was the view of the President in Council, the Hon. J. Dorin. Contemptuous of the 'absurdities' perpetrated by the sepoys, he felt that their future behaviour could not be predicted by the ordinary dictates of common sense. These disarmed Corps in full pay at Barrackpore were a source of perpetual anxiety and disquietude, they could not be trusted with arms hereafter and were encumbrances with the power of doing much harm if kept together in organized bodies. He too had learnt that these men were now in a state of desperation fearing punishment for the general crimes of the native army. 'Yet they commit no outward and visible act of mutiny or disobedience or even negligence that can justify their punishment.' The President then suggested that in view of the disorganized state of the Barrackpore Corps, its members should be discharged gradually.

At the end of these discussions the Secretary of State accepted the recommendations of these advisors, with some modifications. The majority of the disbanded sepoys were discharged and gradually sent home. Others were to be disarmed (except for ramrods) and returned under strict European surveillance. The Commanding Officer was instructed to select a suitable site for the native lines and to release 8 to 10 from each regiment, making sure they were sent home quietly and made regular progress before the others are released (IOR 1858g). About 3,000 were to be deported for life, neither to western Australia nor the Caribbean but rather to the bleak Andaman Islands deep in the southern Indian Ocean. What was the rationale behind the choice of these desolate islands over the more developed west Indian colonies? Primarily, it was much closer to India and could be more easily controlled from Calcutta. The major reason however was strategic. The islands had been captured by the British in 1789 but later abandoned because of their extreme insularity:

The Bay of Bengal is now, as observed by Mr Grant, a British Sea and it is more than ever incumbent upon us to prevent persons not subject to the British government from settling within its limits. That many vessels have been wrecked on the Andaman Islands and many shipwrecked mariners destroyed by the savage inhabitants are of notoriety and to some extent, official record. (IOR 1858g)[5]

The British considered the occupation of the Andamans to be of major strategic importance. The French were active in the area and had to be fended off. Of lesser importance was the fact that escape for these deportees was virtually impossible because of the hostility of the jungle around Port Blair, the major detention centre and the fierceness of the native people in protecting their turf. The initiation of the deportees gave a bleak indication of the terrain. Many of the first set succumbed to malaria and cholera in the fetid swamplands to which they were taken. Thereupon 228 of them tried to escape; of these 20 were killed by fever and by the natives and the rest staggered back to the prison. The reception committee headed by the Superintendent Dr Walker immediately hanged 81 of them. The Hon. J.P. Grant now President in Council ordered the cessation of such British brutality. Escape was a natural impulse, he told Dr Walker 'to which it is impossible to attach more guilt'. A ban on native boats and a good flogging would have solved the problem (account based on Taylor 1996: 13; Ward 1996: 538). Once Port Blair had been suitably brightened up, European prisoners were encouraged to go there in exchange for the reduction of their sentences. But a very high rate of mortality among them ended this experiment; for the Indians however Port Blair was all right.

My final enquiry has to do with the number of disbanded soldiers who may have come to the Caribbean. As mentioned earlier, the policy of vengeance undertaken by the British in the post-1857 period meant that those who wished to indenture themselves as a means of escape had to do so surreptitiously in order to avoid detection. As a result, some passenger records in the post-Revolt period are vague. During 1859 and 1860 for example, the *Bruce* brought 191 immigrants to Trinidad. The detailed caste descriptions and usual personal details are noticeably absent. As such 108 of them are described as Tamil (i.e. from Madras or Tamil Nadu) or Telegu (i.e. from Andhra Pradesh) or gentoo (i.e. Hindu) (Wood 1968: 142). During the 1850s and 1860s the Great Revolt was a major determinant of attitudes in Trinidad:

Cawnpore joined Haiti as a Precedent for a possible massacre of whites and colored men of property. Those in country districts felt that they were 'living on the crest of a volcano...' part of the legacy of the mutiny was a fear that the Indians could no longer be trusted that ... there was a Frankenstein monster in the colony that one day might get out of control. (Wood 1968: 154–5)

During 1860/1 the London-based Baptist Missionary Society sent one of its leaders Edward Bean Underhill to examine the religious condition of Baptist churches in the Caribbean with particular reference to the effects of

Emancipation. A former Baptist missionary to north India, Underhill stopped to talk to some indentured labourers at a plantation in Arouca. His account is most instructive:

> In conversation, I discovered among them some rebel sepoys from India; one had been a follower of Ummer Singh of Judgespore. They were ready enough to talk; said that 'this' was 'good land', that they were well off, and were saving money. But finding that I knew those parts of India from which they came, they quickly walked off, apparently fearing that the discovery of their connection with the mutiny might in some way compromise them. (Underhill 1970: 37)

Underhill hardly understood the significance of this information. His 'Ummer Singh' of 'Jugdespore' was in fact Amar Singh of Jagdishpur. Amar Singh was the able lieutenant of his 90-year-old brother the Rajput Raja Kunwar Singh, a leading zamindar of Bihar. Kunwar Singh's forces were large, at least 7,000 in one battle against the British. He had engaged the British not only in Bihar but had moved as far west as Gwalior and had then returned to defend Lucknow. The British considered him 'the only foreman worthy of our steel' and 'the only leader who has displayed throughout the rebellion either skill or courage'. Even after Kunwar's death in battle in Meerut 1858, Amar Singh had continued to lead until he was cut down by British firepower (Taylor 1996: 186). Underhill's account rings true to the present-day memory of Dr James Boodhoo whose greatgrandfather Anand, was indentured in the Tacarigua/Arouca area in Trinidad during the late 1860s. Anand has escaped from India in the immediate aftermath of the Revolt by serving as a *girmitya.* He brought to Trinidad a sword as a memento of his early years in India; the family remembers it, but cannot now trace its location since Anand's descendants moved from estate to estate in search of work.[6] A recent researcher, looking at the *Trinidad Royal Gazette,* 1882, points out that one *arkatiya* (recruiter) engaged a soldier and a policeman alongside an oil seller, a weaver and a shopkeeper in splitting wood so that they could develop hard hands and corny palms, so necessary to qualify for recruitment as a *girmitya* (Weller 1968: 6). In the Caribbean, those who had come through the sieve of detection set up in India had to keep a low profile.

In the Trinidad Immigration Report for 1865 a frustrated bureaucrat wrote of 'a retired Mohommedan solider or sepoy' who was already unsuitable for agricultural work and was un-Christian in his attitude, but 'the number of sepoys is unfortunately too scanty to admit proof of the latter' (reported in *POSG,* 3 May 1865). During his extended visit to Trinidad in the late 1880s the English evangelist and travel writer Charles Kingsley reported that there were in Trinidad a number of sepoys 'who had found it prudent to emigrate after the rebellion' (Kingsley 1890: 99). This researcher was told by villagers of Barrackpore in southern Trinidad that they too had heard ancestral accounts of their village being thus named (Barrackpore) because it was originally settled by former Indian sepoys from Brrackpore, north of Calcutta, the major centre of revolt of the Bengal army. Again in 1945 a prominent Trinidad Indian, Mahabirsingh claimed that he was the greatgrandson of Echchowsingh, 'killed in action in Indian Mutiny' (Kirpalani et al., 1945).

The last quarter of the nineteenth century was a particularly turbulent period for the Caribbean sugar industry. Britain, through the 1846 Sugar Duties Act, had equalized all duties on all sugar imported from abroad, whether this was slave-grown as in Cuba or through paid labour as in the British colonies. By the 1870s the effects of equalization began to make themselves manifest by pushing down the price of west Indian sugar in the British market. Caribbean producers shifted the burden of economic adjustment to the backs of the workers (Singh 1988: 9).[7] They did this by increasing the amount of the tasks performed but not raising the wage rate. Another device was to increase the number of Indians sent to prison so that maintenance costs of such persons on the estates would be reduced. In addition there were numerous unaddressed complaints from women against drivers and managers. Furthermore, hundreds of Indians saw their savings go up in smoke when in 1883 Archdeacon Richards of the Anglican Church, with whom they had deposited their money and jewellery for safe-keeping, declared bankruptcy and left for England. His former wards could now contemplate their loss of some TT $350,000, a very large sum for that period. These hardships led to numerous disturbances such as those at Jordan Hill in 1872 and at the neighbouring Restates of Cedar Hill and Fairfield in 1882. But these aforementioned real causes of the strikes hardly figures in the assessment of the events by the establishment. Once again 1857 was revived in all its ferocity. Contemporary newspapers recalled the horrors of 1857 was portrayed the Indians as 'a race subject to variety of prejudices easily aroused, and a standing threat to managers, overseers and all non-Asiatic labourers' (Singh 1988: 10). After the 1882 Fairfield riot, one newspaper saw Indian unrest as a 'fermentation of some kind not yet laid bare' (*San Fernando Gazette,* cited in ibid.: 11). When in 1884 the Indians, joined by Africans, sought to assert their cultural space by bringing their traditional Muharram procession into San Fernando they were fired upon by British troops, leaving some 16 dead and at least 100 wounded. Reflecting on this incident a Trinidad newspaper was quick to warn the population of the 'possibility of the atrocities of another Cawnpore (Kanpur) being re-enacted here' (*New Era,* 3 November 1884, cited in Singh 1988: 9).

After much deliberation, the Secretary of State appointed a commissioner to enquire into this Muharram Massacre. He made sure to appoint Sir Henry Norman, then Governor of Jamaica who had previously spent 35 years in India as a soldier and had survived the Great Revolt. In his report the good knight indicated that he had spoken to the Indians in their native Hindustani. However he could find no fault with the Government for taking this action which they did. He had, of course, listened to their complaints but these were not in any way connected to 'the attempts to infringe the laws with respect to processions'. He had also heard of the losses suffered by the Indians at the hands of 'a clergyman who had much influence over them.... Other coolies known to have lost money in this way, have with much quiet forbearance, not pressed their claims'. Yet Norman did not recommend any remedial action. As to the question of increased task work 'there is some evidence that the tasks for those who take task work have been increased since the price of sugar fell, but some complaints on this head have fallen through upon investigation'. In any case task work was shorter than a day's work and the worker could always resort to timework if he disliked task work (Norman Commission Report, in Singh 1988: 48). Norman's major recommendations were two-fold. In the first place the Trinidad law regarding processions should be tightened as had been done in India after 1857 and in Demerara in 1871. Secondly the Protector of Immigrants in Demerara and Trinidad should not be a local man but instead, one with Indian experience and 'well-known for his power of influencing natives'. Indians were like little children 'who should be firmly but kindly dealt with and have to look to someone as protector who thoroughly understands them'. Indeed 1857 had not been lost on Norman!

In 1868 a group of Canadian missionaries arrived in Trinidad to begin a mission of evangelization among the East Indians of the Caribbean. Starting in Trinidad, they expanded to Demerara, Grenada, St. Lucia and Jamaica during the nineteenth century. In Trinidad they were particularly welcome and always had the full support of the government of the colony. Gordon, the Governor of the island had every reason to be happy since he had no other fear for the security of the colony than that of Chinese or Indian insurrection:

> The only danger of disturbance to the public tranquillity (so long as Great Britain is at peace with other powers) that I can see is that of serious outbreaks among the Chinese or Indian migrants. (PRO 1869)

The Canadian missionaries more than repaid the trust confided in them by the British administration. They strongly supported the suppression of the Muharram celebrations in 1884 and remained in constant vigilance against any recurrence. The disturbances on the sugar estates which lay in the Presbyterian sphere of influence was particularly disturbing to Kenneth Grant, missionary based at San Fernando. He now warned his congregation that unless moral forces were strengthened 'we should be exposed to the tragedies of 1857 in India' (Grant 1923: 94). The local newspapers blew this admonition into a dire warning of another Indian mutiny and the Governor, himself, upon reading some, had started enquires. Grant then requested and obtained an interview with the Governor and assured him that there was in fact no threat of a recurrence of 1857 and that the whole matter was 'a tempest in a tea-pot'. And so the mission continued with its job of conversion of Indians through preaching and teaching under the safe protection of the colonial administration. The deteriorating economic situation, describing Trinidad in the 1870s can be applied to Demerara as well. Again planter reaction to the overall depression in sugar prices was an increase in size of tasks without a corresponding rise in payment. Not only were many Indians unfamiliar with the task system 'but many could hardly adjust to the rigorous, regimented life on the plantation' (Mangru 1966: 69). To this oppressive regime, a series of draconian laws and regulations were added.

Indians could be arrested at will for a variety of offences under the immigration laws, they could not choose an employer or bargain for wage increases, neither could they strike for increased pay. In that colony the Indian response was certainly more violent than in Trinidad. In July 1869, for example, some 40 labourers on the Leonora estate complained when their wages were withheld for their non-completion of task work on waterlogged soil. Armed with hackia sticks or lathis—what the British had called ramrods in 1857—they confronted soldiers armed with Enfield Rifles. Their leaders were then arrested, convicted and jailed. In 1870 violence again erupted, this time in many places: Plantations Hague, Uitullught, Mon Repos, Nonpareil, Zeelught, Vergenoegen and Success. In 1872 the most violent disturbance broke out in October at plantation Devonshire Castle in Essequibo; the confrontation ended after five Indians had been fatally shot. In this protest it was noted that women actually participated in the action since they too had had enough. In 1873 again there was an uprising at Plantations Eliza and Mary. Once more leaders were arrested. In their profuse speculation about the causes of these disturbances many planters in Demerara, traced the origins of these disturbances in the Revolt of 1857. This theory 'asserted that there were actually little or no grievances in the immigrant camp and the disaffection was instigated by a few sepoys who had arrived in disguise' (ibid.: 77). At the enquiry into the uprising at the Devonshire Castle Estate an Indian policeman stated that among the demonstrators there were 'Calcutta fighting men, and some were sepoys or other people. There were six or seven sepoys among them' (Tinker 1974: 228).

In conclusion, there seems to be no doubt that the Revolt of 1857 had far-reaching consequences, some 10,000 miles away, in the Caribbean. It was indeed a major push-factor in the migration of many thousands of Indians who felt constrained to leave their homes in search of a less severe environment. There also appears to be reliable evidence that many of those who came did in fact participate in the turbulence of 1857. There is a strong coincidence between the major areas of revolt and the main recruiting areas Kanpur, Lucknow, Azamgarh, Faizabad, Ghazipur, Basti, Gorakhpur and Allahabad in Oudh as well as Arrah, Chhapra, Patna, Gaya and Hazaribagh in Bihar. In 1858 George Campbell, Lieutenant-Governor of Bengal, toured some of the affected areas to see how the disbanded soldiers had been settling in their various villages; what he reported was significant:

> After much inquiry I am satisfied that the mass of the mutineer sepoys have not yet returned to their homes and it is very difficult to find what has become of them. (Campbell, cited in Mangru 1987: 71)

Some years later about 25 to 30 sepoys were reportedly involved in an attempted mutiny on board the *Clasmerden* bound for Demerara. They had concealed their identity at embarkation in Calcutta (ibid.). Revolutionaries of 1857 had, of necessity, to use every device of concealment as was possible but many appear to have made it to a better life in the Caribbean. This better life was possible because they were able to utilize efficiently the many prospects of a society that was far less developed than India. In this new world, the most precious requirement was their labour, badly needed to transform jungle and swamp into prosperous fields of sugar. This labour was combined with that of their African predecessors, now fellow travellers to convert much of the southern Caribbean. A considerable part of this effort was inwardly directed, that is, to their own enterprises as they struggled to create their own new spaces in the Caribbean environment. The better life which they enjoyed here was very much their own creation.

NOTES

1. Cotton adds that 'we may date modern Calcutta from 1757'. By today's reckoning 76 lakh would be £110, 000.00 and 40 lakh, £60,000.00.
2. This was written a full year before 1857.
3. See also, Canning to Secret Committee of the Court of Directors where he speaks 'of the revolt of the native army of India'.
4. The rest of the account is drawn from this source.
5. See Grant, Peacock and Dorin to court of Directors: East India Company, 10 March 1858.
6. Interview with Dr Boodhoo, 4 June 2000 at Trincity, Trinidad.
7. The rest of this section is based on this source.

REFERENCES

Aschroft, N.D. (1968), *Land Use and Trade: The Processes of Economic Change in British Honduras,* Ph.D. Thesis in Anthropology, Brandeis University.

Cotton, H.E.A. [(1909) 1980], *Calcutta, Old and New,* Calcutta: General Printers and Publishers.

Davis, F. (1968), *The Population of India and Pakistan,* New York: Russell and Russell.

Grant, K.J. (1923), *My Missionary Memories,* Halifax: Imperial Publishers.

Henning, C.G. (1993), *The Indentured Indian in Natal, 1860–1971,* New Delhi: Promilla & Company.

India Office Records (IOR) (1851/8), Secret dispatches of the Board of Commissioners, 1851/8, L/PS/5/590.

——— (1856), Board Collections 1857–8, Memo by Grant, 3 April 1856, F/4/2724.

——— (1857a), Board Collections 1857–8, Fort George Consultation, 20 October 1857, F/4/2720.

——— (1857b), Board Collections 1857–8, F/4/2720, John Hutt to Lord Canning, 26 November 1857.

——— (1857c), Board's drafts of secret despatches 1851–8, Third series. Memo dated 19 September 1857.

——— (1858a), Bengal and India Secret Letters 1858–9, L/PS/5/63. Canning to Elign, 20 January 1858.

——— (1858b), Fort William Military Consultations, F/4/2724, 2 March 1858.

——— (1858c), Bengal and India Secret Letters 1858–9, L/PS/5/63, Canning to Court of Directors, 9 January 1858.

——— (1858d), Bengal and India Secret Letters 1858–9, L/PS/5/63, Canning to Court of Directors, 4 March 1858.

——— (1858e), Bengal and India Secret Letters 1858–9, L/PS/5/63, Canning to Secret Committee, 30 June 1858.

——— (1858f), Major Gen. J. Hearsey to Ag. Sec., Govt. of India, F/4/2724, 11 May 1858.

——— (1858g), Sec., Govt. of India to Major Gen. J. Hearsey, 14 May 1858.

Jha, J.C. (1973), *The Indian Mutiny cum Revolt of 1857 and Trinidad,* Research Paper, UWI Library, St. Augustine, Trinidad.

Kingsley, C. (1890), *At last a Christmas in the West Indies,* London: Macmillan.

Kirpalani, M. et al. (1945), *Indian Centenary Review,* Port-of-Spain, Trinidad: Indian Centenary Review Committee.

Laurence, K.O. (1994), *A question of labour: Indentured immigration into Trinidad and British Guiana, 1875–1917,* Jamaica: Ian Randle Publisher.

Llewellyn-Jones, R. (1985), *A Fatal Friendship: The Nawabs, the British, and the City of Lucknow,* Delhi: OUP.

Majumdar, P.C. (1905), *The Musnud of Murshidabad, 1765–1793,* Murshidabad: Sarodar Ray.

Malik, D. (1988), 'Political Economy of Indian Indentured Immigration', Paper at the International Conference on Origins and Development of Indo-Guyanese, University of Guyana.

Mangru, B. (1966), *A History of East Indian resistance on the Guyana Sugar Estates 1869–1948,* New York: Edwin Mellen Publisher.

——— (1987), *Benevolent Neutrality: Indian government policy and labour migration to British Guiana, 1854–1884,* London: Hansib.

Mansingh, L. and A. Mansingh (1999), *Home away from home: 150 years of the Indian presence in Jamaica, 1845–1995,* Jamaica: Ian Randle Publisher.

Nath, S. (1980), *Terrorism in India,* New Delhi: National Publisher.

Oldenburg, V.T. (1989), *The Making of Colonial Lucknow,* Delhi: OUP.

Omissi, D. (1994), *The Sepoy and the Raj,* London: Macmillan.

Port-of-Spain Gazette, 17 October 1857.

Public Record Office (PRO), London (1858a), Co. 123/96, vol. 1 Correspondence.

——— (1858b), Co. 123/96, vol. 1, Correspondence. Seymour to C.H. Darling, 16 February 1858.

——— (1869), Co. 295/247, Gordeon to Newcastle, 24 May 1869.

——— (1862a), Co. 123/109, Seymour to Eyre, 10 February 1862.

——— (1862b), Co. 123/111, Eyre to Newcastle, 23 December 1862.

Singh, K. (1988), *Bloodstained Tombs: the Muharram Massacre 1884,* London: Macmillan.

Taylor, P., ed. (1996), *A Companion to the Indian Mutiny of 1857,* Delhi: OUP.

Tinker, H. (1974), *A New System of Slavery: The Export of Indian Labour Overseas,* London: OUP.

Underhill, E.B. [(1862) 1970], *The West Indies: Their Social and Religious Condition,* Connecticut: Greenwood Publishing.

Ward, Andrew (1996), *Our Bones are Scattered: The Cawnpore Massacre and the Indian Mutiny of 1857,* New York: H. Holt and Company.

Weller, J.A. (1968), *The East Indian Indenture in Trinidad,* Castilla: University of Puerto Rico.

Wood, D. (1968), *Trinidad in Transition,* London: OUP.

6

Resistance to Enslavement and Oppression in Trinidad, 1802-1849

Bridget Brereton

No major rebellion by the enslaved people occurred in Trinidad during its short experience of plantation slavery (1780s to 1830s). This is a contrast to Tobago, which experienced several significant rebellions between 1770 and 1802, as well as Barbados, Demerara and Jamaica, each erupting in large-scale uprisings in 1816, 1823 and 1831 respectively. Nor did Trinidad have large, organized Maroon communities such as those in Jamaica and Surinam indeed, Alvin Thompson's comprehensive study of *Runaways and Maroons in the Americas* (2006) makes no mention of Trinidad.

Of course, many of those enslaved in Trinidad did seek to escape from bondage, maroonage was endemic, and there were many small maroon camps scattered throughout the island right up to the early 1830s. There is some evidence of collective and organized resistance by groups of the enslaved, and Trinidad's free coloureds and free blacks, as is well known, also organized themselves to protest against oppression under the British regime after 1797. This article examines some aspects of resistance to enslavement on the island, concentrating on the period between 1802 (when Trinidad was ceded to Britain) and 1834 (when slavery was formally abolished). The analysis is extended to the post-Emancipation period with a brief discussion of the 1849 riots in Port-of-Spain. One purpose of the article is to assess the impact of events in—and people and ideas from—the French Caribbean islands on these various kinds of resistance in Trinidad.

MAROONAGE IN TRINIDAD

According to B.W. Higman (1984: 387–8), 'the largest proportion of maroon slaves identified in the initial registration was found in Trinidad'. In 1813, when the first detailed returns of the enslaved population were mandated by the British government, 0.78 per cent of the island's rural slaves, and 0.73 per cent of its urban slaves, were listed as 'deserters', a higher proportion than in any of the other British Caribbean colonies when registration was extended to them a few years later. The returns fail to indicate how long these 'deserters' had been absent, only that they were still regarded as their 'owner's' property. In 1827–8, Higman (1984: 387–8) shows, 516 persons, 2.1 per cent of the enslaved population, were punished for 'absconding'. Because of its late development as a plantation colony, Trinidad had a high proportion of African-born people well into the 1820s, and extensive forests and mountainous or remote areas not under cultivation which could serve as places of refuge for maroons. Port-of-Spain, with its fairly large black and mixed-race population relative to that of the island as a whole, was also a focus for internal maroonage, and the gateway for escape to the nearby mainland (see Toussaint 2000: 77–113). There is no evidence of a decline in the incidence of maroonage after 1824, when ameliorative measures were enacted by Order in Council (Higman 1984).

Many maroons fled to the eastern part of Trinidad, then remote and sparsely settled. At the end of 1805, a white cotton planter Walsh and one of his slaves were killed by a 'band of Wretches' from the 'Woods' behind his small estate on the East Coast. According to Governor Hislop, this event 'produced the greatest Alarm among all the Settlers of that distant part of the Island', leading him to send troops and militiamen to the coast 'with orders to scour well the Woods for the discovery of Brigands', under the command of Colonel Soter (from Martinique). Twenty years later, the authorities were still concerned about maroon camps in this area. In 1825, a camp of 'runaways' was discovered in the marshy area on the East Coast, between the Nariva and Ortoire Rivers; 14 persons were captured, two were shot for trying to escape, others got away. The following year, a 'survey' of the interior was carried out at the orders of the governor, and four maroon camps, hitherto unknown, were found in the woods near the coast in the Nariva area. On the very eve of emancipation, the Governor noted the existence of a 'maroon camp' in Mayaro, also on the East Coast, and announced that he had 'raised a Militia' there, in 1833, to forestall possible 'disturbances'.[1]

Maroons were also to be found much closer to the colony's capital. The hills surrounding the Diego Martin Valley, just opening up for plantation settlement in the early 1800s, provided refuge to many escapees. One plateau to the east of Diego Martin, Cameron, derived its name from 'Camp Maroon' or 'Cimaron', the Spanish equivalent. 'Maroon hunts' were held regularly in these hills in the 1820s and early 1830s. In 1805, there were reported to be many 'Runaways' in the Quarter (district) of St. Ann's, close to Port-of-Spain, and several deserters from the Seventh West India Regiment were said to be hiding in a valley behind an estate in Carenage, west of the capital. Advertisements for enslaved persons who had 'absconded' appeared in the newspapers of the island right up to 1834, and the same year in July, the Governor issued a Proclamation, in English, French and Spanish, 'exhorting Runaways' to return to their 'Owners' before the first of August, promising no punishment should they do so (de Verteuil 1987).[2]

Pain nous ka mange: The 1805 'Plot'

In December 1805, the authorities and the entire white population were agitated by the discovery of a slave plot or conspiracy in the Carenage district, west of Port-of-Spain. Coming as it did soon after the declaration of Haiti's Independence and the news of widespread killings whites which followed, this event was guaranteed to terrify the mainly French elite on the island and, indeed, all its slave-owners. The links between the conspiracy and the events in the French Caribbean since the early 1790s seemed all too clear to them.

Just before its discovery, Governor Hislop wrote that most of the free coloureds and slaves on the island were 'French', and that many had arrived 'engrafted with those Principles of insubordination and disorder through which the French Revolution had been brought about'. Some, he continued, disappointed in not enjoying the promised 'Liberty and Equality' in Trinidad, 'became consequently impressed with no other idea but those of Vexation and Revenge'—carried out by poisoning people and livestock, among other methods. In 1801–2, his predecessor, Governor Picton, had conducted 'trials' of enslaved persons for alleged crimes of poisoning and had imposed savage punishments on those found guilty. Now with the discovery of the Carenage plot, Hislop had no doubt that his declaration of martial law and timely arrests had averted 'the most Dreadful Event': 'The approaching Christmas would otherwise ... have brought with it in this Island the diabolical Scenes which led to the same sort of Government now existing in San Domingo'. A rising planned for Christmas Day was 'to begin by a General Massacre of Whites & Mullattos not even sparing those of their own Colour (it being determined there should be but *one*) who should refuse to join them'. The general panic was heightened by an alleged plot to poison the 'Garrison' in Tobago, causing the declaration of martial law there too at around the same time, and—so Hislop wrote—'a plan of an Insurrection among the Negroes in Guadeloupe has fortunately been discovered ... and six of the Chiefs (have been) burnt alive.—They were said to be from St. Domingo'.[3]

The plot in Trinidad, Hislop reported, was 'confined to the French Negroes'. The great majority of those enslaved persons who were cross-examined in the 'trials' following the discovery, and of those actually punished, gave their evidence in 'French' (Creole) and were described as 'French Negroes'. But the lengthy reports of the cross-examinations make it clear that the term was used freely to describe persons who spoke Creole and came from a Creole-speaking island (such as Grenada), not simply persons born in the French colonies; indeed, at times it was apparently applied to persons born in Trinidad and speaking Creole—the majority of the enslaved population in 1805.[4] We should not conclude, therefore, that the people involved in the plot were mostly born in Martinique, Guadeloupe or Ste Domingue/Haiti, though a few probably were.

The evidence taken from the enslaved and other people who were cross-examined and 'tried' by the Council showed that the slaves and some free blacks of the Carenage district, and areas in and around Port-of-Spain, had formed associations called 'Convois' (convoys) or 'Regiments' for the purpose of holding dances and dinners. These had kings, queens, dauphins, princes and princesses, treasurers, judges, captains and 'capitaines des dames', generals, aides-de-camp and so on.[5] Among the 'Convois' were 'Guadeloupe and Martinique Convois', but these two (along with the 'Convois La Fantasie', 'Convois Danois' and others) were said not to be involved directly in the plot. However, a few Creoles of Martinique and Guadeloupe were members of other 'Convois'; Noel, a Grenadian Creole and king of the 'Convoi Sans Peur' of Port-of-Spain, testified that his 'Convoi' included people from Martinique. One was Gabriel, who had come to Trinidad in 1792 during the Spanish regime. He claimed that the 'Convoi Sans Peur' to which he belonged had been established by 'Rosette Smith, alias Picton, who was for some time Queen'—a free woman who had been Governor Picton's mistress and notorious 'housekeeper' during his time in Trinidad (1797–1803). Gabriel was given 'a very bad character' by his owner, who testified that he had been heard to say 'that his Master was not all powerful, and would not always be his Master'.[6]

One man said to have been a 'ringleader', who was never found, was Old Michel. According to Marie Louise, formerly queen but now princess of the 'Macacque Regiment', he 'was an Old Soldier in Colonel Soter's Corps and had seen a good deal of Service in Martinique'. Picton had jailed him for being the accomplice of Mathew L'Engagne, 'an old runaway from Grenada in the Spanish time'; the two of them were 'at the head of the runaways of St Ann's Quarter, intending to incite an Insurrection'. It was Old Michel who was heard to say 'there were plenty of Musquets' at Rochard's house in Carenage. His military experience in Martinique obviously excited suspicion against him, especially when an officer testified that several deserters from the Seventh West India Regiment were being harboured in a valley behind Rochard's estate.[7]

But the most sinister link between the 1805 plot and events in the French Caribbean was the famous Creole song which the conspirators were said to have sung. Testimonies given during the cross-examinations, and recorded in the reports of these proceedings, as well as other contemporary sources, yield varying versions of this song or chant. Before any arrests had been made, Dr Metivier, the Surgeon to the Garrison, stated in a letter to Hislop that a Carenage planter (Melville) was told by his driver *Nous ete a un trop belle. Fete, euxvanous Pain et puis Yin … nous Pain la c'est Viande Beqye et Vin la c'est Sang Beque.*[8] On the basis of this letter, and other information, several alleged plotters were seized and examined; naturally, this song, and other 'seditious' utterances, formed an important aspect of the questioning. Jeanette, also one of Melville's slaves, denied 'any knowledge of a Song respecting Bread and Wine'. Dr Metivier himself, under examination, said he had heard several 'Negroes' from the window of his Port-of-Spain home singing *Pain nous mange c'est viande Beque.*

The chorus of the whole song was Cora and it continued *Vin nous Boire c'est Sang Beque Cora.* When the group saw Metivier one called *Paix, Paix Donc*, the song ceased and everyone ran away. De Gannes, a Maraval planter, testified that two weeks before the plot was discovered, he met about twelve women in the woods en route to the Maraval market. Striking flower pods for percussion, they were singing: *Pain c'est viande beque, Vin c'est sang beque, nous va mange pain beque, nous va boire sang beque*—'and their companions answered with the chorus "St Domingo"'.[9]

The chorus referring to Haiti, was, of course, of particular concern and seemed to seal the fate of the alleged plotters. In pronouncing the guilt of many of the arrested persons, special mention was made of the 'Enigmatical Songs' preparing the minds of the plotters for mayhem; the refrain 'St Domingo' showed how the minds of the enslaved population in general were being prepared for an island-wide insurrection. In sum, the song 'clearly alluded to the approaching annihilation of the Whites' on the lines of the Haitian Revolution.[10] The version of the song reproduced by L.M. Fraser in his history of Trinidad, published in 1891, is this: *Pain nous ka mange/C'est viande beke/Di vin nous ka boue/C'est sang beke/He St Domingo songe St Domingo.* Fraser further claimed that the plotters held a 'blasphemous Mass': as the bread and wine were administered, they said: *Songe, pan z'autes ka mange c'est viande beke; di vin z'autes ka boue c'est sang beke*, which he translates as 'Remember, the bread you are eating is white man's flesh; the wine you are drinking is white man's blood'. In this latter refinement Fraser goes beyond the reports of the cross-examinations (which he may have seen), for the tribunal failed, despite its best efforts, to obtain any testimony that such a 'Mass' was ever held. Yet there remains a strong possibility that some of the Trinidad enslaved did, indeed, celebrate their knowledge of what had happened in Haiti, and their dream of a world turned similarly upside-down in Trinidad, in song and even in a parody of the mass (Fraser 1971: 268–72; see also Brereton 2006: 128–9).

The conspiracy, real or imagined—for E.L. Joseph, who lived in Trinidad around 1820, wrote his history of the island only three decades after the event, and had read the reports of the examinations and 'trials', and was very sceptical about its significance or even its reality—was brutally suppressed. As Fraser points out, 'some of the members (of the Council) had actually witnessed the horrors of servile insurrection (in Grenada or the French colonies); to all, the details of the revolt of the slaves in St. Domingo were familiar'. None was in doubt, like Hislop, of the need to save themselves from 'fire, pillage and rapine'. A contemporary wrote from Trinidad about 'the explosion of a volcano here as well as in San Domingo which would have completely overwhelmed not only the British but all the other Colonies'. Swift 'trials' were followed by savage punishments, all endorsed by the British government, which congratulated Hislop and his Council for their swift action to save Trinidad from disaster. So did the free coloureds, ever anxious to 'prove' their loyalty to Britain and devotion to order and hierarchy. Partly because of the links to events in the

French Caribbean—and these links were symbolic rather than actual—the reprisals were brutal even though not a single person had been harmed, not a stalk of cane had been burned, by the 'plotters'.[11]

'AMELIORATION' AND RESISTANCE, 1823–5

The new policies on slavery adopted by Britain after 1807, especially after 1815, created a climate of anxiety, hope and uncertainty for both the enslaved and their masters, which was the main factor behind the major rebellions in Barbados (1816), Demerara (1823) and Jamaica (1831). Nothing comparable took place in Trinidad, but there is certainly evidence for unrest and resistance on the part of the enslaved people during this period, especially in 1823–4 when the island was at the centre of the new 'amelioration' measures, first enacted in the Trinidad Order in Council of March 1824.[12]

News of the Demerara revolt reached Trinidad just as heated public discussions among the planters (sanctioned by Governor Woodford) about the new amelioration proposals were underway. 'No public demonstration by the Slaves has hitherto taken place', Woodford informed London, 'although it must be allowed that great uneasiness prevails among the Slaves, and serious dissatisfaction among the Proprietors'. Towards the end of 1823, several enslaved persons from Diego Martin and Carenage (the same area where the 1805 events took place) were committed for 'seditious conversation'. Secret meetings were held, which were to climax on All Saints' Night, an important event in the Catholic calendar: 'a general impression was created of the intention of the Slaves to rise in revolt on the above-mentioned night', and Woodford became convinced that 'erroneous impressions' about the content of the new policy existed widely among the enslaved, especially the notion that they were to be given three free days each week. Such was the panic of whites in and around Port-of-Spain that Woodford took precautionary measures on All Saints' Night, calling out the regular troops and the militia. The judge who examined the arrested slaves from Diego Martin and Carenage felt that their committal was fully justified, for 'in a community composed as a West India Community, the appalling consequences, which experience has taught to follow from the Commission of this offence (intention to revolt), have superadded to the consideration of its enormity'. But no evidence emerged to justify sending any of them to trial and they were released with an 'exhortation' from the Governor. It turned out that the meetings were to plan a prayer, sacrifice and dance organized by an Ibo woman for her dead daughter, to be held on All Saints' Night.[13]

This generalized panic, no doubt reinforced by the Demerara rising and its aftermath, soon spread throughout the island, and the events in the French colonies in the revolutionary period, now over 20 years in the past, clearly lay behind the language and images conjured up by the planters and others. The 'Gentlemen of South Naparima' in the south of the island called for a military post there, for 'it is evident that the greater part of this fine Country might be laid Waste before the Militia could be assembled, and long before any information could reach or assistance be derived from Port-of-Spain'. Such a post would be a safe refuge for women and children and arms could be stored there. And the Commandants of the Quarters (lay magistrates for the districts of Trinidad, invariably landowners) inundated Woodford—who had permitted them to hold public meetings to discuss the amelioration proposals—with reports using very similar language and images. In San Juan (Aricagua) planters claimed to have noted 'an incipient State of Contumely, prevailing amongst the Negroes, since the murmur has got abroad of the proposed innovation in their Situation'. They believed that the king had ordered the three free days, 'and it is a Question among them, *why Bacckra no do that King bid him*' [emphasis mine], a belief which, if unchecked, 'may lead to disagreeable consequences'.[14]

Planters recognized the discontent and rebelliousness of their enslaved labourer clearly and memories of the revolutionary era reinforced their sense of danger, especially in the remoter districts in the colony's southern areas. The Commandant of Erin, for instance, believed that the enslaved 'have all the ambition to become Monsters, and only now want some active head to assist them in throwing off or destroying both the name and person of Master'. He claimed to fear that T.F. Buxton (demonized as the man behind the amelioration proposals) might be

> the cause not only of anarchy for a time, in the West Indies, but probably of many murders. The name of Freedom ... to the uninstructed and ambitious Slaves, is united with the idea of murder; what will he say or imagine? Our friends at home now wish for our liberation, our masters here will not grant it to us, let us force it by their destruction.

His colleague in nearby Icacos felt sure that the slaves, well aware of the ultimate intention of Parliament (Emancipation), 'will think of accelerating it by the destruction of those whom they will consider as the only obstruction to it'. In the remote and sparsely settled quarter of La Brea and Guapo, the language of the planters was especially apocalyptic: 'Ruin and entire Destruction' of proprietors would be the inevitable outcome of the proposed law to prohibit most corporal punishment and the use of the whip in the field, claimed 'Inhabitants of Guapo'; it was calculated 'to provoke a Rebellion against us'; the enslaved in this quarter believed the three free days had been granted and intended, if it was not bestowed by the end of 1823, 'to obtain it by force'. The Commandant solemnly endorsed his constituents' fears: without some mode of punishment in the field, 'there will be an end to all subordination, and then there will be nothing to be expected but, Devastation, Blood and Fire'. Unless the slaves' 'spirit of insubordination' was checked, he concluded, 'a scene of desolation and bloodshed may be the result, and the Lives and Properties of many Persons, fall a Sacrifice to the late attempt at ameliorating the condition of the Slave Population'. The 'Proprietors of Pointe-a-Pierre' believed that any attempt to restrict punishments was 'likely to produce disaffection and bloodshed, a catastrophe we have too much reason to apprehend from the impolitic interference in the management of our Slaves', and their Commandant claimed that it would put Trinidad 'in as wretched a state as if the Emancipation of the Slaves was at once proclaimed, when Anarchy and Bloodshed must ensue' and 'this fine Country' be reduced to 'Barbarism'. [15]

In a more measured tone, Trinidad's leading owner of slaves and most effective defender of slavery, W.H. Burnley, attacked the amelioration proposals in the Council as it would surely produce 'a Catastrophe similar to that which has recently hazarded the existence of a neighbouring colony' (Demerara) and to 'strike at the root of discipline and subordination'. 'Negroes are Children of larger Growth', he opined, and worked only through fear of punishment; in Trinidad, where 'the principal prop of our labouring strength still consists of native Africans', this was especially true. Woodford declared martial law for the Christmas/New Year season of 1823–4, a practice which had fallen into disuse after the end of the Napoleonic War in 1815, but which he felt was necessary in view of the 'Alarm ... and the extreme apprehension among the majority of the Slave Proprietors'. When the Order of March 1824 was actually issued, and published in the local newspaper, Woodford claimed to fear for the safety of the colony, and requested (and received) a company of regular troops from Barbados to join the garrison in the island. A deluge of petitions, addresses and 'remonstrances' appeared, protesting against the Order in the same kind of language as in the 1823 reports.[16]

There is scant evidence to prove that slaves in Trinidad were in fact planning rebellion, murder or even concerted resistance; the only alleged 'plot' of the 1823–4 period was admitted even by Woodford and his chief judge to be wholly imaginary, and all the 'plotters' were set free. The amelioration proposals, as well as the actual 1824 Order, were quite modest reforms in the slave system, which did not (for instance) prohibit the corporal punishment of males, far less alter the basic features of chattel slavery. It is difficult not to conclude that the lurid fears expressed by the planters in 1823–4, while in part simply strategic attempts to frighten London into abandoning the new policies, were partly the result of memories of revolution in the French colonies and Grenada 30 years earlier.

This is not to argue, however, that the discontent and dissatisfaction among Trinidad's enslaved people were not very real. Frantic discussions of the amelioration plan did, of course, filter down to them, and the role of rumour and deliberate misinformation, such as the three free days notion, must have played a role in Trinidad as we know it did in Demerara and Jamaica. As the powerful Martinique-born planter St. Hilaire Begorrat said in 1825, 'what frequently commences with a trifling disturbance may end unless immediately suppressed in open Insurrection'. It was from this period that a second 'subversive' slave song emerged in Trinidad. A.C. Carmichael, the wife of a Scottish planter in Trinidad, heard it around 1825–6, and described it as 'an insurrectionary song':

Fire in da mountain
Nobody for out him
Take me daddy's bo tick
And make a monkey out him.
Chorus: *Poor John! Nobody for out him, &c.*
Go to de king's goal
You'll find a doubloon dey
Go to de king's goal
You'll find a doubloon dey.
Chorus: *Poor John! Nobody for out him, &c.*

This was the explanation that she obtained:

> when the bad negroes wanted to do evil, they made for a sign a fire on the hill-sides, to burn down the canes. There is nobody up there, to put out the fire; but as a sort of satire, the song goes on to say, 'take me daddy's bo tick' (daddy is a mere term of civility), take someone's dandy stick, and tell the monkeys to help put out the fire among the canes for John; (meaning John Bull).... Then when the canes are burning, go to the goal (gaol), and seize the money.

Interestingly, the song survived in the folk memory, and was recalled by a white Creole born in 1867 when he was writing his memoirs as an elderly man: 'There was an old ditty which we children used to sing when we saw a bush fire in the hills: "Fire in de Mountain/Nobody dey to out urn/Take Daddy Booshon stick/And make monkey out urn".' His explanation was simply that 'Daddy Booshon' was a mythical bogeyman used by nurses to scare young children; he lived in the hills around Port-of-Spain and carried a huge bag in which he stowed the little ones whom he seized and disposed of.[17] Carmichael, of course, was in no doubt of the 'insurrectionary' nature of the song. Resistance and danger were close to the surface.

Point de six ans! Resistance at the Moment of Emancipation, 1832–4

A wave of panic about unrest among the enslaved swept Trinidad in 1832–3, closely related to the planters' agitation about the Order in Council issued in November 1831, which laid down much more stringent rules for slave management, and contained stronger enforcement measures, than the earlier 1824 law. The main organ of the proprietors, the *Port-of-Spain Gazette,* rarely failed to predict dire consequences from any signs of disobedience or 'insolence' from the enslaved. A planned 'strike' on a group of estates in the Naparimas, early in 1832—apparently a group of slaves brought from Tortola around 1820 believed that they had been promised their freedom after a few years in Trinidad, if they agreed to the move—might have led 'to subsequent horrors, which are too well known to require recapitulation and which afford so useful a lesson upon the subject of "delay" and "neglecting to adopt timely precautions"...'. Enormously exaggerated reports of the Jamaican revolt in December 1831 were reaching the editor at the same time, of course only heightening the sense of panic. Two unrelated estate fires in the Naparima district in March 1832 provoked a 'Gazette Extraordinary' published on a Sunday, peppered with hysterical language: 'The die has been thrown—the work of destruction has commenced—Heaven only knows where it will stop!' All in the Naparimas was 'terror and alarm'; Trinidad would soon suffer 'a second edition of the horrors lately enacted in Jamaica'. Subsequent articles claimed that only Providence had averted 'a tragedy ... the bloodiest in the history of Trinidad' and that 'multitudes of our negroes are in a state of mutiny—estates wantonly and maliciously burned—out slave population encouraged to—[*sic*] But the picture is too frightful for contemplation'.

Governor Grant believed that there was little evidence for serious slave unrest in the early part of 1832, and attributed the exaggerated fears expressed in the newspapers to the planters' indignation at the 1831 Order and their concerns about unfavourable seasons, over-speculation and debts. With some justice, he wrote that if any 'mischief' did occur, the planters would have only themselves to blame. But writing privately to Lord Howick, Grant admitted that there was considerable 'insubordination' among the workforce of Plein Palais estate in Carapichaima. He issued a proclamation in May 1832, ordering obedience and subordination on pain of due punishment. When he visited the estate the following month, he found that 23 people had decamped, perhaps to a maroon camp in the woods, or to Port-of-Spain. The insubordination arose because the driver had told the people that they were entitled to three free days. Some of them had behaved 'violently' when the Commandant remonstrated with them, and when he called in the troops, they fled to the woods or hid in the canefields. Many went to Port-of-Spain to make a statement to the Protector of Slaves. The driver was held responsible and duly flogged. Grant heard of grievance that the people had been forced to work in gangs on their provision grounds, contrary to custom; there was a new manager on the estate who had made changes to established work routines. He did not think there was evidence of 'insubordination' on any other estates, though there was a 'vague and general' report that 'the Male Slaves were sullen and the Women insolent'.[18]

By the middle of 1833, a new governor (Hill) reported general tranquillity, but in view of the imminent passage of the Act of Emancipation he promised to do everything necessary 'to provide against any movement amongst the Black Population'; he would call out the Militia if any serious disturbances threatened. In Mayaro, where there was at least one maroon camp and where disturbances might be anticipated because of the remoteness of the region, Hill had raised a Militia company. Early in 1834, he reported that the enslaved people had been generally 'peaceful and well-behaved' over the Christmas and New Year period. While 'discontent' was reported on a few estates, it was found that this was almost always due to the planters withholding gifts and privileges customary during the holidays. This was the case, for instance, on some plantations in the Pointe-a-Pierre district, where 'some excitement' had been reported. But Governor Hill was generally optimistic about the transition to nominal freedom which was to take place in August 1834.[19]

This optimism was largely dissipated by the middle of 1834, as Hill came to recognize that the slaves deeply resented the imposition of a six-year 'apprenticeship' instead of outright emancipation. He visited estates along the south-west coast to explain the 'nature of their situation' in July, and found they 'manifested extreme discontent' and disbelief that the King expected them to work 'for six years more'. Moreover, none of the Special Magistrates provided for in the Act had arrived by the end of July, and Hill recognized that it would be hard to explain to the people the absence of officers who, they had been told, were being sent from England by the King expressly to see that justice was done to them. He made elaborate arrangements for acting Special Magistrates, appointed Adjoint Commandants of Quarters, tried to raise a police force, and generally braced for disturbances. 'From the Spirit of Discontent' which he witnessed during his personal visits to estates in the main sugar districts towards the end of July, Hill reported, he 'saw that it was necessary to take every precaution for preserving the Peace of the Country'. He put the 'Country Militia' in a state of readiness, and, in districts without militia companies, he distributed arms to 'respectable and well disposed Inhabitants'.[20]

Hill's fears were well founded: there was a near-riot in Port-of-Spain on 1 August 1834, when hundreds of apprentices, including many older men and women, converged at Government House to protest against their new status, shouting '*point de six ans!*' and loudly complaining that they had not been given 'full free' status. Hill addressed them, presented the two Special Magistrates who had just arrived, explained the law, and exhorted them to return to their estates; they refused. 'Some of the most prominent characters' were arrested, but large numbers remained in the town and others continued to arrive from the country. On 2 August 'hundreds' again assembled at Government House whereupon the Militia had to 'clear the Streets on the night of August 2'. The 'alarmed Inhabitants' of the town sent 'numerous Deputations' to Hill asking for the declaration of martial law as 'the only means of ensuring the Security of Life and Property'. In language, no doubt influenced by memories of the revolutionary era, one such deputation spoke of the 'present awful crisis which threatens ruin to the Colony and destruction to our Lives and Properties... the Spirit of Insubordination and Mutiny which we consider likely soon to bring on the Horrors of a Servile and Civil War'. To his credit, the Governor, and the colonel commanding the regular troops, refused to declare martial law, thus avoiding (as he put it) 'scenes greatly to be deplored', but earning severe rebukes from the *Port-of-Spain Gazette.*

Hill did, however, agree that the 'ringleaders' who had been sentenced to corporal punishment by the Special Magistrates should receive it in public, and on 5 August, 23 men received 15 to 39 lashes in the Public (Woodford) Square. This, Hill noted, was 'salutary', and the apprentices dispersed to their districts.

But they remained generally 'sullen and discontented', and returned to work reluctantly: 'They say they cannot comprehend that the King would call them "Free" and yet compel them to work for their former owners. That they require no "Apprenticeship" knowing their business perfectly at present.' Moreover, it had not escaped them that the persons freed by the Vice-Admiralty Court (because illegally imported into Trinidad as slaves), and the 'Colonial Negroes' (people owned by the government) had all been freed unconditionally, without an apprenticeship. By mid-August, Hill could report that apprentices all over Trinidad had returned to work. In the sugar districts around San Fernando, in the south, Captain Burns of the regular troops had been placed as Superintending Justice of North and South Naparima, and he had 'swiftly suppressed' disorder in the first days of August 'in that extensive and important part of this Colony'. Hill considered the crisis was over by the end of August, though he noted that on some estates, the apprentices still showed 'sullen unwillingness to work, and perform their work slowly and badly'.[21]

As in other British Caribbean colonies, such as St. Kitts and British Guyana, the newly 'freed' people in Trinidad strongly protested the quasi-slavery of the Apprenticeship Scheme, even at the risk of corporal punishment or worse. Most of the apprentices who protested in Port-of-Spain early in August seem to have come from the estates in the northern part of the island, but there is evidence that urban residents, whether apprentices or free blacks/coloureds, were also volatile. In September 1834, the news that a free black man had been illegally whipped in the town jail, brought on a crowd of some 200 who gathered, demanding to see the Governor, calling for 'revenge', shouting out '*aux armes*' and '*a la Geole*'.

In October, a prisoner was 'liberated' from the San Fernando lock-up, and when the four men convicted of this 'outrage' arrived at the Port-of-Spain wharf, en route to the town jail, a mob gathered to 'rescue' them. Hill was convinced that free coloured/black persons were deliberately working to 'stir up' the apprentices: 'It was painful and disgusting to observe the anxiety with which one or two who influence the agitators exerted themselves to magnify this case into importance and give it a complexion to irritate a portion of the lower orders', he wrote; they were 'Men of desperate fortune and character' who were trying to persuade the masses that Apprenticeship was 'worse than Slavery itself'.[22] Several years later, another Governor would similarly blame 'agitators' for stirring up the urban 'lower orders' when a riot took place in the capital in 1849.

A REVOLUTIONARY SPIRIT? THE 'PRISONER RIOT' OF 1849

Early in October 1849, crowds of up to 4,000 or 5,000 protested in Port-of-Spain for two days against new prison regulations, which seemed to make it compulsory for persons jailed for not paying their debts to have their heads shaved and do hard labour, as was the case for common criminals. Several hundreds protested outside the Red House, where the Council sat, the situation seemed menacing to the authorities, the Riot Act was read and the police fired, killing two persons and injuring several. Though the protest was easily and quickly repressed, a few cases of apparent arson on estates in the countryside and an attack on the house of the Warden (chief magistrate) of Oropouche, suggested that unrest had spread, though very briefly, outside the capital.[23]

Lord Harris, the Governor, was convinced that the 'mob' had been stirred up by a small group of mostly mixed-race, 'French' men, notably G.N. Dessources and that sinister influences from the French islands, especially Martinique, were also at work.[24] Harris wrote that only 'French' (presumably Creole) was spoken by the rioters; the mob repeatedly expressed their 'desire to get rid of the white man', but 'I am happy to say, almost universally in French'. He believed that agitators led by Dessources, and his newspaper, *The Trinidadian,* had for some time been trying to push the people 'in a revolutionary direction', 'men who boast of infidel notions and revolutionary desires, foreigners [with a] professed hatred to Great Britain' who worked on the passions of 'an ignorant and excitable people'. This had been going on for some time, Harris thought, but it had accelerated 'since the late French Revolution' (1848). 'The doctrines adopted by the leaders' of the agitation, he claimed, were to drive the whites out of Trinidad 'by continual annoyance and by burning (arson on the estates), or if those means fail, to exterminate them by violence'. 'I have reason to believe', Harris solemnly concluded, 'that a Revolutionary Spirit is very much fostered in Trinidad by the constant communication with the French Islands and by the visitors imported from thence'.[25]

In two confidential letters to Earl Grey, Harris recommended special measures for the registration, and deportation if necessary, of 'aliens' entering the colony. He told Grey that opposition to his government was whipped up by a 'motley party', some of whom held 'socialistic and communist notions derived from England, and Red Republican ideas introduced from France and Martinique'. Others were simply ambitious for political power through constitutional change, or were motivated by 'colour hatreds'. But he was sure that constant communication with Martinique 'only fanned the flames'.[26] Though the actual rioting was in Port-of-Spain, the authorities and the whites, with their anxieties about and memories (both recent and more distant) of revolution and mayhem, were especially concerned about the evidence of arson and violence in the countryside. Reports reached the capital that canes and megass houses on 'several' (actually two or three) estates east of Port-of-Spain had been destroyed by fire, and that 'bodies of men', some armed with cutlasses and bludgeons, were marching to the town from the country. The magistrate of St. Joseph, a few miles east of the capital, said that about 50 'armed men', many smallholders from the region, had been stopped by him from marching to town to join the rioters. On 4 October, after the riots in town had ended, a mob attacked the house of the Warden of Oropouche, a fairly remote district in the south of the island. Yelling '*a bas le comis de la Ward foutre—tue le*', about 40 persons stormed into the house, began to chop down the steps and posts which supported it, set fire to the building and seemed to be trying to kill the Warden and his family—who however escaped by hiding in the woods. 'A spirit of riot and lawlessness' was abroad in his district, the terrified Warden wrote; 'there are two emissaries from Port-of-Spain, and many of our *would be coloured and black gentlemen* are assisting them' [emphasis mine].[27]

This was an isolated incident, and there is evidence to suggest that the Warden was particularly unpopular. But scenes of this kind, exaggerated as they inevitably were, called forth the deepest anxieties, only a few years after the end of slavery, and one year after the revolutionary events in France and Martinique. They were reflected in the language used by W.H. Burnley, the leading planter spokesman, in the Council debate on the riots:

> What was the situation of the Agricultural Proprietors at the present moment? Why [is it that] they went to bed every night under the apprehension that their estates would be burnt down before the morning.... What was the situation of respectable families in this Town on the night of the 1st of October? Women and children, left alone in their houses, while their husbands and fathers were doing duty as special constables, in the midst of ferocious rioters! In their fears they expected nothing less than being burnt, or assassinated, in their beds.

He painted a lurid (and largely unfounded) picture of island-wide insurrection, the jail issue a mere pretext to 'stir up the passions of the labouring population throughout the length and breadth of the Colony—to have induced ... a body of incendiaries from Port-of-Spain to set fire to canes and burn down houses and works in the rural districts ...'. 'Sinister faces were seen unknown to the Police and inhabitants', Burnley solemnly assured the Council, 'and menacing cries were heard savouring of the worst periods of Jacobinical France.... And among the rioters now under arrest, was one who boasted of being a relative, a brother he (Burnley) believed, of Soulouque, the present Emperor of Hayti!'[28]

Unquestionably, as Dessources argued in several articles in his newspaper, this tirade was carefully calculated hysteria and lurid fiction from a former slave-owner who openly regretted emancipation. But it seems clear that the revolutionary events of the year before, as well as the more distant memories of Haiti, were a powerful influence behind these reactions, however calculated, to a riot during which not a single person was actually harmed by the rioters. Nor is it necessary to doubt that Harris was sincere in his conviction that persons and ideas from Martinique helped to fan discontent. In fact, of course, there were several issues and grievances (some arising from his own policies) which agitated the ordinary people and the educated mixed-race politicians like Dessources, and which lay behind the riots of 1849. But the possibility of a 'French connection' with this post-Emancipation disturbance, as with some of the earlier protests against enslavement, cannot be dismissed entirely.

NOTES

1. National Archives (UK), Colonial Office (hereafter CO), 295/14, Hislop to Castlereagh, no. 15, 8 January 1806; CO 298/6, Minutes of Council, 2 June 1825 and 26 June 1826; CO 295/99, Hill to Stanley, Private, 4 September 1833. There is a 'Brigand Hill' near Manzanilla on the east coast.
2. The Plates IV, 'Cameron' n.p.; CO 298/2, Examination of Witnesses re 1805 Plot, evidence of Marie Louise and Capt. Massey; CO 295/102, Hill to Spring-Rice, no. 2, 20 July 1834.
3. CO 295/11, Hislop to Castlereagh, no. 10, 13 December 1805, Hislop to Castlereagh, no. 12, 17 December 1805; CO 295/14, Hislop to Edward Coke, Private, 8 January 1806.
4. The cross-examinations are in CO 298/2, Minutes of Council, 14 and 18 December 1805, 6 and 13 January 1806, ff. 101-48.
5. For this aspect of the 1805 affair, see Cowley 1996: 12–14; Joseph 1970: 229–30; Naipaul 1973: 291–9; Fraser 1971: 268–72; de Verteuil 1987: 72–3; and The Plates, III, n. p.
6. See note 4.
7. Ibid.
8. CO 298/2, Minutes of Council: Letter from Dr Metivier to Hislop, 8 December 1805. Spelling as in the original here (and elsewhere in this paper).
9. See note 4.
10. CO 298/2, Minutes of Council, 18 December 1805 and Statement to the Public, 20 December 1805.
11. See note 5; also Besson and Brereton (1992: 90–1), and Brereton (2006: 128–9).
12. The best account of Amelioration in Trinidad, see Fergus (1996: 308–33), and Fergus (2008: 75–99); see also Titus (1974).
13. CO 295/59, Woodford to Bathurst, no. 502, 3 September 1823, Woodford to Bathurst, no. 518, 5 November 1823, Woodford to Bathurst, no. 523, 5 December 1823.
14. CO 295/59, Woodford to Bathurst, no. 519, 6 November 1823 Enclosed Gentlemen of South Naparima to Commandant, 9 October 1823; CO 295/60. Reports of Commandants of Quarters, Public Meetings, etc. (1823). Many of these are in French and a few are in Spanish.
15. CO 295/60: Reports of Commandants of Quarters, Public Meetings, etc. (1823). Many of these are in French and a few are in Spanish.
16. CO 295/60: Opinions of Members of Council, W.H. Burnley, n.d. (1823); CO 295/65, Woodford to Bathurst, no. 591, 5 January 1825; CO 295/62, Woodford to Bathurst, no. 545A, 7 May 1824, Woodford to Bathurst, no. 547, 7 May 1824, Woodford to Bathurst, no. 549, 26 May 1824 and enclosures.
17. CO 295/66, Woodford to Bathurst, no. 629, 12 June 1825: Evidence of St. Hilaire Begorrat to Committee on the Negro Character, given 9 March 1825; Carmichael (1833: 301–2); P. Fraser, *Looking Over My Shoulder,* ed. B. Brereton, San Juan: Lexicon Trinidad, 2007, pp. 204–5.
18. For this and the subsequent paragraph, see *Port-of-Spain Gazette* (*POSG*), 15 February, 7 March, 14 March, 25 March 1832 (Gazette Extraordinary), 7 April, 11 April, 18 April, 6 June, 9 June, 9 November 1832, 30 April 1833; CO 295/92, Grant to Goderich, no. 8, 13 January 1832, Grant to Goderich, Separate, 26 March

1832, Grant to Howick, Private, 26 May 1832, Grant to Goderich, no. 27, 8 June 1832.

19. CO 295/98, Hill to Stanley, Private, 2 July 1833; Hill to Stanley, no. 28, 1 August 1833; Hill to Stanley, Private, 4 September 1833; Hill to Stanley, no. 41, 12 October 1833; CO 295/101 Hill to Stanley, no. 1, 8 January 1834.
20. CO 298/9, Minutes of Council, 29 July 1834; CO 295/102, Hill to Spring-Rice, no. 2, 20 July 1834 and enclosures, Hill to Spring-Rice, no. 3, 20 July 1834; Hill to Spring-Rice, no. 6, 30 July 1834; Hill to J.G. Lefevre, 24 July 1834; CO 295/103, Hill to Spring-Rice no. 7, 7 August 1834.
21. For the events of August 1834, see CO 298/9, Minutes of Council, 3 and 6 August 1834; CO 295/103, Hill to Spring-Rice, no. 7, 7 August 1834 and enclosures; Hill to Spring-Rice, Private, 7 August 1834; Hill to Spring-Rice, no. 8, 9 August 1834; Hill to Spring-Rice, no. 9, 14 August 1834; Hill to Spring-Rice, no. 18, 26 August 1834; *POSG*, 3, 5, 8, 12 August, 16 September, 24 October 1834; Besson and Brereton (1992: 169–70); Lt. Col. Capadose, *Sixteen Years in the West Indies*, London: 1845, vol. 1, 66–7; Wood 1968: 47.
22. CO 295/103, Hill to Spring-Rice, no. 39, 26 November 1834.
23. For the events of 1849, see: CO 295/168, Harris to Grey, no. 79, 6 October 1849 and enclosures, Harris to Grey, Confidential, 20 October and 12 November 1849; CO 295/170, Harris to Grey, no. 1, 5 January 1850 and enclosures; *The Trinidadian,* many articles and editorials (by G.N. Dessources) between October and December 1849; *POSG*, 2 and 6 November 1849: Council of Government, 1 and 2 November 1849; Besson and Brereton (1992: 302–4); Wood (1968: 175–7); D. Trotman, 'Protest in Post-Emancipation Trinidad: The Prisoner Riots of 1849', Fifteenth Conference of Caribbean Historians, Jamaica, 1983; Trotman 2005: 118–42. A vivid contemporary account of the riot by the wife of a military officer stationed in Trinidad is in Margaret Mann to Baynes, 2 October 1849, in Delon 2008: 373–80.
24. For Dessources, see Brereton (2006: 137–44); and M. Toussaint, 'George Numa Dessources, the Numancians, and the effort to form a colony in Eastern Venezuela, circa 1850–54', Thirty-third Conference of Caribbean Historians, Trinidad, 2001.
25. CO 295/168 Harris to Grey, no. 79, 6 October 1849.
26. CO 295/168 Harris to Grey, confidential, 20 October and 12 November 1849.
27. See note 25 (with enclosures) and Mann to Baynes, 2 October 1849.
28. *POSG*, 2 and 6 November 1849: Council of Government, 1 and 2 November 1849. See also Brereton (2006: 143–4).

REFERENCES

Besson, G. and B. Brereton (1992), *The Book of Trinidad,* Port-of-Spain: Paria.

Brereton, B. (2006), 'Haiti and the Haitian Revolution in the Political Discourse of Nineteenth-Century Trinidad', in *Reinterpreting the Haitian Revolution and its Cultural Aftershocks,* M. Munro and E. Walcott-Hackshaw, eds., Kingston: University of the West Indies Press, pp. 128–9.

Carmichael, A.C. (1833), *Domestic Manners and Social Condition of the White, Coloured and Negro Population of the West Indies,* vol. 2, London: Whittaker, Treacher & Co.

Cowley, J. (1996), *Carnival, Canboulay and Calypso Traditions in the Making,* Cambridge: CUP.

de Verteuil, A. (1987), *Begorrat-Brunton: A History of Diego Martin 1784–1884,* Port-of-Spain: Paria.

Delon, D., ed. (2008), *The Letters of Margaret Mann,* Port-of-Spain: The National Museum.

Fergus, C. (1996), 'British Imperial Trusteeship: The Dynamics of Reconstruction of British West Indian Slave Society with special reference to Trinidad and Tobago, 1783–1838', Ph.D. thesis, University of the West Indies Press, St. Augustine.

——— (2008), 'The *Siete Partidas:* A framework for philanthropy and coercion during the Amelioration experiment in Trinidad, 1823–1834', *Caribbean Studies,* vol. 36, no. 1, pp. 75–99.

Fraser, L.M. (1971), *History of Trinidad (1891)*, vol. 1, London: Frank Cass.

Fraser, P. (2007), *Looking Over My Shoulder,* ed. B. Brereton, San Juan: Lexicon Trinidad, pp. 204–5.

Higman. B.W. (1984), *Slave Populations of the British Caribbean 1807–1834,* Baltimore: John Hopkins University Press.

Joseph, E.L. (1970), *History of Trinidad (1838)*, London: Frank Cass.

Naipaul, V.S. (1973), *The Loss of El Dorado,* Harmondsworth: Penguin.

Titus, N. (1974), 'Amelioration and Emancipation in Trinidad, 1814–1834', M.A. thesis, University of the West Indies, St. Augustine.

Toussaint, M. (2000), 'Afro-West Indians in Search of the Spanish Main', Ph.D. thesis, University of the West Indies, St. Augustine.

Trotman, D. (2005), 'Capping the Volcano: Riots and their Suppression in Post-Emancipation Trinidad', in *Contesting Freedom Control and Resistance in the Post-Emancipation Caribbean,* G. Heuman and D. Trotman, eds., Oxford: Macmillan, pp. 118–42.

Wood, D. (1968), *Trinidad in Transition: The Years after Slavery,* London: OUP.

7

General Elections of 2007 in Trinidad and Tobago

The Indian Factor in the People's National Movement

Benjie Mahabir

As the twin island republican state in the Caribbean, Trinidad and Tobago is noted for its many attributes including carnival, calypso, its multi-ethnic population and a relative abundance of its reserves of natural gas and petroleum. With an area of 4,828 sq. km. and a population of approximately 1.3 million, Trinidad and Tobago has practised a system of parliamentary democracy for over 50 years with general elections constitutionally due every five years. The last general elections held on 4 November 2007 and the People's National Movement (PNM) was successful, capturing 26 of the 41 constituencies.[1] The other main parties in the 2007 elections were the United National Congress (UNC) which captured 15 seats and the Congress of the People (COP), which failed to win a seat but nevertheless had the support of 1,48,000 voters. Historically, parties in Trinidad and Tobago usually had a political base among the different ethnic groups of the country.[2] The PNM, for example, has always been considered a party of the Afro-Trinbagonians while the UNC was considered an Indo-based party. It must be remembered that both races are almost of the same number, close to 49 per cent each. The COP was seen as a combination of people who supported neither the PNM nor the UNC but mostly it was a breakaway faction of the UNC. This article would explore the contribution of Indo-Trinbagonians in an Afro-based Party, the PNM, in 2007 and briefly examine the campaigning in the election.

FOUNDING PRINCIPLES OF THE PNM

All evidence emanating from the general elections of 1956 to the present day indicate that the PNM is the only viable and enduring political organization in the history of Trinidad and Tobago. The Party, which was founded in 1956 by the Father of the Nation, Dr Eric Williams has remained committed to democratic principles, basic human rights and dignity, morality in public life, maintenance of the rule of law and to constantly improve the standard of living and quality of life of the people of Trinidad and Tobago. In its history since 1956 it has only been defeated twice in general elections, i.e. in 1986 and 2000.

PNM CANDIDATES IN THE 2007 GENERAL ELECTIONS

The PNM fielded 41 candidates in the 2007 elections. Of these the racial profile was as follows with Indians comprising 20 per cent, Blacks 19 per cent and others 2 per cent (see Table 7.1).

TABLE 7.1: Indian Candidates in the PNM in the 2007 General Elections and Constituency Represented

Name	*Constituency*
Christine Kangaloo	Pointe-a-Pierre
Frankie Ramjitsingh	Chaguanas West
Geeta Rampersad	Naparima
Harold Ramoutar	Caroni East
Heeralal Ramparatap	Tabaquite
Indra Sinanan Ojah-Maharaj	Toco/Sangre Grande
Kennedy Swaratsingh	St. Joseph
Lennox Sirjuesingh	Cumoto/Manzanilla
Marlon Mohammed	Princes Town North
Mustapha Abdul Hamid	Chaguanas East
Nadra Nathai-Gyan	St. Augustine
Nairn Ali	Couva South
Nal Ramsingh	Couva North
Neil Parsanlal	Lopinot/Bon Air West
Paula Gopee-Scoon	Point Fortin
Raghunath Mahabir	Oropouche West
Rampersad Lutchman	Siparia
Roger Joseph	La Horquetta/Talparo
Shafeeq Mohomed	Oropouche East
Shivanan Narinesingh	Caroni Central

SUCCESS AND FAILURES

Of these 20 candidates (see Table 7.1), 13 were placed to contest hard core opposition seats and as *apanjhat*[3] politics would dictate, they all failed to win from their respective constituencies. The other seven were successful since they were placed either in hard core PNM areas or benefited from the splitting of votes between the UNC and the COP. Today, as Members of Parliament, six of them are Ministers in the Government while Indra Sinanan Ojah-Maharaj sits as a backbencher and in various Committees of the Parliament.

These 13, it must be noted though, did not simply leave the political scene altogether. Being a mixed bunch of university lecturers, public servants and independent business people they still work with the political party at various levels. This includes helping the Government to shape its policy. In all cases the 13 defeated Indian candidates still play an important role in the decision making of the workings of the respective constituencies and are seen as shadow Members of the Parliament. Some of the Indian Ministers of the PNM Government are listed in Table 7.2.

TABLE 7.2: List of Indian Ministers in the Government of Trinidad and Tobago

Name	*Portfolio*
Paula Gopee-Scoon	Minister of Foreign Affairs
Neil Parsanlal	Minister of Information
Kennedy Swaratsingh	Minister of Public Administration
Mustapha Abdul Hamid	Minister of Public Utilities
Christine Kangaloo	Minister of Science, Technology and Tertiary Education
Roger Joseph	Minister of Works and Transport
Jerry Narace	Minister of Health
Lenny Saith	Minister of Trade and Industry

The first six fought the elections as candidates while the last two were brought in as Senators.

In many ways the PNM has been an Afro-based party with the majority of its supporters being the lower and middle class Afro-Trinidadians. Nonetheless, since its inception in 1956 it always had some support from the Indo-Trinidadian community, especially from the Muslims in the San/Juan Barataria area and the Presbyterians of San-Fernando West, among other areas. Some well known Indo-Trinidadian politicians who served in the PNM as Ministers and Members of Parliament before 1991 included the Mohammed brothers, Kamaluddin and Shamshudddin, Errol Mahabir and Hardath Hardeo. The period beginning from 1991 saw new Indo-Trinidadian faces such as Lenny Saith, Christine Sahadeo, Jarette Narine, Diane Seukeran and others. Numerous Indo-Trinidadians have served as PNM senators since its inception.

PARTICIPATION IN THE ELECTIONS OF 2007

In Trinidad and Tobago, as in many other democracies, a defining characteristic is universal adult suffrage: everyone who is a citizen of Trinidad and Tabago and over the age of 18 has the right to vote. However, not everyone exercises this right and voter turnout varies both over time and across constituencies. This variation is not random; it is a stylized fact of the empirical voter turnout literature that better educated individuals participate more frequently in elections, as do those with greater wealth and higher incomes (Wolfinger and Rosenstone 1980).

In Trinidad and Tobago, both the PNM and the UNC attempted to cross the racial divide by encouraging non-traditional supporters to support them in the 2007 elections. In the case of the PNM one can safely say that the PNM was more successful in doing so looking at the election results.

Unequal participation especially in the general elections has important implications: first political participation is an instrument of representation, and can distort the pattern of representation necessary for democratic responsiveness leading to real effects on policy outcomes. According to Lijphart, 'unequal participation spells unequal influence' (1991: 13).

In Trinidad and Tobago the average voter turnout over the last five elections has ranged between 65 and 83 per cent with 2007 having close to 80 per cent.

Second, inequality is a problem if democratic participation is seen as an intrinsic good in addition to its role as a representational instrument. Also, it may create doubts about the democratic legitimacy of a given political setting. In the 2007 elections a number of Indian voters were in a dilemma since the main opposition parties, the UNC and the COP failed to unite and it was obvious that because of this and other reasons that the PNM would victorious. Many Indian voters who had planned to support the COP changed their minds close to the elections and voted either for the UNC or did not vote at all.

Efforts to understand the determinants of voter turnout often take observed empirical regularities as their starting point. The key finding of Wolfinger and Rosenstone (1980) that information and education is the most important predictor of voting, forms the basis of recent innovative work by Fedderson and Pesendorre who argue that informational differences among voters can help explain variations in political participation.

In their models of single issue elections, uninformed citizens' optimal choice can be to abstain from voting even if they prefer one alternative to the other. Instead, they effectively delegate decision making powers to better informed/educated voters, thereby increasing the likelihood of the optimal policy being chosen.

In the general elections of 2007 a total of 3,42,466 voters voted for the UNC and COP. The general break-up is as follows:

PNM	UNC	COP
2,99,813	1,94,425	1,48,041

Thus, the PNM which won the elections, took 26 of the 41 constituencies and was able to secure the highest amount of votes. Together, the opposition parties, the UNC and the COP were able to secure 3,42,466, definitely a higher number than the PNM. Translated into votes though, the opposition parties would have been able to secure five more seats, if they had united. Then it was possible for them to secure 20 seats, though still not enough to form the Government. However, there is the perception that had they united earlier, the country would have given them a chance to form the Government. Many people did not want the PNM or Basdeo Panday to be part of the government.

Interestingly, these five seats which could have been won had the opposition parties united were: Barataria/San Juan, Chaguanas East, Pointe-a-Pierre, Princes Town/South Tableland and St. Joseph. For the PNM which won these seats, the last three constituencies listed in Table 7.3 were represented by Indo-Trinidadians.

TABLE 7.3: Votes Polled by Constituencies (2007)

Electoral district	*PNM*	*UNC*	*COP*
Barataria/San Juan	7,179	5,358	3,917
Princes Town/South Tableland	8,929	7,908	1,437
Chaguanas East	6,757	4,993	4,086
Pointe-a-Pierre	7,427	6,136	3,740
St. Joseph	7,965	4,945	4,145

THE IMPACT OF CAMPAIGN INTENSITY AND EFFECTIVE CAMPAIGNING

Undoubtedly, a more effective and intensive campaign strategy played a major role in deciding the elections results, for the PNM in 2007. Based on the 2002 results, one can theorize that campaign intensity altered the criteria individuals use when evaluating candidates. Campaign intensity can be defined as the culmination of the interplay among the candidates, media reports and the perceived closeness of the race. As the intensity increased, some people adjusted their decision making criteria. Different people reacted differently to the intensity of the campaign and as the race moved to the finish, people (including the first-time voters) not only relied on party identification, but also on the issues as they saw them while some were told in no uncertain way, as to which way to vote.[4]

Studying the interplay among the competing candidates, the media and the perceived closeness of the race for the next general elections, it must be understood that these forces represent a dynamic reciprocal process wherein the strategies of the candidates, news coverage and the closeness of the race are causally interdependent.

Candidates, with their parties when developing campaign strategies (e.g. the amount and type of political commercials, selections of campaign themes, songs, and punch lines) must take into account their standing in the polls as well as press coverage of their campaign. Likewise, the media coverage of a race (e.g. amount, tone, substance) is often affected by the competitiveness of the contest and the type of strategies adopted by the candidates. Also, the candidates' standing in the polls might change in response to campaign strategies and media coverage, especially if information favours one candidate/party over another (e.g. negative commercials by party/candidate and scrutiny of a candidates/parties prior action by the press).[5] In both 2002 and 2007, for example, the PNM constantly harped on corruption in the UNC and identified key party figures including its then political leader and several of its principal financiers. In 2007 the PNM was able to allege corruption and bribery by top elements in the UNC, as there were by then a few cases in the High Courts of Trinidad and Tobago in which top members and financiers of UNC had been charged.

In every PNM meeting across the country during the campaign it was ensured that Indian entertainment was a priority. Numerous local Indian artistes, especially chutney singers and Indian dancers were on the stage night after night making sure the Indian community was well represented.

It was the simultaneous interaction of these forces that produced the environment in which voters evaluated both the parties and the candidates. It was observed that if any campaign includes interesting candidates, engaging commercials and an abundance of news stories enmeshed in what is considered a close race, voters would not only have access to more information, they would be motivated to process this information. As the intensity of the campaign increased, voters would have more information about the campaign and a greater opportunity to make more sophisticated decisions about competing parties/ candidates.

Having said so, it is important to reflect on the view by the Commission of Enquiry in the functioning of the Elections and Boundaries Commission in Trinidad and Tobago, which was appointed in January 2002. Having concluded that voting behaviour is based on racial preference and that marginal constituencies, where the parties had almost the same amount of support, determine general elections, the commission expressed the view that

> there is a strong perception that the pattern of voting in Trinidad and Tobago is based largely on race and as such each party is assured of a number of 'safe' seats in Parliament. The marginal seats are those in which relatively few voters in some cases only in the hundreds can steer an election to one party or the other. Thus, the marginal seats are very important in the electoral process and the reason why the two major political parties concentrate so much on them in election campaigns.[6]

Although predictions had been made by writers such as Ghany and Maraj that the majority of seats would have been secured by the UNC and COP, it was shown that this did not happen (Ghany 2005). The party that secured most seats would have been the one to get the voters out on Election Day to vote for it. This was clearly one of the main strengths of the PNM which had its Election Day machinery working very smoothly. To ensure this success, the party had to come up with a highly effective campaign strategy which will be discussed below.

An effective campaign strategy must be designed by (1) treating information, (2) diagnosing problems or opportunities, (3) searching for options, (4) forecasting or estimating outcomes, (5) assessing options, (6) selecting a strategy by identifying values, setting goals, principles, and core ideas, (7) selecting tactics,

(8) implementing strategy by identifying tasks, (9) rank-ordering those tasks, (10) assigning them to various members of the campaign team, (11) monitoring them, (12) confirming, adjusting or changing tactics, and (13) finally confirming, adjusting or changing strategies. The PNM was able to hire at least three foreign firms dealing with intelligence gathering, informing public opinion and propaganda to assist it to win the elections.

In researching the composition of a winning campaign team for the 2007 general elections, the questions raised were:

- How and what do potential team members contribute?
- What are potential team members' interests in a victory?
- What does a potential team member's record of action and decision say about his/her willingness/contribution/effectiveness?
- Is that team member's willingness harmonious with that of the rest of the teams?
- What tactics does that potential collaborator use?
- Are those tactics something the rest of the teamwork with?

The PNM ensured that the best possible candidates were chosen by asking the executives of the various constituencies to locate suitable individuals. After this process the potential candidates went through a closely scrutinized interview with the leadership of the party and then a thorough check was made on their background. Especially in the case of the Indian candidates, many of them were either highly qualified, some with a Ph.D. level and some were successful business people with a proven track record.

The design of research questions to obtain information was key to the quality of the PNM strategy. Generating questions that needed to be answered was usually quite easy. Once a wish list was established, each question was reviewed for its importance to achieving the goal and ranked accordingly. Among the research questions asked were those about other political actors and their supporters (Khan and Kenney, 1995). They included:

- Who has run in similar elections in the past? Who has won?
- How will voters react this time? What will be similar? What will be different?
- What has changed since the last elections?
- How is the voter list controlled? How are candidacies made official within parties? Is it according to election law?
- Who controls the processes of voter and candidacy registration?
- According to what procedure is this done: deadlines/criteria?
- Who controls the information the voters get?
- Where does the voter get his or her information? Are there any individuals whose voting preferences are broadly influential?
- Are there voting blocks? What are they? How do they vote?

Sources of information included political operatives, past and present, whose biases and judgements were to be expected, but also those whose expert opinions had to be taken into account. They also included media and academic sources. Media reports are not unbiased, but at least they are usually first-hand. Academic sources often provide more technical or arcane information, although it was occasionally useful. Common problems with information included: (1) an unknown degree of completeness; (2) an unknown degree of accuracy; and (3) an unknown range of validity. If crucial information from an open and accessible source comes to you through another actor, that is a red flag. Candidates and their managers in the PNM were encouraged to be very eclectic in what information was used and the sources normally had to be confirmed for accuracy.

According to John La Guerre (1983), 'Race in Trinidad as elsewhere will always have a part to play. But racial appeal will increasingly have to compete with other factors such as economics, patronage, changing perspectives of voters and generational differences'. Arguing in 1981, that these other factors were able to seduce many voters from the traditional allegiances, he further asserts, 'changes in constituency voting are never abrupt and sudden'. They take place over decades, almost imperceptibly.[7]

In the case of Pointe-a-Pierre which was won by the PNM candidate Christine Kangaloo, the author contends that this constituency was won because both the PNM and the COP were able to woo the voters, especially the first-timers and those whose allegiances were not fixed. Many people who formerly supported the UNC either voted for the PNM or for the COP which also had an effective campaign strategy and as such voting was split. The figures clearly indicate that due to an intense campaign first by the PNM followed by the COP, the UNC lost many of its voters, having secured almost 10,000 in the previous election of 2002. Also it showed that had the opposition come together they would have won this seat.

CONSTITUENCY OF POINTE-A-PIERRE: NUMBER OF VOTES IN 2007 ELECTIONS

The figures for the number of votes polled in the 2007 elections in Pointe-a-Pierre were as follows:

PNM 7,427; UNC 6,136; and COP 3,740.

People of this constituency argued, for example that though they had voted for UNC in the last elections, especially 1995, 2000, 2001 and in 2002, the UNC did not provide adequate infrastructure for the area in terms of needs, such as hospitals, playing grounds, nor did it provide the basic amenities of water and electricity in many areas. Many former Caroni workers whose allegiance had been to the UNC blamed the party for not doing enough to either save Caroni Ltd., or to ensure that the former workers would have gotten a sweet deal with the closure of Caroni. Many believe also that Panday, once he had become Prime Minister was more apt at helping the business classes rather than those who had traditionally been his core supporters.

In planning the PNM strategy for the 2007 elections it was recognized that the party needed to consider not just rivals and voters, but other actors like leaders of pressure groups, social movements or political commentators. The strategists in the party needed to consider what was the agenda of the other actors, where they came in the election process, how far along in their own plans or strategy they were, and how they might have been able affect their own strategy as it proceeded. In determining and planning an effective strategy campaign the successful party had to have sufficient resources, namely, money, people and time.

In every constituency the amount of money needed depended on three factors:

1. How high the essential expenses were,
2. What expenditures could have made a significant difference to success or failure of the strategy, and
3. Expenses which might, but were not assured of making a difference at all.

The PNM was successful in raising large amounts of money and I estimate that it spent no less than 50 million in its campaign. Of this money, a substantial amount, at least 20 per cent would have originated from Indian financiers.

Once the funds were acquired, they needed to be managed properly. Proper management of money was not limited to its judicious use; it also included maintaining credibility by decisions which were likely to be closely watched.

Faced with the prospect that the party which had the better campaign strategy would have won the elections, the strategists in the PNM understood that in their plans, people mattered, even more than money. Thus it was necessary to select, recruit and motivate not only members of the party but also other actors who may have power, influence or information essential or helpful to the strategy. This required assessing skills and contributions as well as the creation of good working relations. In the 2002 elections, for example, the UNC was able to secure the assistance of well known doctors in the area, the leadership of temples and some churches, chutney soca artistes, sportsmen and market vendors, among others, while the PNM found support and received assistance by some religious leaders (both black Muslims and Christians), sportsmen, farmers, youth leaders and women leaders.

The fact that in the 2002 elections, for example, the PNM beat the UNC by a mere 318 votes in the Ortorie/Mayaro constituency is reflective not only of the intensity of the campaign but also of the hard and detailed work of the strategists and helpers of the PNM. In 2007 the PNM failed to win this seat having secured 8,133 votes while the UNC was able to garner 8,583 votes.

Many argue this very point, that in 2007 the PNM campaign in Mayaro was less intense than in 2002.

CONCLUSION

Sound constituency campaigning and the planning and execution of an effective campaign strategy are key determinants in winning elections. Having recognized that without the support of a substantial number of Indian voters in certain constituencies, the PNM could not have won the elections. The PNM ensured that it was well represented by Indian candidates, made a concerted effort to expose the Indian presence in the party and assured its Indian supporters of key benefits to be gained from supporting the party, especially in terms of jobs, financial assistance and other forms of social assistance. Together with this, there were the Indians who were fed up with the opposition parties and their leaders. Some Indian families were also traditional supporters of the PNM and as such on election day were the ones who were key in assisting the PNM in winning the elections of 2007.

What mattered was that on election day, people went out to vote. The party that succeeded in getting the people out on election day to vote for them emerged victorious and in the case of 2007, it was the PNM that was successful in doing so.

NOTES

1. In the previous six elections there were 36 constituencies, 34 in Trinidad and two in Tobago. In 2007, for the first time there were 41 seats, two being in Tobago and 39 in Trinidad.
2. The main ethnic groups in Trinidad and Tobago are the Indians (Indo-Trinidadians), the Negroes (Afro-Trinidadian), the Chinese (Sino-Trinidadians), the Whites, the Syrian/Lebanese and a rapidly growing mixed population.
3. *Apanjhat*, mean voting for your own kind.
4. People were told in certain places such as Mayaro and Laventille that if they voted for any party other than the PNM then they were nothing more than traitors. *Daily Express,* 12 October 2007.
5. In the case of one PNM candidate, she had to be excluded from the line-up since she was exposed as having stolen money from at least three individuals.
6. According to Ghany (2005) the possible marginal seats for the next general elections could be:

   (i) Princes Town/South Tableland
   (ii) St. Joseph
   (iii) Tunapuna
   (iv) Chaguanas East
   (v) San Fernando West
   (vi) Pointe-a-Pierre
   (vii) Mayaro
   (viii) Cumuto/Manzanilla
   (ix) Lopinot/Bon Air West

7. Report of the Commission of Enquiry into the function of the Elections and Boundaries Commission of Trinidad and Tobago, p. 11, section E, 30 May 2002.

REFERENCES

Feddersen, Timothy and Wolfgang Pesendorfer (1997), 'Voting Behavior and Information Aggregation in Selection with Private Information', *Econometrical,* vol. 65, no. 5, pp. 1029–58.

Ghany, Hamid (2005), 'Understanding Marginality in the Electoral System of Trinidad and Tobago: The Search for a Fair Electoral Formula', *UWI Today,* St. Augustine: University of the West Indies, 21 August.

Kahn, Kim Fridkin and Patrick J. Kenney (1997), 'A Model Candidate Evaluation in Senate Elections: The Impact of Campaign Intensity', *The Journal of Politics,* vol. 59, no. 4, pp. 1173–205.

Kahn, Kim and Patrick J. Kenney (1995), 'The Nature and Consequences of US Senate Campaigns: How Competition Influences the Candidates Discussion of Issues', paper presented at the annual meeting of the American Political Science Association, Chicago, Illinois.

La Guerre, John Gaffar (1983), 'The General Elections of 1981 in Trinidad and Tobago', *Commonwealth and Comparative Politics,* vol. XXI, no. 2.

Lijphart, Arend (1991), 'Unequal Participation: Democracy's Unresolved Dilemma', *American Political Science Review,* vol. 91, no. 1, pp. 1–14.

Paquette, Laure (2004), *Campaign Strategy and the Key to Political Longevity,* Nova Science Publishers Inc.

Randall, Vicky (1988), *Political Parties in the Third World,* London: Sage Publications.

Report of the Commission of Enquiry into the Functioning of the Elections and Boundaries Commissions of Trinidad and Tobago, Friday, 31 May 2002.

Ryan, Selwyn (2003), *Deadlock! Ethnicity and Electoral Competition, in Trinidad and Tobago 1995–2002,* Trinidad and Tobago: Zenith Pointing Services.

Ryan, Selwyn, Eddie Green and Jack Hareward (1978), *The Confused Electorate: A Study of Political Attitudes and Opinions in Trinidad and Tobago,* St. Augustine: University of the West Indies.

Ryan, Selwyn (1996), *Pathways to Power: Indians and the Politics of National Unity in Trinidad and Tobago,* University of the West Indies.

Wolfinger, Raymond E. and Steven J. Rosenstone (1980), *Who Votes?,* New Haven: Yale University Press.

REFERENCES

Feddersen, Timothy and Wolfgang Pesendorfer (1997). 'Voting Behavior and Information Aggregation in Selection with Private Information', *Econometrica*, vol. [illegible], no. [illegible], pp. [illegible].

Ghany, Hamid (2006). 'Understanding Marginality in the [illegible] System of Trinidad and Tobago [illegible]', [illegible], University of the West Indies, [illegible] August.

Kahn, Kim Fridkin and Patrick J. Kenney (1997). 'A Model of Candidate Evaluations in Senate Elections: The Impact of Campaign Intensity', *The Journal of Politics*, vol. 59, no. [illegible], pp. [illegible].

Kahn, Kim and Patrick J. Kenney (1999). 'The Nature and Consequences of US Senate Campaigns: How Competition Influences the Candidates' [illegible]', paper presented at the annual meeting of the American Political Science Association, Chicago, Illinois.

[illegible]

[illegible] (1999). [illegible], vol. [illegible], no. [illegible], pp. [illegible].

[illegible] (1993). [illegible]

[illegible] (2002). *Report* [illegible] of Enquiry into the Functioning of the Elections and Boundaries Commission of Trinidad and Tobago, Friday, 31 May 2002.

Ryan, Selwyn (2003). *Deadlock: Ethnicity and Electoral Competition in Trinidad and Tobago, 1995–2002*. Trinidad and Tobago: Ameeth Printing Services.

[illegible]

Ryan, Selwyn (1999). *Winner Takes All: The Westminster Experience in the Caribbean*. [illegible]: [illegible], University of the West Indies.

[illegible] and Steven J. Rosenstone (1980). *Who Votes?* New Haven: Yale University Press.

When we [illegible]
the world [illegible]
and Tobago [illegible]
concentrated [illegible]
such a process [illegible]
born. This [illegible]
processes which [illegible]
institution [illegible]
Contrary [illegible]
between [illegible]
evolved [illegible]

8

Nationalism and Education

Dr Eric Williams' Vision for Trinidad and Tobago

Rattan Lal Hangloo

> To your tender and loving hands, the future of the Nation is entrusted.
> In your innocent heart the pride of the Nation is enshrined.
> On your scholastic development the salvation of the Nation is dependent.
> — DR ERIC WILLIAMS (1981: 329)

THE PROCESS OF global structurization and the rise of nation states in the world started in the sixteenth century.[1] Although the English were credited with being the first nation, nationalism did not remain confined to the old world, it travelled to the new world, especially to the North American British colonies (Kedourie 1971; see also Lipset 1963). The national movements that appeared in Latin America and Balkans during the 1820s provided a major thrust to the societal reorganization (Roudometof 2001). This adaptation of nationalism to contexts that did not share the historical legacy, socio-economic and cultural features of Western Europe and North America was a major step towards reorganization of the globe into the 'world of nations'. Among these many nations, Trinidad and Tobago also carved out with considerable difficulty her place of pride as a nation (Ryan 1972).

When we look at conceptual presuppositions for the rise of nationalism in the world the case of Trinidad and Tobago is a very specific one. In Trinidad and Tobago nationhood implies a complex set of ideas and mentalities concerning the politicization of multicultural life (Braithwaite 1960).[2] When such a process created social bonds, a different kind of national identity was born. This entire development was the outcome of varied historical forces and processes which were understood, articulated and guided by one individual institution: Dr Eric Williams.[3]

Contrary to the interpretations that emphasized historical continuity between pre-modern and modern forms of national identity, Dr Williams evolved a mechanism that connected the manner in which the Caribbean region

*My thanks to Dr. Erica Williams, Professor Dominic Shellard, Pro-Vice-Chancellor, International Affairs and Dr Jennifer Lavia, University of Sheffield for their suggestions.

and its people experienced their transition to modern world as a nation. He posited a direct relationship between politics and culture. To him nationalism was largely the outcome of the processes and complexities of capitalism and colonization.[4] As a result he perceived nationalism as a cultural idea diffused across what became national boundaries. He felt seriously that much of the growth of nationalism rested in part on collaboration among nationalists from different cultural, ethnic, social and even territorial roots and this could be facilitated by education (Williams 1961). He made a distinction between nationalism within the world and nationalism against the world.

Through most of his speeches and writings he rightfully emphasized the ways in which the discourse of nation and statehood was institutionalized within a wider global framework (Williams 1961). His condemnation of colonization was not restricted to its expression in the Caribbean but he was equally consistent in his criticism of colonial rule in Asia and Africa as well. He said, 'The colonized people regardless of their ethnicity and location were his brethren, his partners in suffering and brothers and sisters in struggle for justice and independence' (as quoted in Palmer 2006: 15).

His deployment of multidimensional nationalism is striking in his attempt to come to terms with the problems of the Caribbean and its contextualization. There is a frequent tendency in him to regard the Caribbean as a more or less unique phenomenon (Ryan 1972: 1–13).[5]

Within the Caribbean region the evolution of Trinidad and Tobago into a nation has gone through varied historical processes. The roots of nationhood of Trinidad and Tobago lie deep in its history and in its experience of struggle for existence. Despite Trinidad and Tabago's immense cultural diversity, Dr Williams evolved strands of a common cultural heritage, knitting people together and giving them a sense of unity even while inculcating tolerance of diversity and dissent (Williams 1981). In one of his addresses he says, 'You have come here in Trinidad with people like myself and others. We have all messed out of [the] same pot and tried to develop something on our own so that we can say, it may not be wonderful, it may not be big, but it is our own' (Williams 1974: 7–8).

A major asset of his political ideology was that he believed in accommodative politics and was very sensitive to popular sentiment on linguistic, racial, cultural, ethnic and other issues. The national consolidation involved territorial integration, mobilization of political and institutional resources, economic development and adoption of policies which would promote social justice, remove glaring inequalities and provide equal opportunities (Ryan 1972: 140).

He was surrounded by a society which did not have an indigenous middle class or a bourgeoisie. It had several layers of distinctive social classes with an outlook and origin different from each other, not united by a common ethos unlike West European society or the nations in Asia (ibid.). True that the country was not very big as compared to many colonized regions in the world but it was not devoid of the complex problems that had to be judged in terms of how they affected the lives of people. He knew that his people needed a compassionate understanding of their plight and his task of nation building did not lack humility. Colin A. Palmer observes, 'As a professional historian he gives the members an understanding of their origins and view of their future. He can scold, exalt, lead marches, burn documents, turn himself 180 degrees. In view of the rank and file there is almost only one thing given Williams cannot do; he cannot do wrong.'[6]

By the time he came on the scene, there was a serious lack of political, administrative and economic unity (Klass 1991: 42–4). Even though people were divided by language and ethnicity he made them share common economic and political interests. He played a pivotal role in integrating them into a common framework of political identity and loyalty to the nation that he evolved. He knew that the making of a nation was a prolonged and continuous process, open to continuous challenges, interruption and disruption. Since common people had less experience and knowledge about such problems, it might have been the reason why some people were critical of him at times (Palmer 2006: 11). But we should not ignore the fact that he was well qualified to consider in detail the growth of nationalism in the Caribbean region which made him more popular among his people.

As Edwin Moline rightly says:

> He is the subject of adoration in photos, articles letters studding the pages of 'The Nation'. He is member of every important committee in the upper reaches of party, and no one wants to make a decision without direct or indirect evidence of his approval. The rank and file looks to him for education, inspiration and authority. He formed the party, lead it to unexpected victory in its first political effort and speaks for it in government and in international affairs. More effectively than any other single member he articulates its tactics and strategy, its practical objectives and its philosophy. (Palmer 2006: 10)

Perhaps because of this immense popularity his critics sometimes accused him of harbouring dictatorial tendencies (ibid.).

However, the criticism he received did not distract him, he remained seriously committed to democratic principles and wanted total progress at the societal level. He gave economic issues their due and related them to social, cultural and political developments for his nation and conceived them as a long-drawn process to be carried on in future. He was well aware of and deeply involved in sophisticated discussions of a world society as well as other frames of reference for analysis of long-term global change (Williams 1981: xxiii–xxxiv).

Dr Williams demonstrated the falsity of the colonial construct that the so-called backward people were incapable of ruling themselves in the conditions of modern world. He said, 'Familiar with the disparaging ways in which colonized people had been depicted by imperial scholars we will call upon them to reject the histories written by those who sought only to justify the indefensible and seek support for preconceived and outmoded prejudices' (Palmer 2006: 17).

It was a tough task for him to nurture national sentiment and modernize the nation while retaining its multicultural identity. To him national development was a tool of legitimacy for the Government and an alternative to the legitimacy of colonialism (ibid.). The problem was how to articulate national development for which he felt that the growth of consciousness as a nation was an essential element in his scheme. To him the evolving new nation and its development demanded the ideal of progress, education and struggle to transform the inherited cultures in order to make it suitable for the conditions of the modern world. It required the destruction of archaic forms of authority and creation of conditions for growth of a certain degree of individual initiative and understanding of his own position and the circumstances in which he was situated (Chatterjee 1986: 3; Plamenatz 1976). He left this task to intellectuals and educationists to examine.

After the transfer of power from the British, he had to grapple with the overwhelming and challenging task of national reconstruction. While the deeper maladies like poverty, illiteracy, unemployment, disease and socio-economic development called for sustained effort, there were certain problems arising out of the problem of integration. He genuinely tried to address the issue of racial conflict. With a sustained effort he introduced a public discussion to educate people about the racial climate (Williams 1955b).

He gave a lecture on 25 February 1955 before his formal entry into politics wherein he stated,

> insofar as the history of federal system indicates any thing at all, it suggests that differences of race, religion, language or nationality, far from encouraging hostility to federation, strengthen the sentiment for it, as the only means of securing the advantages of union whilst retaining separate allegiances (Palmer 2006: 262).

He said,

> Here in the British West Indies we have our insular differences and our racial distinctions. We are Barbadian and white, Trinidadian and Indian, Jamaican and Negro. We now face the problem of imposing a common nationality upon these differences. The very existence of differences suggests the desire for separation within the union. The Indians, for example might be as vociferous as a minority as the French Canadian, but demanding federation.... They could be tenacious of their own identity as the Swiss cantons, as the majority group in British Guiana, as a powerful minority in Trinidad they could be insistent on states rights. The position in many respects suggests that they can be excellent federations. (ibid.)

However, in any national development, the relationship between the ideas of the intelligentsia and the social conditions and consciousness of the masses have always varied according to the stage of general economic and cultural development. He was aware of the fact that the societal format in Trinidad and

Tobago was vulnerable to events in Africa and Asia. In Africa and Asia the development was, of course slower. The most modern provinces of Egypt, India and China bore resemblance to the backwardness or primitiveness of medieval times. In large parts of Africa things were much more primitive still. In these countries the twentieth century educated people were cut of from the mainstream by a deep divide thus resulting in revolts. When he saw similar symptoms growing in his Trinidad that was bound to be vulnerable to such issues, he contained it with his own efforts by informally and formally educating the public on these issues and without resorting to any violence. He clearly admitted:

> Our West Indian societies with their special history traditions and institutions are particularly vulnerable to all these world forces, but particularly to the black protest. The history of West Indies has been the long history of deprivations and injustices for the two numerically dominant racial groups of African and Asian origin ... our government has fully appreciated all these world currents and its whole policy has been directed towards a restructuring of society which we inherited. Political power and independence was the key to everything, and so we concentrated on those first. We consciously sought to promote multiracial society with emphasis on economic and social upliftment of the two major disadvantaged groups. Our goal has been Afro-Asian unity. (Williams 1981: 163)[7]

He involved people in the development process, trained them in self-government at grass root level and educated them (both for an understanding of their position in the world and for acquiring the skill and appropriate knowledge which was necessary for handling the affairs of their own nation).[8] He knew that his country could make progress only when progress itself embraced the whole society. In fact it is interesting to remember what Jawaharlal Nehru (the then Prime Minister of India) said in 1957 around same time when Dr Williams was also grappling with somewhat similar problems. Nehru said, 'Personally I feel that the biggest task of all is not only the economic development of India as a whole, but even more so the psychological and emotional integration of the people of India' (Chopra 637; see also Gopal 1979: 22).

But it was not an easy task for Dr Williams. In many nations language was the principal instrument for strengthening the process of nationalism and modernization but in this case language did not help because as in India and West African nations, the population of his nation was multilingual and therefore he could not emphasize language as the foundation of national feeling (Dookeran 1985; see also Braithwaite 1974). He had no prejudice against any particular language but retaining English for the conduct of government business was a historical inevitability. Assertion of linguistic identity has been one of the most divisive issues determining or inhibiting the consolidation and progress of some of the nations in the world but in Trinidad Dr Williams did not allow it to cause any strong political current at that crucial moment (*Trinidad Guardian*, 2 August 1956; see also Singh 1993). He emphasized that the feasible option was to accept and live with multiplicity in a manner that disallowed the emergence of conflicting situations (Ryan 1972: 140). It is assumed here that he was very well aware of the developments and debates about issues in India, where the language issue had become virulent in the form of an opposition to Hindi and tended to create a conflict between Hindi speaking and non-Hindi speaking regions of the country at that time (Chandra 1999: 89; see also Gopal 1984: 352).

It was after independence that he built nation and nationality sentiment anew by constructing institutions that identified nationality with national interest. He designed developmental programmes to make economic prosperity a national project and evolved a government education system that turned social and other identities into national identities (Ryan 1972: 140). He states very proudly,

> Every struggle by Indians or by Africans for the improvement of labour relations and for embracing the dignity of labour in British West Indies is a step in the direction of modernization of Caribbean society. Every step in education of Indians is a step in production of well informed body of citizens on which British West Indian Democracy depends. Every Indian admitted to the professions and the civil service is a further victory in the cause of that participation of local men in administration of British West Indies without which self government is delusion. (ibid.)

A broad feeling of public participation in the activities of the state had to be created to shape the national government which was positioned to establish itself in the institutional framework in which education figured prominently (ibid.). Prior to his planning, no well defined effort was ever made towards the moral training of the students in schools (ibid.: 25). Problems such as these continued among certain schools throughout Trinidad and Tobago and it was increasingly becoming necessary to reform the education system of the country. Education would be the key to ensuring a greater nation and Dr Williams set about implementing such strategies as erecting a new type of school education system which he thought would benefit the nation (ibid.).

To reach out to a larger audience he renamed the 'Woodford Square' in Port-of-Spain 'the University of Woodford Square' creating a large open air lecture room for students who came in thousands to hear his speech (Palmer 2006: 9–11). This was an extraordinary experiment in public education and literacy programme going on in many developing countries today. Williams mission was to create a citizenry that was well informed about its history, conversant on topical matters, educated and politically conscious (ibid.: 9). He spoke from the perspective of a West Indian nationalist who was seeking to destroy all vestiges of colonialism (ibid.: 10). Yet he had profound appreciation for the achievements of the English like Mahatma Gandhi who carried out a long-drawn non-violent struggle against colonialism but always recognized whatever was good in the English people (Gandhi 2007: 46).

He also gave greater emphasis to vocational education and training in technical and agricultural sciences because he found that these fields had been neglected in the colonial system of education. He envisaged a massive industrialization programme (which gathered momentum in the 1970s) and could not be carried out without technically trained professionals (Williams 1974). He outlined the difference between political, education and technical or professional education clearly in facilitating national development.

Dr Williams had his own vision about education in the West Indies. He felt that education in West Indies was not directed to serve the interest of the imperial power or the small colonial intelligentsia. He made it serve the interest of the masses in strengthening the cause of cultural autonomy, political self-determination and Caribbean identity (Campbell 1997: 60). As a result he formulated different approaches and ideas for reforming the then secondary education system. While, delivering a lecture at the graduation ceremony at the University of the West Indies Mona campus he clearly stated:

> Your degree, ladies and gentlemen, qualifies you, whatever it might be, qualifies you to work for the community. It would be great misfortune if that qualification were to be regarded by you, or by others, as nothing more than an opportunity or the basis for getting on an official guest list and getting your names in the social columns of our newspapers.... We in various West Indian countries need very badly people whose preliminary training at Mona represents the beginning and not the end of their career ... there is nothing in the world to stop you from cultivating [an] independent mind. (ibid.: 254–5)

To him, the future of the nation depended on the scholastic achievement of the children of Trinidad and Tobago. The late 1960s marked an era when Dr Williams and his administration decided that it was time to reform the education policy and reinforce what was already being put in place in the education sector (ibid.).

Within the first five years of his regime (1956–61), education was acknowledged as the most successful aspect of government policy (Campbell 1992: 67). Dr Williams facilitated the setting up of the Maurice Committee on Education (*Trinidad Guardian,* 1968(a); see also Trinidad and Tobago Educational Report 1959: 24). The Maurice Committee of 1959, recommended the Comprehensive School system as the main type of secondary school; but there were also central schools, secondary modern schools, and technical schools. The existing secondary grammar schools, whether denominational or government, were to be converted to central schools or secondary modern schools. According to the Maurice Committee, the central school was to provide better opportunities for the education of post-primary classes but it would also lead to the social integration of the pupils drawn from the various primary schools (Government of Trinidad and Tobago 1968; see also Trinidad and Tobago Educational Report 1959; *Trinidad Guardian,* 1968b). The Committee also recommended that the central schools be of the secondary modern type in areas wherever the grammar schools existed. These comprehensive secondary schools provided a five-year course leading to the Cambridge School or an equivalent certificate. It was recommended, however, that junior secondary schools and comprehensive schools should be adopted, along with the existing secondary grammar schools and technical/vocational schools. The difference, however, was that the comprehensive school would be a continuation of the junior secondary schools in the sense that children could move from the junior secondary schools to the higher forms of the comprehensive school (Government of Trinidad and Tobago 1968; see also Trinidad and Tobago Educational Report 1959; *Trinidad Guardian,* 1968). As a result, the first breakthrough in the evolution of the two-cycle secondary education system was made, with comprehensive schools following the junior secondary schools. The schools set up under the new scheme were free secondary schools to be maintained by the government; the curriculum was based on the Modern School Curriculum (Government of Trinidad and Tobago, 1968: 17; see also Trinidad and Tobago Educational Report 1959: 24; *Trinidad Guardian,* 1968c).

The Government liked the idea of the central schools and accepted it as the main model to work on. Although the scheme did not register adequate progress in its initial stages, its comprehensive school system resulted in combining the academic and technical/vocational subjects under one roof and recommended itself socially as the common melting pot of the races and the classes (Government of Trinidad and Tobago, 1968; see also Trinidad and Tobago Educational Report, 1959: 24; *Trinidad Guardian,* 1968a). The comprehensive school or common school according to the Committee was an institution which was directed to preserve the unity of the school society by providing a common and equal opportunity for all pupil to develop their personalities by sharing certain physical and social activities in an interactive space that was vital to the integration of the society. A part of Dr Williams' main aims was also to achieve a large scale expansion of free secondary school education.[9]

One of the concerns of Dr Williams in initiating the new education policy was to construct a nationalist education system that would be receptive to the force of the local sovereign government and not to that of clerics of foreign heads of churches (Campbell 1992: 71). This was because at that time in Trinidad and Tobago he was dealing with a society both ethnically and politically and devoid of patriotism.

Williams was critical of the old system and characterized those schools as 'breeding grounds of disunity' (ibid.: 72). He did not mean any disrespect for any religion or community but he upheld national interest above all sectarian interests. As a result a number of measures were initiated at various levels.

The Concordat of 1960 was implemented.[10] This pertained to the educational upliftment of people of Trinidad and Tobago whose ancestors had came from India, Africa and China. The Committee on General Education set about formulating a new education policy that Dr Williams as Premier got endorsed by the colonial heads. The Committee therefore decided that six postulates should be adopted; they believed that these ideas would help ensure a better and more organized education system for Trinidad and Tobago. The following general principles were agreed upon that:

- the education is essentially a national affair;
- there comes a stage in the growth of a colonial territory to democratic self-government when the education system must be the responsibility of the people of the territory;
- political and administrative changes had already taken place to show that education was fast becoming a movement rooted in West Indian soil;
- a full and comprehensive system of education cannot be planned and worked on in isolation;
- in a moral and spiritual sense, a nation's citizen can grow and develop in goodness only so far as its education system makes this possible; and
- education policy is not something that can be laid down once and for all (Trinidad and Tobago Educational Report 1959: 24).

The governing bodies of those schools were not discontinued. The Government aid was generously made available for their administration, maintenance, repair and furnishing (ibid.). The Principals of assisted secondary schools had to provide a minimum of 80 per cent of the First Form entry places to those who passed the qualifying test for the Common Entrance Examination for free secondary education (Trinidad and Tobago Educational Report 1959: 24). Therefore a new sort of education system was evolved to facilitate the advancement of the country.

As a result, this policy document served as the benchmark for the government to lay down the foundation of a national educational system to promote nationalist ideology (ibid.). Dr Williams took up the challenge and saw to it that this new education system would not only educate more citizens but also brought about social transformation and national integration that finally promoted and assisted the country's economic development (ibid.). On 22 April 1959 he said:

> We are here today as West Indians—the new nation born out of [an] amalgam of disparate cultures and different racial stocks. Our demonstration today demonstrates national unity. Let us go forward in national unity, the country of all and for all, with a career open to talent, without racial discrimination of the past and social sycophancy nurtured thereby. Let us march united, resolved to recognize the equality of all West Indians, moral, religious, political and legal resolved to expunge from West Indian vocabulary the nomenclature of colonialism—niggers and coolies, chinks and limeys. A demonstration such as this is not only a political leap forward. It is also a spiritual purification. As we surge forward confidently to meet the future we bury the past. (ibid.: 315)

Dr Williams knew that people could never develop their own national pride and consciousness without using education to organize all possible human resource. Therefore the Committee conducted its debates on a far wider framework of moving the newly founded nation towards their own independent thinking.[11]

He believed that the new pattern of education in a developing society should not be envisaged only in terms of properly educating the children. It must also embrace procedures designed to teach and influence all individuals who had already left school, including those who had never been to school. Once this was achieved, it would ensure a more enlightened and knowledgeable society as an incentive of higher standards of conduct thus creating a more developed society at the national level—which was only possible through education.[12]

His government also produced highly trained workers to widen representation on the Board of Education, and raised the status of teachers. A greater number of years in school were promised to children.

The other two important developments in this direction were the independence of University of the West Indies in 1962 and starting of its campus at St. Augustine. Another achievement was to start medical school, to teach medicine—a task that was earlier only taken up by denominational schools. For Dr Williams, while executing these measures, his nation and its independent outlook came first. While outlining the graduate's obligations to the country, he states:

> The first one is to defend the national independence at all times. The university has benefited from extensive benefactions, from the friendly foreign governments and friendly foreign philanthropic foundations. Those we gratefully acknowledge. This must not blind us, and you, to the fact that we live in a world of nations who have no particular love for you and/or for the West Indies, who place their interests first, who will seek to use you when ever they can for their own military or economic or political purposes and who when they assist you and/or likely to do so for prestige reasons or because of the benefits that assistance to you brings to them. (Government of Trinidad and Tobago 1968: 17; Government of Trinidad and Tobago 1984: 11; see also Trinidad and Tobago Educational Report 1959: 23; The Education Concordat 1960)

An increase in secondary school enrolment took place from 30,000 to 43,000 in 1973. The average annual capital expenditure of over 8 million Trini Dollars was set apart between 1967 and 1973 with an annual recurrent expenditure of 54 million Trini Dollars (ibid.). Another major feature of this new policy was that it disallowed the Government to relinquish responsibility for education to the churches as stated in the Concordat of 1960 (ibid.). The first order of business in the reformation of secondary education was the abolition of intermediate schools. These schools covered both the primary and secondary stages with an extraordinary age-range of pupils from 5 to 19 years of age.[13] The intermediate school did not fit in with the new pattern of proposals and the Committee on General Education agreed that it should go out of existence to be replaced by the secondary modern school. As a result, immediate steps were taken to provide all intermediate schools with laboratories (Trinidad and Tobago Educational Report 1959; see also The Education Concordat 1960).

Dr Williams knew that his nation could not stand for economic and social development in multifarious ways, especially in fields of communication, education, medicine, technology and agriculture. In this regard he laid down certain broad guidelines for governmental policy from which the modern Trinidad has stemmed (Palmer 2006: 16–17).

The Committee agreed that the regular secondary schools should be more comprehensive, where there would be separate grammar and modern schools. The system of the single comprehensive school or the bipartite system of the grammar and modern school could provide an academic and technical education at a junior level adequately (Trinidad and Tobago Educational Report 1959). The pupils of the modern or comprehensive school whose special aptitude was along practical lines were offered the opportunity to blossom and could then proceed to the polytechnic at the age of 15, at a time when their technical skills were more accurately determined (Trinidad and Tobago Educational Report 1959: 24). Or later, at the age of 17 or 18, with a grammar school background and a greater knowledge of science and mathematics, they could proceed to the senior division of the polytechnic or senior technical college or school of technology.[14] The Committee also recommended steps to establish government grammar schools for girls in both provinces.

In Dr Williams' vision, since Trinidad and Tobago was a self-sufficient and industrialized society, new measures should be implemented to ensure the success of the students of the country (Williams 1981: 247–50). At this time, Williams and his team were trying to create ways to raise the standard of education. Ironically, it was at the same time when the principals of secondary schools in the Caribbean region were indicating that they wished to lower academic standards by making it easy for pupils who fail to get certificates.[15] This is how the modern schools come into being, as the grammar schools were geared for teaching those who intended to make a career in engineering or technology. Pupils at the grammar schools who had a technical aptitude, but could not reach the higher level in science and mathematics were supposed to be better off at the modern school (Trinidad and Tobago Educational Report 1959: 79). The modern schools were turned into the junior secondary schools, more geared towards educating pupils who could be placed in other sectors of the industry. Since there were no modern schools within Trinidad and Tobago at that time, Dr Williams immediately saw to it that the provisions were made for these institutions as this seemed to be the solution for removing the outstanding weakness in the school system. The secondary modern school represented the required provision that was needed for the improvement and expansion of the school system of the country (ibid.).

As the discussions on education raged, a more influential description of the two-cycle secondary system was provided by the local planners of the Draft Education Plan 1968–83. The Plan stated that all children were to be educated up to age 14 in the junior secondary schools. The junior secondary school was to be followed by the senior comprehensive school which would provide a broad range of academic and practical/agricultural/technical/commercial courses with the option to specialize in one aspect of the curriculum (Trinidad and Tobago Educational Report 1959: 110). In actuality both the junior secondary school and the senior comprehensive school had a comprehensive type of curriculum, the difference being that the comprehensive range was intended to discourage specialization in the junior secondary school, but to facilitate it in the senior comprehensive school. In 1967–8 the Government at last had a definite model of the secondary school system which the Parliament endorsed (ibid.: 79).[16]

In educating people and in nation building Williams' calibre that of a professional historian, gave him an added advantage. He knew that capitalism stood in contrast to slavery/indenture or feudalism where the individual in each group was a link in the chain of that group and was submerged in that group to one degree or another (Government of Trinidad and Tobago 1961: 49). In a capitalist society the individual leaped out upon the historical stage in an extraordinary way. The very type of this capitalist society—anarchic, bound together only by the bonds of exchange and characterized by conflict of competition—brought this free individual to the forefront. Even though his countrymen were having freedom unlike slaves or indentured labourers, Dr Williams knew that the Trinidadian was not only freed from feudal fetters but was also against other analogous individuals in cruel competition. He knew that in such circumstances he could not speak for individuals in general because in a growing class society individuals were defined in terms of class. It is because of Dr Williams that the impulse the nation's technological development became more powerful (ibid.).

Was it not Dr Eric Williams who put forward tremendous plans for the electrification, mechanization, chemical and other aspects of industrialization of the country? He was a tremendously powerful concentrating force breaking down a variety of conservatisms single-handedly, always insisting on high standards and quality in an unparalleled technological reconstruction of the country (Williams 1974: 7–8, 44).

When he was appointed a member of the Council of the United Nations University Dr Williams laid a great stress on inclusion of the subject of coexistence between peoples of different cultures, languages and social systems. He was aware of the fact that the efforts to make people aware of coexistence were necessary for maintenance of peace, security, realization of human rights and universal human values related to the quality of life. To him the institutions were also agencies for facilitating peace like Mahatma Gandhi. He said,

> The United Nations University with that charter becomes one of the principal agencies for not only avoiding the typical confrontations but bringing together cultures and systems that have up to now been struggling and for giving some dignity and enhancing the position of peoples and cultures that have been steadily denigrated and depreciated by European civilization in the age of modern civilization (Williams 1981).

People who are capable of seeing the long view of history, people who suffer over the painful and difficult problems of today's world, people who sincerely want to rebuild, who feel that human progress is dearer to their hearts, must understand that the prime condition for their decisive victory over future problems is to have a fresh look at Dr Williams' vision and explore his perspectives for not only this nation but the entire Caribbean region.

NOTES

1. The Ottoman expansion into Eastern Mediterranean and North Africa gave impetus to the European 'Age of Discoveries'. The Italian city states responded to these developments by searching for alternative commercial routes to the 'Orient' and financed Spanish expeditions into what was characterized as the New World. The consequence of these developments was cross-cultural interactions between Westerners and their newly discovered and subjected people of Americas, India, Africa and South-East Asia (Kedourie 1971), for details see also Mukerjee (1986).
2. The kind of society that evolved in Trinidad in the nineteenth and twentieth centuries was forced to perceive accommodation in which separate ethnic social entities each with their own distinctive institutions (African and mixed European, and Asian descent) met and interacted only in economic and political areas. It grew bonds of solidarity on political plane when the constraints of their geographical roots began to recede (Alleyne 1972).
3. Dr Eric Williams, the first Prime Minister of Trinidad and Tobago, is a teacher, historian and philosopher. Born on 25 September 1911, he was educated at Queen's Royal College and won the Island Scholarship to Oxford University. At Oxford, he received his Doctor of Philosophy degree in 1938. In 1939, Williams migrated to the United States to teach at Howard University. In 1955 he returned to Trinidad and Tobago and became more involved in politics (http://users.rcn.com/alana.interport/eric.html). Eric Williams' entry into politics was hardly surprising development after his ties with Caribbean Commission were severed in June 1955. In the previous year he had begun to give a series of lectures at Trinidad Public Library in Port-of-Spain to educate people about their history and to promote a sense of West Indian nationalism (Palmer 2006).
4. There was neither a freedom struggle nor a protest against the British in this region. This is clearly spelt out by Dr Williams in his writings (Williams 1994: 210).
5. He invokes and utilizes transnational relation or existence in strictly conceptual way as opposed to the then rhetoric contemporary politics.
6. Palmer (2006: 11) (based on) Edwin Moline to US Department of State 12 July 1961 Central Decimal file Trinidad, NA-DS, boxl670, folder74Eoo/6-261.
7. The party that he founded created structures of local politics and power through which the masses put forward their demands, their needs and requirements in regard to a countless specific improvements in conditions of life, whether in the broader economy or just in domestic life as well as in questions of administration and education. The policies of the party in almost all decisive spheres, with the exception of internal party policies passed through public eye. There are lots of similarities with Nehru, for instance, not accepting complete socialism or capitalism. Although as the founder of PNM Dr Williams employed a stridently nationalist rhetoric, the party was reformist in its ideology. It adopted a firm anti-colonial stance, supported a Federation of the West Indies, a reorganization of territories economy with special emphasis on the development of agriculture, and industrialization. His vision was

that of a harmonious multiracial society. Eschewing socialism, the party also avoided any formal association with trade unions, unlike the British Labour Party and the People's National Party in Jamaica (Palmer 2006: 10).

8. Sir Stephen Luke, the British official who led the committee responsible for handling matters relating to the inauguration of West Indian Federation scheduled for 1958, observed in January 1957 that Williams had extraordinary personal qualities. He said: 'His energy is inexhaustible He is one of the most remarkable public speakers I have ever heard he is of course exceptionally intelligent.' Luke clearly perceived why the PNM is a movement and not a party, why so many people feel since 1956 general elections some sense of national revival. He had detected none of the prejudices for which Williams has been criticized. Williams was criticized for harbouring dictatorial qualities (Palmer 2006: 11). Similarly Nehru was also criticized for a similar approach.
9. His government struggled to gain greater legislative control over the education system. Before 1950 the authority of the government was already sufficient in relation to denominational elementary schools; therefore the government planned to upgrade its authority by establishing secondary schools which were separate from the already established denominational secondary schools (Campbell 1992: 67).
10. One of the clauses stated that the existing relationship between Government and the Governing Bodies and teachers in assisted secondary schools would remain (ibid.: 72).
11. Williams felt that one of the main problems with the education system was that the colonial schools had been built for children of a particular section, religion and race. Therefore it became an issue when people had major problems gaining admissions in some of these schools. He sought to rectify this by asking the Committee to devise a public system of education that would remove these suspicions from the minds of the people. This new education system would be a system of integration which would be suitable and adaptable to the local conditions (Government of Trinidad and Tobago 1968; Government of Trinidad and Tobago, 1984; see also Trinidad and Tobago Educational Report 1959; The Education Concordat 1960).
12. Some of the main directions of government policies in education in the first term of office (1956–61) were already adumbrated by the writings of Dr Williams before he entered politics. In 1956, his party made two types of promises in respect to education: there was a promise of reorganization and a promise of expansion. Even though these promises were treated by some as an effort to gain political mileage no body could deny that the goal of Dr Williams' was to raise the academic standards and establish an education system that suited the political, social and economic needs of the country (ibid.).
13. There were eight intermediate schools: two run by the Government (1 boys', 1 girls'), five Roman Catholic (2 boys', 3 girls') and one Anglican intermediate school. The fee in these schools ranged from 60 cents in the primary division to $1.80 in the secondary division (Trinidad and Tobago Educational Report 1959; see also The Education Concordat 1960).
14. In 1957, two more secondary schools (1 boys' RC, 1 girls' RC) with the same fee structure were given aid by the government (Trinidad and Tobago Educational Report 1959).
15. There was a general notion that the granting of a certificate to students as a concession for failing was not acceptable, as it would only serve to further weaken

the character of pupils. However, the new compromise certificate was described as the General Certificate of Education which was to be issued to candidates who had failed the School Certificate. For some years now it has been the policy to progressively reduce the academic standard of the School Certificate as a test of a good general education. There was the abolition of compulsory group subjects and group requirements and not this reward for failures. In the grammar school, the General Certificate of Education, was not generally regarded as an improvement. The Committee was content that the substitute certificate to be awarded to candidates who had failed their School Certificate was not in the best interest of education, and recommended that it was necessary for the Government to set up its own standard of matriculation for Trinidad and Tobago, so as to indicate what is expected of the grammar schools. The grammar school was expected to provide a certain type of training and maintain a certain standard of scholarship and as a result it should not be too tolerant to mediocrity. The grammar school curriculum had a special syllabus which was adapted to overseas areas in some subjects, for example, the Agricultural Science for School Certificate. History was another subject to be taught in grammar schools as it was a great cultural subject. The Committee recommended that the history of the last hundred years of West Indian, British and European existence should be taught. The inclusion of woodwork classes in the grammar school curriculum was thought unnecessary and undesirable (Trinidad and Tobago Educational Report 1959: 66–7).

16. Interestingly one finds that a large number of students was attracted not only to government schools but even the schools run by Roman Catholics, Hindus and Muslims made great progress and this would not have been possible without state patronage. The number of students (both boys and girls) in Roman Catholic schools rose from 42,532 in 1954 to 57,109 in 1961. The number in Hindu schools rose from 8,507 in 1954 to 17,298 in 1961 and in Muslim schools it rose from 2,443 in 1954 to 5,133 in 1961 (Government of Trinidad and Tobago 1961: 49).

REFERENCES

Alleyne, Michael H. (1996), *Nationhood from the Schoolbag: A Historical Analysis of the Development of Secondary Education in Trinidad and Tobago,* Organization of American States, New York.

Alleyne, J.M. (1972), *The Creolization of Africans and Indians in East Indians in Caribbean: A Symposium on Contemporary Economics and Political Issues,* Institute of African and Asian Studies, University of the West Indies.

Braithwaite, Lloyd (1960), 'Social stratification and cultural pluralism', in *Social and Cultural Pluralism in Caribbean: Annals of New York Academy of Sciences,* V. Rubin, ed., vol. 83, no. 5, pp. 816–36.

——— (1974), 'Problems of Race and Colour in the Caribbean', vol. I, no. I, New York.

Campbell, Carl (1992), *Colony and Nation: A Short History of Education in Trinidad and Tobago (1834–1986),* Jamaica: Ian Randle Publishers.

——— (1996), *The Young Colonials: A Social History of Education in Trinidad and Tobago, 1834–1939,* Jamaica: University of the West Indies.

——— (1997), *Endless Education: Main Currents in the Education System of Modern Trinidad and Tobago, 1939–1986,* Barbados: University of the West Indies Press.

Chandra, Bipan et al. (1999), *India after Independence,* Delhi: Penguin.

Chatterjee, Partha (1986), *Nationalist thought and the Colonial World: A derivative discourse,* London: The United Nations University Press.

Dookeran, Winston (1985), 'East Indians and the Economy of Trinidad and Tobago', in *Calcutta to Caroni: The East Indians of Trinidad,* John La Guerre, ed., University of the West Indies, Trinidad.

Gandhi, Raj Mohan (2007), *Mohandas: A True Story of Man, His People and Empire,* Viking.

Gooding, Kimberly Marie (2008), 'The Legacy of Eric Williams: A Critique of the Secondary School System in Trinidad and Tobago', unpublished document, Caribbean Studies Project, University of the West Indies.

Gopal, Sarvpali, ed. (1984), *Selected Works of Jawaharlal Nehru,* vol. 2, Delhi.

——— (1979), *Jawaharlal Nehru: A Biography,* vol. 3 (1947–52), London and Delhi.

Government of Trinidad and Tobago (1968), *Draft Plan for Educational Development in Trinidad and Tobago 1968–83,* Trinidad: Government Printery.

Government of Trinidad and Tobago (1961), *Central Statistical office: A digest of Statistics on education,* Government Press, Port-of-Spain, Government of Trinidad and Tobago.

Government of Trinidad and Tobago (1984), *Ministry of Education: Assessment of the Plan for Educational Development in Trinidad and Tobago 1968–83,* Trinidad: Government Printery.

Kedourie, E. (1971), 'Introduction' in *Nationalism in Asia and Africa,* K. Kedourie, ed., New York, pp. 1–15.

Ken, Boodoo (2002), *The Elusive Eric Williams,* Jamaica: Ian Randle Publishers.

Klass, Morton (1991), *Singing with Sai Baba: The Politics of Revitalization in Trinidad,* Westview Press.

Lipset, S.M. (1963), *The First New Nation,* New York.

Mukerjee, C. (1986), *From Graven Images: Patterns of Modem Materialism,* New York: Columbia University Press.

Palmer, Colin A. (2006), *Eric Williams and the Making of the Modern Caribbean,* University of North Carolina Press, USA.

Plamenatz, John (1976), 'Two types of Nationalism', in *Nationalism: The Nature and Evolution of Idea,* Eugene Kamenka, ed., London: Edward Arnold, pp. 23–36.

Roudometof, Victor (2001), *Nationalism, Globalization, and Orthodoxy: The Social Origins of Ethnic Conflict in Balkans,* London: Green Wood Press.

Ryan, Selwyn D. (1972), *Race and Nationalism in Trinidad and Tobago,* University of the West Indies Press, Trinidad.

Samaroo, Brinsley (1985), 'Politics and Afro Asian Relations in Trinidad', in *Calcutta to Caroni: The East Indians of Trinidad,* John La Guerre, ed., Trinidad: University of the West Indies, pp. 63–94.

Singh, H.P. (1993), *Indian Struggle for Justice and Equality: Black Racism in Trinidad and Tobago (1956–1962),* Chaguanas: Indian Press Review.

The Education Concordat (1960), *Approved by the Cabinet and signed by Hon. J.S. Donaldson.* Minister of Education on 25 December 1960, Port-of-Spain, Government Press, Government of Trinidad and Tobago.

Trinidad and Tobago Educational Report (1959), Committee on General Education, Port-of-Spain, Government Press, Trinidad and Tobago.

———, Committee on General Education, *'Maurice Report'*. Trinidad and Tobago: Government Printery.

Williams, Eric [(1944) 1994], *Slavery and Capitalism,* North Carolina Press, USA.

——— (1955a), *An Analysis of Recommendations of Education Commissions and Experts in Trinidad, 1869–1954,* 20 January.

——— (1955b), Lecture 'Federation in world today', 25 February, Port-of-Spain, Trinidad and Tobago.

——— (1974), *The International Significance of Asia and the Far East from the intellectual and cultural stand point,* Port-of-Spain: Key Caribbean Publications.

——— (1981), Message to the Youth of the Nation, 30 August 1961, in *From the Love of Liberty: Selected Speeches of Dr Eric Williams,* Paul K. Sutton, ed., Trinidad: Longman.

NEWSPAPER ARTICLES

Rupert V. Baptiste. 'Government and the Draft Plan for Education', *Trinidad Guardian,* 26 June 1968.

Hollis, Boisselle, 'Teachers' College, 19 New Schools by 1972', *Trinidad Guardian,* 25 September 1969.

'Camacho Raps Teachers', *Trinidad Guardian,* 22 January 1969.

McNeilly, Russell, 'Education Plan Not Thorough', *Trinidad Guardian,* 24 June 1968.

'Teachers: Shift System Should be Avoided', *Express Newspapers,* 28 August 1968.

'Tell Me If I am Wrong About the Draft Plan', *Trinidad Guardian,* 9 September 1968.

Excerpt from 'A Shake up in the Education System', *Trinidad Guardian,* 1 April 1968.

'Valdez Points To "False Economies" in Education Plan', *Trinidad Guardian,* 1 March 1969.

9

Breaking the Glass Ceiling

East Indian Women and Educational Mobility in Trinidad and Tobago

Ann Marie Bissessar

IN DISCUSSING THE mobility of any group, it is necessary to first understand the historical and cultural environment from which it emerged. In the case of East Indian women, for instance, one of the critical obstacles to their entry into the arena of education, and later the workforce, had to do with the way they were assimilated during the period of indentureship. There can be no doubt that the entry by East Indian women, first in the schools and later into the workforce, was to a large extent determined by the cultural traditions of this group as a whole. However, an important factor that has often been overlooked, particularly during the immediate post-indentureship period had to do with the relatively small number of women who had emigrated. A tangential to this could be issue the caste of the emigrants. Indeed, it can be surmised that since many of the women who migrated came from underprivileged castes they would later show a reluctance to send their offspring, particularly their daughters to schools, mostly schools which were 'foreign' to their group. Rather, their orientation would be directed towards land and husbandry. The discussion which follows will accordingly present a brief historical overview of the indentureship experience and try as far as possible, given the absence of literature, to focus on the experience of East Indian women during this period.[1]

THE EAST INDIAN WOMEN AND INDENTURESHIP

During the period 1845-1917, approximately 1,43,000 indentured labourers left the Indian subcontinent to work in Trinidad and Tobago (Jha 1985). According to Reddock (1984), however, when indentureship commenced in 1845, what became known as 'the Indian Women Problem' had already reared its head. Indeed, it was found that one of the central concerns raised during the first prohibition of East Indian immigration in 1839 was that a small number of women had migrated. In November 1844, when the Government of India lifted its ban on indentured Indian migration to the Caribbean, one of the conditions that accompanied it was that at least 12½ per cent of the emigrants should be women. By 1845, however, the ratio between men and women had not increased significantly.[2] A number of explanations have accordingly been put forward to explain why the male : female ratio was uneven. Jha (1985: 2) for instance, suggested that women were not willing to emigrate in large numbers. Other reasons offered by Jha (1985) included the following factors:

1. The method of recruitment was faulty;
2. The recruiters wanted to earn money and presented a false picture of the conditions of the country to which the Indians were emigrating and therefore many left their families behind;
3. The privacy of a normal family life was non-existent in the depots and the boats; and
4. The living conditions in the barracks were poor.

While all these factors contributed to the small number of women leaving India, one of the more critical factors, however, lay with the nature of the recruitment process. The planter class was reluctant to cover the additional cost of attracting and transporting women to the West Indies. According to one writer, they felt that the importation of Indian women was an unnecessary burden and they were perceived as a financial disability particularly when work time was lost as a result of child bearing and child rearing. However, this was later revised since the colonial administrators considered the system of indenture a 'blessing' with one 'blot' being the shortage of women. The Acting Governor of Guyana, Young, trying to convince the planters to undertake the cost of importing more women commented:

> It is a gratifying sight in this Colony to witness the numerous instances of industry and thrift to be found among the free Coolie women and to observe their intelligence in the management of the little property they and their husbands may have acquired. In many cases their husbands seem to leave all business details to their wives and the wives seem well worthy of the trust. It is the women in most cases who are to be seen paying in money to the savings bank or making lodgments of money for remittance to India. (Tinker 1974: 266)

While Young pointed out that East Indian women were not physically capable of strenuous plantation exertion, he argued that they were industrious and exerted a civilizing and humanizing effect on those around them. There was no doubt that a number of factors that seemed to limit the participation of women in indentureship. At the same time, however, there were also pressures that made an overwhelming case for their inclusion. For instance, one major argument was that it would have been cheaper to maintain a local labour force rather than rely on the importation of labour. In addition, it was felt that there was a need to stabilize the male labour force and the problems incurred in securing the 'right kind of woman' (Reddock 1984: 8). Given a proactive policy by the colonial administrators to encourage emigration of women, by 1857 the ratio of female to male was one to three and in 1859 this was further reduced to a one to two ratio (ibid.: 9).

In July 1968, however, the Government of Bengal, a primary depot from which the indentured labourers were recruited, complained that the increase in the number of women would lead to the recruitment of women from the underprivileged caste, mainly prostitutes. Accordingly the ratio once more reverted to one to three but finally, as Brereton pointed out, it was fixed by the Colonial Office at two to five (Brereton 1974, cited in Reddock 1984). Thus, there was always an unequal distribution of male to female.

Apart from the small number of female immigrants it was also found that the majority of East Indian women who came to the Caribbean came as individuals without attachments. Reddock (1984) noted that as late as 1915 the Commissioners McNeill and Lal described the composition of women indentured labourers thus:

> The women who came out consist as to one-third of married women who accompany their husbands, the remainder being mostly widows and women who have run away from their husbands or who have been put away by them. A small percentage is ordinary prostitutes. Of the women who emigrate otherwise than with their husbands and parents the great majority are not, as they frequently represented to be shamelessly immoral. They are women who have got into trouble and apparently emigrate to escape from a life of promiscuous prostitution which seems to be the alternative to emigration.... What appears to be true as regards a substantial number of women is that they ran away from home alone or accompanied by some one by whom they were abandoned that they drifted into one of the large recruiting centers and after a time were picked up by the recruiter. (Reddock 1984: 12)

It is interesting to note that the women who left India were not 'married'. Rather some were widows, others had either left their husbands or had been deserted by them, while a smaller proportion comprised those who were pregnant or prostitutes. In other words, the 'structured' East Indian family that existed in India was not exported to the colonies. By 1870, however, new Indian village settlements along the lines of the traditional Indian concept of 'family' were introduced. Intra-family relationships were governed by regard for age and kinship status. Strong subgroup loyalties were built around the 'family' and family members were expected to cooperate in the plantation work, save money and acquire property. In short, East Indian women were subsumed within the milieu of the larger group. More importantly, though, the East Indian woman was able to adjust easily to this kind of domestic environment since it was a situation to which they were accustomed.

THE INTRODUCTION OF THE CANADIAN MISSION SCHOOLS

In 1868 with Trinidad as a base, Canadian missionaries established schools throughout Trinidad with the main purpose to educate and convert the children of East Indian immigrants. Hamel-Smith suggests that the proportion of boys to girls attending primary school in Trinidad changed very slowly between 1900 and 1956. She observed that, until World War I there were approximately 44 girls to every 56 boys on the school registers. During the inter-war period and continuing into the 1950s there was a slow but steady improvement in the proportion of girls attending primary school. By 1950 there were 48 girls to every 52 boys on the school registers (1984). The statistical data, however, was not subdivided along ethnic lines. In the 1891 Census when interpreting the information regarding children, sex, numbers and occupations it was recorded that:

> ... females are occupied at an earlier age that the males, and a comparison of the ... different sections of the population, will show that this is almost entirely confined to the Indian section of the population ... many of the females among whom become wives and mothers at an age when those of other sections are still attending school. (ibid.: 1)

Indeed, it was evident that the East Indians as a group had maintained the tradition of marrying their children, particularly the girls at an early age. The average Hindu or Muslim girl, for example, was betrothed while barely an adolescent and thus entered into a relationship which dominated and set the pattern of her life. As Hamel-Smith observed, if 'by twelve or thirteen one was married, then the skills which the school imparted were regarded as unnecessary' (1984: 3). Another educator, Kenneth Grant also complained that 'in the earlier years of our work it was almost impossible to get the girls to school' (1923: 84).

A number of reasons can accordingly be offered for this seeming 'reluctance' by the East Indians to send their children 'especially the girls' to school (Bushe 1968: 190). One of the reasons already in this article was that of early marriages. Other reasons had to do with the need for help with domestic tasks, which of course was considered a critical social skill if the girl was to maintain a successful marital relationship. Thus, the tradition of early marriages accorded the formal education of girls a very low priority.

Another explanation might well have to do with the way that women were perceived. Indian men, like many others during this period, shared the general view that the female mind was 'incapable' of learning non-domestic skills. According to Brereton (1985) the 'idea' grew that Indians held their women in contempt and that 'chopping' was their national way of resolving differences. Indeed, one mission teacher went to considerable lengths to convince parents that their girls were capable of learning. He recounted:

> ... A little girl is reading the Second Book. When any of the parents visit the school, Mr McDonald shows them the cleverness of this little girl in reading and arithmetic as proof that their doctrine of female stupidity is false. (Morton 1916: 159)

It could be argued, though, that while this perception was held widely by the less privileged and working classes, the upper classes sent their children including their girls to schools, though there was a different curriculum for boys and girls. Part of the explanation, in this case then, for the low attendance by East Indian girls in the case of colonies such as Trinidad, was due to the caste of their parents, the majority of whom were of the underprivileged and working class. They felt that the girl was not part of the family but would eventually be the property of some other man. Sarah Mortorn had complained in her notes about a Brahmin stepfather who had removed his two small girls from school and in response to her protests had retorted:

> ... If you teach a boy you will get some good of it, but a girl is not yours. She is some other man's, why should you trouble with her? Girls are to cook, wash and keep the house.... Sometimes to worship God. (Morton, 1916: 257)

However, the need to educate their offspring in general, was not a priority since in addition to the cultural orientation of the East Indian group; the economy at this period was largely based on agriculture. Because of this, employment policies as a whole did not place emphasis on formal education but rather was directed to skills, craftsmanship and agricultural-type employment.

While culture was indeed one of the obstacles in the move to educate East Indian women, another more critical factor, perhaps, was religion. Indeed, it should be recalled, particularly among the Hindus that a very rigid and endogamous system based on colour and profession was adhered to. Racial endogamy was observed and inter-racial marriage was frowned upon. Thus, the early 'mission schools' were perceived as institutions that undermined the religious belief of the East Indian population and indeed the major aims of these schools was conversion rather than education. On the other hand, the missionaries were of the view that the Indians were 'heathens and morally degraded'. According to Brereton (1985: 29), Morton thought Hinduism an unclean religion which fostered a sense of the untruthful, revengeful and avaricious, with an obsessive respect for their sinister rites and traditions. In addition, many East Indians were afraid of their children mixing with other 'elements' of the population since they felt that would lead to a general decay of their culture and value systems. It should also be recalled that according to Hindu philosophy the devil 'Ravan' was symbolized as 'black'. Thus, contact with the 'negro' was to be avoided at all possible costs.

By the late 1860s, then, when the Indian population was over 20,000 there were only a handful of Indian children in the public primary schools. Education for the East Indians began with the establishment of the Canadian Presbyterian Mission for the Indians in 1868. From the beginning the missionaries stressed on education and it was this rather than conversion which the Indians valued. By 1878 there were 15 Canadian Mission state-aided primary schools; there were 52 in 1891, 59 in 1901, 61 in 1911; in 1890 the children of indentured labourers were exempted from fees. The number of Indian children at the Canadian Mission schools grew slowly, and secondary institutions were established: Naparima College for boys, a teacher's training college at San Fernando and a girls' high school (see Table 9.1).

TABLE 9.1: Enrolment in Canadian Mission (Presbyterian Schools) in Random Years by Sex 1899-1956

Year	*Boys in CM schools*	*% of total enrolment*	*Girls in CM schools*	*% of total enrolment*	*Total enrolment*
1899	3,012	71.9	1,175	28.1	4,187
1905	4,102	68.1	1,922	31.9	6,024*
1910	5,425	67.8	2,576	32.2	8,001
1914	6,473	69.9	2,788	30.1	9,261
1919	6,929	68.7	3,154	31.3	10,083
1923	9,084	66.8	4,520	33.2	13,604
1927	9,719	66.2	4,968	33.8	14,687
1931	10,811	64.9	5,845	35.1	16,656
1935	11,318	63.0	6,641	37.0	17,959
1938	11,776	60.9	7,568	39.1	19,344
1947	*	*	*	*	26,020
1951	*	*	*	*	28,986
1952	14,910	52.8	13,322	47.2	28,232
1954	14,185	53.3	12,440	46.7	26,625
1956	14,693	52.6	13,234	47.4	27,929

Note: *only summary totals printed in 1940s.
Source: Hamel-Smith (1984). Taken from Brereton (1985: 29).

INDIANS AND EDUCATION: PRESSURES FOR CHANGE

As Table 9.1 indicates while enrolment of both boys and girls were low during the early 1900s, by the end of World War I, the number had increased significantly. In addition, a number of schools for girls were introduced, such as the Iere Girls' Home in Princes Town (1905) and the Archibald Institute which was opened later in Tunapuna but which was intended both to provide suitable wives and partners for young Presbyterian converts.

While Hamel-Smith (1984) suggested that 'time' slowly eroded the 'cultural values' which were hostile to the education of East Indian women, other factors were also at work. Singh (1985) has observed that during the indentureship period, Trinidadians evolved certain ideas and judgements about the East Indians which by repetition became stereotypes. As Indians began settling down and were gradually perceived by other groups as constituting an integral part of society, they were inevitably assigned a social position or status. In the society into which the Indians had entered, occupation, was the main basis of social status, and in this case agricultural labour was generally regarded as the lowest or most undesirable occupation. Indeed Singh's account offers a brief insight into the perception of groups at this time. He wrote:

> As one witness observed before the Royal Commission of Enquiry of 1897, 'to call a man a "gardener" here is at once to class him with the Portuguese jobber, who is of a low type. There is much "in a name", especially in a mixed community like ours, where the people are supersensitive to social standing'. (1985: 35)

According to Singh the most prestigious occupations at this time were those connected with the ownership and management of estates, large commercial establishments or the upper rungs of the civil service. The professions of law and medicine came next, followed by the 'genteel' but poorly placed teaching and lower positions in civil service. The terms on which the Indians had entered the society had automatically relegated them to the lowest status. But Singh maintained that while the terms of entry of this group into the society was the main reason of their low status, there were other important (though subordinate) reasons as well. For example, the acceptance of Christianity, in particular, was felt to be a prerequisite for advancement in civilized life. Perhaps it was the desire to raise their status or standing in the society that eventually persuaded the East Indians to send their children to school.

In addition to changing values, however, it was found that the environment was also changing. After 1885 when working and living conditions on the sugar plantations began to deteriorate, East Indians began drifting into Port-of-Spain and to a lesser extent San Fernando, the two principal cities in Trinidad, to find other sources of livelihood. However, there were few openings for unskilled agricultural labourers and though the Indians managed to make a living by selling grass and coconuts, the majority could survive only by taking up occupations that the other underprivileged groups of the city spurned. Groups which did not go to the cities remained within the sugar belt and engaged in farming. Two major factors were thus placing pressure on the East Indian group to either accept some of the dominant values of the society or remain at the bottom of the socio-economic ladder. The factors included the need to change their occupation in keeping with the rapidly shifting economic environment of the country. But while there were pressures for change, at the same time there were also impediments against accepting the values of their adopted society. Language, for example, was a critical barrier since the majority of the East Indians at this period spoke Hindi or some derivative of this language. Another impediment was of course the professional or occupational segregation of the group. As Jha observed the '"East Indian" could not be on equal terms with the "West Indian" for the former had to carry a passport, was denied full civil rights and modern education and treated as a stranger, a "heathen" or a "barbarian"' (1985: 17).

By the time the system of indentureship was terminated, Indians comprised one-third of the population. By the early 1920s, East Indians demanded a proportional representation of their community in the Legislative Council and by the 1930s they became more vocal in airing their grievances. Since many East Indians had sent their children to schools, it was found that this middle class intelligentsia was now emerging to lead the group as a whole. East Indians now had their own 'clubs', including the India Club in Port-of-Spain, as well as the Plimalaya Club in San Juan which was an exclusive Indian club. By this time, as Mahabir (1994) observed, the value of education as a lever for social mobility and as a bridge for crossing over from the rural-agricultural occupational 'sector' to the urban and modern occupational 'sector' was recognized by the Indian population. In addition to this, compulsory education was introduced in 1950 so that by the early 1950s there were 47 girls out of every 100 children on the roles in the Canadian Mission schools. What is interesting to note is that in the 1950s the pattern of enrolment in the newly established Hindu and Muslim schools was also very similar to that in the Canadian Mission schools (see Table 9.2).

TABLE 9.2: Enrolment of Hindu and Muslim Schools by Sex 1952–6

Year	*Hindu*		*Muslim*	
	Boys	*Girls*	*Boys*	*Girls*
1952	196 (45.5%)	235 (54.5%)	491 (55%)	403 (45%)
1953	3,369 (51.6%)	3,158 (48.4%)	1,204 (53.5%)	1,046 (46.5%)
1954	4,425 (52%)	4,082 (48%)	1,344 (52.7%)	1,199 (47.1%)
1955	5,931 (51.3%)	5,625 (48.7%)	1,667 (52.8%)	1,490 (47.2%)
1956	6,178 (51.1%)	5,902 (48.9%)	2.043 (53%)	1,810 (47%)

Source: Hamel-Smith (1984: 7).

There can be no doubt that the East Indian community was increasingly using a number of avenues to ensure that they became socially as well as economically mobile. One of these was, of course, their entry into the arena of politics which was further aided by the introduction of Universal Adult Suffrage in 1946 as well as free secondary schooling which was introduced in 1960. As the society moved away from plantation economy to an oil-based economy, this led to the creation of numerous new occupations. Increasingly many East Indians moved away from the plantations and were exposed to and assimilated many of the values and aspirations of the 'creole' society. But according to Mahabir (1994), expansion of the economy meant not only increased mobility for men but also for women. For instance, the establishment of the textile industries proved to be an important source of employment for East Indian women since the level of skills needed was relatively low. In addition the establishment of secondary schools for girls at La Pique in the second capital city of San Fernando, and later a vocational school at St. Augustine provided educational opportunities for girls whose families had been converted to Presbyterianism.

From the 1950s to the 1970s, it was evident that the males far outnumbered the females so far as educational mobility was concerned, particularly in the tertiary and technical fields. Mahabir (1994) suggests that a major factor that kept the Hindu woman in her appointed place was that she did not possess adequate qualifications. Education, she noted caused disturbance to the equilibrium of the household of the East Indian women since it led not only to a questioning of authority relationships within the home but also impacted as well the system of arranged and early marriages.

There were, however, some critical factors, that led to a re-thinking of the education policy insofar as the East Indian group was concerned. A major development was the conversion of many Hindu families to Christianity, more particularly Presbyterianism. While this conversion did not lead to a disintegration of the extended family at the time, it exercised a demonstration effect with other family members. Since conversion was translated into an increase in social status, educating one's children, boys as well as girls, it was perceived as an indicator of one's rise in the social ladder. Those who could afford it also sent their children to schools abroad to become 'professionals' either in the fields of medicine or law. Another development was the expansion of the economy which led to increasing opportunities for many, induding women. As more East Indians achieved economic mobility this became a powerful stimulus for families lower down the economic ladder. It was found, however, that in districts where groups were primarily as lower in the socio-economic category, there was an under-representation of women at both the secondary as well as at the university levels (Table 9.3).

TABLE 9.3: East Indian Women with Secondary and University Education in Selected Areas

District	*Secondary*	*University*
Caroni	1,194	0
Chaguanas	355	6
Couva	4,222	42
Victoria	2,139	13

Source: 1970 Population Census of the Commonwealth, UWI, Jamaica, 1973. Taken from Mahabir (1994: 25).

As Table 9.3 indicates, in Caroni and Chaguanas, which were mainly cane-farming areas as compared to the more industrial regions of Couva and Victoria, it was found that the number of women attending both secondary as well as tertiary institutes was significantly lower.

Apart from economic and social changes, other factors were at work. With the advent of electricity and with it the introductions of radio and television, men as well as women were 'bombarded' by what were considered to be the norms and standards of the developed countries. The media conveyed the idea of freedom and independence of individuals which was later reinforced by the Women's Rights Movement in the 1960s. It presented the message of equality between the sexes and the liberation of women via education. Even in the 'Bollywood' movies it was evident that the female 'stars' were not the 'crying' matriarchs of the fifties but rather beautiful, independent, well-established, assertive young women. These were the standards that became the symbol that even the most illiterate would aspire towards.

These cumulative developments over the years persuaded an increasing number of families to send their children, even their girls to secondary and even to tertiary level institutions. Indeed, increasingly it has been found that women have been asserting themselves and entering even the more male-dominated areas such as medicine, engineering and natural sciences (see Table 9.4 for Faculty of Engineering).

TABLE 9.4: East Indian Females in the Engineering Faculty

Years	2001	2002	2003	2004	2005	2006	2007
Engineering Faculty	129	151	145	159	203	225	259

Source: UWI, St. Augustine, 2007.

It is evident that, as Table 9.4 indicates, the number of women who entered the Faculty of Engineering has increased significantly from 2001 to 2007. The entry of East Indian women, in what were once considered male-dominated areas suggests that increasingly, as the economy shifts what emerges is the fight for occupations of one's choice by both sexes. Apart from this, one partial explanation that can be advanced to explain the entry of females in what were once areas of male dominance, is that much of the manual labour has been replaced by technology and machinery, thus replacing 'muscle power' with 'brain power'.

In addition to these factors women have increasingly been asserting themselves and psychologically their strength and individuality have been reinforced by a number of women's movements and 'declarations' all over the world. Myths and taboos associated with what were formerly considered 'female illnesses' such as menstruation, and pregnancy no longer results in isolation and indeed, modern medicine has found ways of alleviating the 'discomforts' associated with these occurrences. One of the most important developments, was the advent of free tertiary education in 2006. Since many of the male-dominated faculties were those where the fees were extremely high, it was found that families increasingly preferred to send their boys rather than their girls to them—girls were sent to faculties such as education, arts, and humanities for which fees were significantly lower. The non-payment of fees have in a sense therefore literally opened up the more expensive faculties and increase in the number of students has been accompanied by an expansion in the number of East Indian women students as well.

CONCLUSION

In short, what this article has attempted to do is to look at some of the impediments that prevented East Indian women from accessing educational opportunities. What emerged in the article was that to a large extent, factors such as culture, norms and traditions were obstacles particularly during the period between the 1920s and the 1970s. However, with the introduction of the Canadian Mission Schools, data revealed that the number of women students increased significantly. By the 1970s, as a result of economic and social changes, along with the advent of compulsory and free educational opportunities, more and more women sought access to not only the secondary but also the tertiary level institutes as well. The article contends the media along with increasing the number of spaces available at tertiary level institutes had a critical part to play in the upward mobility of East Indian women so far as educational mobility was concerned.

NOTES

1. As it has been difficult to divide into the religious categories of Muslims and Hindus I have opted to generalize according to gender rather than religion.
2. Reddock for instance noted that when the Fatel Rozack brought the first 227 Indian immigrant labourers to Trinidad on 30 May, 206 were male and 21 were female (Reddock 1984).

REFERENCES

Brereton, Bridget (1985), 'The Experience of Indentureship: 1845–1917', in *Calcutta to Caroni: The East Indians of Trinidad,* John La Guerre, ed., University of the West Indies, Extra Mural Studies Unit, pp. 21–32.

Bushe, R.G. (1968), 'The System of Education in Trinidad and Tobago', in *Special Reports and Educational Subjects,* D.H. Simpson, ed., vol. 12, part 1, London.

Grant Kenneth (1923), *My Missionary Memories,* Halifax: Imperial Publishing.

Hamel-Smith, Angela L. (1984), 'Primary Education and East Indian Women in Trinidad 1900–1956', Paper presented at the Third Conference on East Indians in the Caribbean, 28 August to 5 September, University of the West Indies, Trinidad, WI.

Jha, J.C. (1985), 'The Indian Heritage in Trinidad', in *Calcutta to Caroni: The East Indians of Trinidad,* John La Guerre, ed., 2nd revd edn, University of the West Indies, Extra Mural Studies Unit, Trinidad, West Indies, pp. 1–20.

Mahabir, Bindimattie (1994), 'The Changing Role of the East Indian Woman in Trinidad: The Family in Perspective', in *The East Indian Odyssey: Dilemmas of a Migrant People,* Mahin Gosine, ed., New York: Windsor Press, pp. 20–7.

Morton, Sarah (1916), *John Morton of Trinidad,* Toronto: Westminster.

Reddock, Rhoda (1984), 'Indian Women and Indentureship in Trinidad and Tobago-1845-1917: Freedom denied', Paper presented at the 'Third Conference on East Indians in the Caribbean', 28 August to 5 September, University of the West Indies, St. Augustine, Trinidad.

Singh, Kelvin (1985), 'Indians and the Larger Society', in *Calcutta to Caroni: The East Indians of Trinidad,* John La Guerre, ed., University of the West Indies, Extra Mural Studies Unit, pp. 33–62.

Tinker, Hugh (1974), *A New System of Slavery: The Export of Indian Labour Overseas 1830–1920,* London: OUP.

10

Market and Field

The Workplace of the Indian Women in Trinidad, 1900–1940

Shaheeda Hussain

THROUGHOUT THE CARIBBEAN there was a movement of people away from estates and into ex-plantation labour since the 1840s. Women in the Caribbean played a central role in economic activities outside of plantation labour. They were, for example, the primary group involved in huckstering and in the inter-island trade of agricultural produce, or trafficking, that developed and flourished in the latter part of the nineteenth century and well into the twentieth century. This essay looks at the general history of people who had made a living away from plantation labour. It adds to the ongoing story of economic and labour activities independent of the dominant plantation sector; of informal economic activities engaged in by ex-plantation workers, specifically Indian women in Trinidad, and the role of these women in the economic diversification and development of the island.

By 1940, almost 100 years after Indians first arrived in Trinidad and some 20 years after the system of indenture had ended, it had become well established that they were no longer transient labourers, but had emerged as permanent settlers on the island. For a small minority of Indians who had risen through the ranks and become part of an intellectual middle stratum, access to, and perhaps acceptance by, the wider society was possible through education and the adoption of the dominant Euro-centric cultural norms. This was facilitated by the presence and activities of the Canadian Mission schools and the Presbyterian church, which catered almost exclusively to the education and conversion to Christianity of the Indians (see Malik 1971). It was clear however, that for the vast majority of Indians, their lives existed outside the periphery of the mainstream Trinidad culture.

Most Indians in Trinidad lived in the rural areas well into the 1940s. The population census for 1946 showed that there was a total of 1,95,747 Indians living throughout Trinidad and Tobago. It also showed that most Indians lived in Victoria and Caroni, both rural counties. Aproximately 61,000 Indians, 52.03 per cent of its population, lived in Victoria. In Caroni, there were approximately

43,000 Indians, or 68.22 per cent of its total population (Population Census 1946).[1] In both these counties, agriculture was the main economic activity. Like other areas in rural Trinidad, these counties had poor infrastructure which made communication and transport difficult.

Indians were subjected to severe limitations and privations in Trinidad, first through restrictive immigration legislation specific to them and second by the socio-economic conditions in which they found themselves. In spite of all this, once they became a permanent presence in Trinidad, the Indians set about carving a niche for themselves, within the proscribed limits of their situation. Their initial marginalization as a group within Trinidad society must have inspired Indians to go in for independent economic activity. Their search for a sound economic status can be viewed as a reaction to the wider society and a means towards compensating for their marginalized status.

In general, agricultural labour remained their main economic activity. A substantial number, both male and female, worked as estate labourers. As the twentieth century progressed however, an increasing number of Indian women withdrew from estate labour. The 1891 Population Census for Trinidad revealed that there were 13,944 female Indian estate labourers. In 1946 this figure stood at 11,342. These figures reveal that there was a decline in female Indian estate labourers and consequently, an absolute decline in Indian women as wage labourers. Where did these women go? Indians had always engaged simultaneously in estate labour and private economic activities. The Report of the Wages Committee of 1919–20 revealed that:

> ... many ... have other sources of income than their actual earnings from labour on the public works or on an estate ... (their) own garden ... or goldsmith ... or have a cocoa contract or rent rice land. And it is common knowledge that many ... supplement their earnings in many other ways.[2]

As the Indian village system became more established in early twentieth century and an increasing number of Indian men and women became landowners, a thriving Indian peasantry evolved. The majority of Indian women who withdrew from estate labour, did so to participate fully in independent economic activities. Five such activities included: the production and sale of milk, charcoal production, market gardening and vending, rice production, and the retail trade of shopkeeping. This article examines each of these activities in detail. It relies heavily on the oral testimonies of women involved in these occupations. The oral testimonies provided data which is not available in written records, and facilitated the emergence of a more complete picture.

PRODUCTION AND SALE OF MILK

The 1891 Population Census for Trinidad showed that there were 68 Indian milk sellers, out of which 40 were women. Milk selling was usually associated with Indians in general and Indian women in particular. It was an important economic activity up to the 1940s, since milk was usually sold fresh and there was a ready market for it, particularly in the urban areas. One way in which the Indian woman earned an independent income was by selling milk:

> I use to sell milk in Rio Claro Junction and in the police station. In those days you have to be licensed for you to sell milk. Remember when they take milk from you, they carry to analyse in Town—to see how much water it have in it.... We use to go from house to house to sell. I, my uncle and my brother use to carry. Each of we [*sic*] had we different part to carry it to. We had twenty-one cows. I was not yet ten years old. Then people use to come home for the milk too. We use to put in bottles and carry it in a basket and cover it. It was six cents a bottle.[3]

For the women who lived in the rural areas and were dairy farmers, the day began early:

> We use to get up four o'clock in the mornin' and first thing we make some coffee. We brush we teeth and ... and then we go and milk the cow. And then we had to carry the milk—7 o'clock was the latest we had to go and carry the milk to the Junction. When we come back then we eating breakfast ... I had to cut grass ... from small.... We use to have to go in the river for water. We use to carry the cow and them in the river. We didn't live far from the river. Then we have to clean out the cow-pen and them. And in the evening we had to milk them again.[4]

In addition to taking care of the cows, she had to complete her other household chores.

Diluting the milk remained a problem, both for the vendors and the authorities. The problem was frequently highlighted in the daily newspapers.

Watered Milk

> An attempt has been made to check the sale of adulterated milk in Port-of-Spain. Some days ago Police Sergeant Hanly stopped several coolie milk sellers and performed the peculiar ceremony prescribed by law, by taking from each of their cans, three samples, one for the analyst, one for himself and the other to be returned to the seller. Each of the phials had to be sealed up and marked for identification and the process had to be carried out on the pavement, exciting the curiosity of a large crowd. When the government analyst has reported on his tests, it will be known whether the parties ... will be brought before the magistrate for 'selling' their customers by watering their milk too freely ... the milk that is daily hawked about the streets, by coolies principally, is generally too bad for honest folks to drink ... but the great bulk of the population can hardly avoid buying it. The coolie justifies his tricks of trade by ... the measure makes it imperative that the milk should be well watered in order that the supply should be adequate to the demand.... Even the pitiful appeal once made by a medical

> man was not mercifully received when he implored them for God's sake, if they would sell milk like that, to put the milk and water in separate vessels.[5]

The issue of adulterated milk was a very real one, since there was a genuine health risk involved in the improper watering of the fresh milk, as it was not unlikely that contaminated water could be used in the process. Therefore the health authorities were particularly vigilant, especially in those early years when there were outbreaks of diseases like cholera and dysentery. If found guilty of selling adulterated milk, milk sellers were charged with profiteering.

Heavy Penalties for Watered Milk

> That they bought milk from other vendors to sell by retail, was the defence advanced by several milk vendors in the Auxiliary Court yesterday, when they were accused ... of selling milk which contained 17 per cent of extraneous water some time ago. 'We buy milk and sell'... (ordered) to pay a fine of $25 and $2.56 costs and compensation or 30 days hard labour.[6]

Indian milk sellers also ran the risk of physical injury, particularly in urban areas. In the 1940s for example, the *Port-of-Spain Gazette* reported that one of the favourite games of black children was to pelt stones at Indian milk sellers, who, with cup in one hand and large, covered milk pan precariously balanced on their heads, steadied by the other hand, became easy, largely defenceless, targets for these children. Whatever the risks involved however, milk selling remained an invaluable source of income for Indo-Trinidadian women well into the 1940s.

PRODUCTION AND SALE OF CHARCOAL

Another occupation in which Indian women were involved was the production and sale of charcoal. There was no initial investment of capital necessary in charcoal production as the raw material, large forest trees, were usually available from the virgin forested lands that Indians acquired through purchase for eventual market gardening or other agricultural activities. When the land was being cleared, the trees would either be sold to sawmills, or burned to make charcoal, which would then be sold as fuel for cooking. The only skill required was that involved in burning the trees to turn them into charcoal.

Up to the 1940s, charcoal remained an important source of cooking fuel, especially as in most homes the coalpot was used in cooking. In 1891, the Population Census indicated that, out of a total of 65 charcoal burners/sellers, there were 13 Indian females. This proportion would remain more or less the same up to the 1940s. One of the women interviewed for this article was a charcoal burner-seller, and another was a charcoal seller.

Charcoal production was a long, slow process which required some skill. If it was not done properly, the result would be a heap of useless ash. The charcoal burner-seller in this article became one when she got married:

When I did first married me husband use to burn coals and sell.... We use to get wood in the forest, real high wood you know.... The day he put fire, whole night he go remain in the forest. And then in the morning early, after I done cook and thing, I use to put in me cart and I gone. Then we go have to take out the coal. We have to out the fire, and then we go full the bag and load it on the cart, and then we go home. We use to carry the coals in town (the capital city) and wholesale it in the market. You know everything was coal then. Some fat, fat tree and we have to dig a big coal pit and junk the tree and put it in the pit, then put fire. And is whole night we use to have to turn that and turn that coal. He didn't have no help, so is me and he one who use to do it. I use to help him cut down the tree and thing. And I know about the fire to put. When it done bag and thing, then we setting out for town. Midnight we use to have to start to go to town. But it was plenty coal cart, plenty cart coming. All man have they lantern and they going; so we never really 'fraid.[7]

The vendors bought large quantities of charcoal wholesale, then retailed it in their own shops for use in households and eating establishments. Like other essential items, charcoal was sold in almost all retail shops:

I carry on the shop for them two uncles of mine. I sell all the goods in the shop ... everyday people buying two, three measures of coal. We use to measure with a scoop make with a pitch oil tin what we cut in a slant-half and half. And that we shove in the flap and get the coals out. We never weight it, just use the scoop to measure it out.[8]

PRODUCTION AND SALE OF MARKET PRODUCE

Through market vending, Indian women were able to earn an independent income. In fact, after estate labour, market vending engaged more Indian women than any other economic activity. Many vendors bought produce from the major market centres throughout Trinidad. A significant number also engaged in small-scale subsistence agriculture and market gardening; and either became wholesalers or retailers of their produce. This economic activity became a viable alternative to estate labour. For most of the women interviewed, market gardening and market vending were the chief occupations, ensuring the economic well-being of their families. These women felt that working their own gardens was both more rewarding and less arduous than estate labour:

Estate work was too hard and somebody encourage me to make market. I make market when I find work too hard on the estate. Then when I tired and I can't-make no good money (on the estate), I make garden. When I turn out in garden I make money and build here (her house)... I plant peas, okra, tomato, sorrel on the hill....[9]

This independent economic activity also enabled the women to be sole breadwinners in their families, when their husbands refused to work:

When he (her husband), left Orange Grove Estate and he ent want to go back, so I have to look for work. I make the garden and I start to sell market. We use to sell in the street in Tunapuna, in front the big store and them. I buy bicycle for he (her husband), and I tell he sell in the bicycle. He want to gamble and he ent want to work. So I have to take it up from there. But is something we do from small eh. I use to work in my father garden; we had plenty garden. He use to have a carter-man to take the goods to the Port-of-Spain market, and when the carter-man ent go, I use to drive the cart with two donkeys.... We use to leave home about 9.00 or 10.00 in the night and when we go, we reach about 12.00 in the night.[10]

Not only did market vending have economic benefits, but for those women who transacted business in the capital, Port-of-Spain, there were distinct social advantages as well. Through market vending these women came into contact with people from the wider Trinidad society, both vendors and customers. Over time these Indian women were able to speak, not only their Hindi dialect and English, but also the French patois, which, up until the 1940s was the common language of the Creole working class. This ability to speak several languages that were prevalent in Trinidad at that time enabled them to better communicate with and understand the wider Creole society in a way that the Indian men lacked.

Retail vendors had to go into the major market centres in time for the opening of the market. This could be as early as 1.00 a.m. They would then purchase produce and proceed to the retail markets where they sold, to set up their stalls. Sales normally began about 6.00 a.m. They would usually ply their trade until midday, by which time most customers would have bought their produce and sales would have slackened off. For those who had secured stalls for which they paid a fee, starting to sell was easy. For the majority who did not have their own stalls the situation was more difficult. They competed for limited space along the roadways and pavements surrounding the market, or within the market compound itself. The main market, the Central Market in Port-of-Spain, was a particularly difficult one for those without a paid stall, since both wholesalers and retailers competed for precious space. There was always a competition for the limited available space:

Saturday morning we use to take the cart, load up with bags of peas which we fill the evening before, to the George Street market (in Port-of-Spain). Then we waiting, me mother and me and plenty other marchands (vendors). As soon as the market open, everybody rushing in to find a space. My mother use to leave me with the peas and she running in to put down ah empty bag on any space she find. Then she will call me to stand up where she put the bag and she gone quick to find a man to bring the peas. Then we spreading it out. Sometimes we wholesale by the bag, but mostly we use to retail it. It always have big cuss out when people trying to thief other people space.[11]

RICE PRODUCTION

After market gardening, production of rice was the most important and large-scale agricultural activity in which Indians, in Trinidad were engaged up to the 1940s. Rice production remained largely at the subsistence level. It was grown mainly for consumption within the home and any surplus was sold locally. But there was never any real effort at rice production for export purposes.

It was a useful first crop as the time between planting and harvesting was short—approximately three months:

> If you throw seed in ending of June, July we go plant and then say October, November month we go cut that rice. We use to have rice sometimes for Divali, we rice cut and come. Long time they say when you have rice coming in your house for Divali time, you going to be lucky. You see, food coming. That is a lucky thing.[12]

More important than the short-term of the crop was the fact that rice provided food for the family, sometimes for two to three years to come:

> Planting rice was good, very good. You get food to eat, you could give somebody a pan (a container of a certain measurement).... If you didn't have money to buy flour and thing, then you go cook rice with you talkari, you not starving. And you have the rice going from one year into the next ... when you don't have money and you feel you could sell two bag of rice ... that time money was hard. [13]

One reason that rice production remained popular amongst Indians was that it provided them with food and something to fall back on.

Until the 1900s, rice remained a crop that could earn money for the farmer. The quality grown in Trinidad was very good. Superintendent of the Botanical Gardens in Trinidad, J.H. Hart, spoke of its high remunerative value before the West Indian Royal Committee of 1897, describing the rice grown by Indians as '... a premium rice ... better than imported rice...'.[14]

Rice cultivation by Indians involved the entire family. It was in rice production that the Indian woman played a significant role. It was normal for families to employ labour, particularly during the planting of the rice. Preparing the fields was done by the family members. Rice plots were generally small in size and although there appeared to be labour specialization based on gender, men prepared the land for planting by ploughing and building small embankments which surrounded each field and kept the water in and women sowed the rice nursery and transplanted the seedlings, it was usual for females to help in ploughing:

> I use to do everything. We had to plough the land first. He (husband) use to plough with a bison, with a piece of wood attached to the bison, the plough or 'hengaway'. Well then, sometimes I stand up on that and ploughing too ... and everybody used to clean the land, man, woman, everybody. To clean a piece of land to plant, you have to take a cutlass and cutlass the land and then we digging it and ploughing it.[15]

Indian rice farmers formed themselves into a cooperative work group called a 'hur', which provided assistance for ploughing and planting the rice fields:

You coming to help me clean and plant, I coming to help you. Is so we work; one set of people and all of we going in rounds to help out one another. That way, all of we get the work done, and then it save we money. We don't have to pay for that, we helping out.[16]

In addition to these cooperative work groups, rice farmers also employed labour, at higher wages than the estates. To plant the rice, women were generally preferred because they worked faster and their fingers were believed to be more nimble than that of the men but for preparing the land, both women and men were employed:

They have to level the land first so that the water will spread even ... then you have to pick up the green grass, heap it up and clean all that ... then you flood the clean fields and transplant the nursery ... I use to do it myself ... sometimes me husband help out. But we didn't have money, so is two of we use to plant. It was a little piece.[17]

For larger acreage, labourers were hired; preferably women.

I use to take five ladies to plant because we had one and a half acres. So me and me husband there planting, and we take five ladies. They use to plant one acre and we use to plant the rest.... They use to sing and thing and plant very fast.... You bending down because you have to go down and plant the rice in like that, by the row. When you put your hand you just sticking the rice seedling with you thumb. The ladies use to plant the acre in one day. People did prefer ladies to plant because they was faster ... you pull out the nursery and tie it in faggot and then you scatter it and plant.[18]

The task of maintaining the fields also fell to the women, as the men were usually employed elsewhere:

Don't let grass grow in it, see that it have water, clean and cutlass the meṛhi (embankment enclosing the rice paddy fields). All the time I was in it. When he gone to work, soon as I get little chance from doing my work, is right there I have to go....[19]

The Indian women also played a central role in harvesting and processing the rice:

The rice, when it ripe you going every day, you watching it. But once, when you see the rice on the stem looking kind of yellow, then you say that it good to cut. By the time that you cut it and you pack them and it stifle, they all get brown, like the real paddy rice. So that go remain for two days or three days, whatever, until you ready to beat it.[20]

Threshing the rice was necessary to separate the paddy from the stalk. This was done by hitting a bundle of stalks against a table made of slats of wood, through which the paddy fell on to a bag spread under the table. The paddy was then fanned:

When you beat it, all the grains falling under the machan (table) and you throwing away the stalk. Then you rake up all those things and you heap up the rice. And now you take the same machan and you pull it one side and you take the sowp and you climb on the machan and you start to fan that rice. The flow one (chaff) going far and the solid rice remaining right there. So you do that till you clean up all, then you full in bag and tote it out and bring it home.[21]

After the rice was brought home, it was spread out to dry, a long process that depended on dry weather:

So you bring it home. Then ... we have two ladies cleaning, put your hand and take out all the big one. When we done clean it, we turning it all the time for it not to grow rotten. And then we get good weather, we carrying it out to dry ... and we fanning it. Then we put it to dry. When we see rain coming we go bag it up quick and bring it home. When it well dry properly, then we bag it and put it in a big box.[22]

Two types of rice were produced, white rice and parboiled rice. White rice was easier to produce and was therefore less expensive than parboiled rice:

When we make white rice, you just have to spread it out, let it dry and then mill it —carry it to the mill. Before they had mill we use to have to pound it at home. After it dry, we use to put the rice in a big (mortar), we use to call it 'okrhi', to pound it. Then we take a big piece of wood, a 'musar' (pestle). When we pound it with the musar, get out the shell and take the rice. Ladies use to do that. That is how we used to get white rice. [23]

White rice was most often used for home consumption. Parboiled rice, which required a more involved process, was the type usually sold:

With parboiled rice now, you use to have to soak it, two days it go soak ... then you have to put it in a pan and stifle it with a wet bag. Then you let it steam.... When you feel like it steaming on top, then you open the bag a little bit and you see one rice grain burst on top. The husk will crack, a little slight crack in it. Then you know that rice good to take down. You empty it out and let it get cold a little bit; then you turn it one or two times with your hands and then you mill it. For everyday use we cook white rice. When I want to sell, we use to sell the parboil rice. It was more expensive than the white rice.[24]

The rice was sold within the village to those who did not produce their own. Usually larger producers sold to people who would then retail it to others. Buyers came to the homes of the rice farmers to purchase the rice. Rice production was undertaken in conjunction with other agricultural activities as its main aim was to feed the families of the rice farmers and to have a means of income when times became hard.

Rice production played a significant role in the economic lives of Indians in Trinidad. Indian women provided much of the labour involved in rice production, whether as part of the family work unit, or hired wage labour on someone else's rice fields. Not only was rice production an alternative to estate labour, but it also provided families with food and earned them cash; although Trinidad continued to import rice throughout the period, Indians produced enough rice to satisfy local consumption.

For Indian women it meant an income earner and an employment opportunity. She considered it a benefit:

From rice planting, people have rice to eat. From the same rice, we plant again and we have to sell to others. We plant rice to do better for weself. Because if you don't have work and times hard, rice give plenty work. And when you sell a barrel, you have money. So all how it good.[25]

Like other agricultural enterprises, rice production gave Indians, particularly Indian women, an alternative to estate labour, and one more lever to be used attaining autonomy within the Indian community.

RETAIL TRADE/SHOPKEEPERS

The 1891 Population Census for Trinidad showed that there were 165 Indian shopkeepers in the island who were women. By 1946, it was clear that of the 2,943 Indian women who were indicated as 'Own Account' occupation and 860 who were employers, a significant number were shopkeepers. Shopkeeping had been one of the preferred economic activities that Indians had turned to when their terms of indenture had ended. Protectors of Immigrants Reports at the turn of the century reflected that the more prosperous ex-indentures generally tended to go into shopkeeping. These shops would have sold items necessary for daily life—from foodstuff to general merchandise such as soap, matches, kerosene and charcoal. In some rural areas, shops would have also sold household wares and haberdashery.

To the women who were shopkeepers, this occupation provided a steady and regular income, and for some, a comfortable lifestyle:

I use to help my father in his shop. I never had to go outside and look for work like other women. My father shop always busy. So I hadn't to go outside and work, I see about the shop. My father use to work outside while I run the shop.[26]

Running a shop meant long hours, many of which consisted of waiting for customers. The inactivity and tedium was relieved by the responsibilities involved in running one's household:

I work hard in the shop. My husband would only get up in the morning, open the shop, by the time I cooking for him. He eat and thing and he gone to work. Then I have to see about the shop now and the children. So I didn't have no time again ... he say housework is more for the wives so he didn't use to do nothing at home. I use to have to do everything by meself—cooking and washing and seeing about the children, and on top of that, seeing about the shop. He say that is not his work.[27]

From this account, it is clear that shopkeeping was a supplementary activity to whatever the wife and husband were doing. In the case of the woman, household duties were of equal, or more importance to her shopkeeping activities. Yet shopkeeping afforded a better social and financial standing to those women who were involved in it:

When I get married and started to run my shop, then I learn to experience more. My husband teach me to count and write ... and then he never drunk and get on. I know how other women had it. Some of them, they life hard right round. They don't have money and then they husband only making they life hell.... [28]

Many Indian women engaged in trade in this period, could count without being able to read, write or recognize numbers. It was not unusual for these women to keep accounts of amounts in their heads until someone, whether husband or child at school, came home and wrote down what they had retained mentally.

Despite the fact that this shopkeeper sympathized with her customers who were in a less fortunate position, she did not compromise her business. Although like all shopkeepers she sold goods on credit to customers, she was very clear as to whom such privileges were to be extended:

People use to trust goods from we, but you use to have to know who to trust. You can't trust everybody because it would be very hard to get the money back. Who you know working, have a steady job, you could trust them, because you know when they get pay, you will get the money. But who you know not working, you cannot give them too much of trust because you wouldn't get the money. So you have to know the people you trust.[29]

It was clear that credit was extended only to those who could repay their debts. Detailed accounts were kept of each customer's debits and credits.

The ability to repay debts was only one criterion for the extension of credit. In a village situation, the status of the customers was also taken into consideration. The higher one's status in the village, the easier to obtain credit. Status was not necessarily linked to wealth. The perceived caste of the customer was also a deciding factor. Even if the actuality of caste distinction as in India did not exist, the idea of caste persisted to a very large extent in these villages. Consequently, someone of a perceived higher caste would, in all probability, have the respect of those of the underprivileged castes despite their economic standing. Then too, lower caste people could have received goods on credit as it was understood that they paid through the rendering of services for the so-called higher castes, for example cleaning out pit latrines, or through strenuous manual labour, payment being rendered in kind.

Shopkeeping was an economic activity that allowed Indians to retain a certain independence from the State. This independence was not total however, since there was the need for obtaining licenses to sell certain commodities, such as alcohol, the necessity to adhere to price control through a Schedule of Prices, the routine and unannounced visits from price inspectors and police and the constant threat of prosecution. Notwithstanding all this, Indian shopkeepers, like others, found ways of circumventing these official restrictions and supervision, through practises like hoarding, particularly prevalent during the period of the two World Wars when goods were scarce and fixing scales and other measuring instruments. It was a very significant fact that the formation of small business, of which the retail trade of shopkeeping was a forerunner, insulated the Indians from the rest of society at a point of time when they had not fully consolidated their position in Trinidad. It also enhanced their economic base from which they could negotiate with the wider society, by providing them with the means of self-sufficiency and the ability to provide employment opportunities of their own. Through shopkeeping, Indian women ensured that both their own economic independence and that of their community was being consolidated.

Up to the 1940s, the vast majority of Indians in Trinidad were faced with limited choices for material and social progress. One of the ways open to them was engaging in economic activities which were independent of the state structure and the established pattern of estate/plantation agriculture. None of the women interviewed had any fears about withdrawing from being a wage earner, into becoming a self-employed person. Generally they regarded such employment as being of greater benefit, both to themselves and their families. As one woman reflected:

> When you work for a wage, then that is all you have. When the wage done, you done. But when you work for yourself, well then, you always have a little something to fall back on. You make garden, you have food; you have cow, is milk. And then you is your own boss. So, if only is food, you have that too...[30]

This emphasis on being self-reliant was dominant among the Indian women engaged in independent economic activities. Since they grew most of what they needed, their expenses were minimal. The acquisition of money was not the most crucial element in their equation of survival. To these women, security and well-being of the family were the main concerns. Up to the 1940s, the family played a vital role as a buffer against the wider, often times, hostile Trinidad society. Within the Indian family, the woman played a pivotal role; and although she was exposed to the hostility and unrelenting demands of the family, she was crucial to its survival.

The economic activities that were discussed here established the economic importance of the Indian woman within her family, and by extension, the Indian community. A direct consequence of these activities was the strengthening of

Indians in Trinidad, so much so that, by the end of the 1940s, the group as a whole was able to take on the challenges of the wider Trinidad society.

NOTES

1. Population Census, Trinidad, 1946.
2. Report of the Wages Committee, 1919–20.
3. Mrs W., personal interview, Rio Claro, Trinidad, 14 February 1997.
4. Ibid.
5. *Port-of-Spain Gazette,* 19 July 1884.
6. *Port-of-Spain Gazette,* 29 January 1942.
7. Mrs H.A., personal interview, Dinsley Village, Tacarigua, Trinidad, 14 March 1997.
8. Mrs G.M., personal interview, Maracas, St. Joseph, Trinidad, 4 February 1997.
9. Mrs D,. personal interview, Paradise, Tacarigua, Trinidad, 14 March 1997.
10. Ibid.
11. Ibid.
12. Mrs S.D., personal interview, Cunupia, Trinidad, 27 November 1997.
13. Mrs B.M., personal interview, El Dorado, Trinidad, 19 December 1997.
14. Parliamentary Papers vol. L (C 8657), p. 814: Evidence of J.H. Hart before the WIRC, 1897.
15. Mrs R.M., personal interview, Cunupia, Trinidad, 11 January 1998.
16. Ibid.
17. Mrs S.D., personal interview, Cunupia, Trinidad, 27 November 1997.
18. Mrs B.M., personal interview, El Dorado, Trinidad, 19 December 1997.
19. Mrs S.D., personal interview, Cunupia, Trinidad, 27 November 1997.
20. Ibid.
21. Ibid.
22. Mrs B.M., personal interview, El Dorado, Trinidad, 19 December 1997.
23. Mrs R.M., personal interview, Cunupia, Trinidad, 11 January 1998.
24. Mrs B.M., personal interview, El Dorado, Trinidad, 19 December 1997.
25. Mrs R.M., personal interview, Cunupia, Trinidad, 11 January 1998.
26. Mrs R., personal interview, Guaico Tamana, Trinidad, 7 February 1997.
27. Ibid.
28. Ibid.
29. Ibid.
30. Mrs B.M., personal interview, El Dorado, Trinidad, 19 December 1997.

Index